THOREAU'S WORLD

Thoreau's World

MINIATURES FROM HIS JOURNAL

Edited by Charles R. Anderson

PRENTICE-HALL, *Inc., Englewood Cliffs, New Jersey*

Thoreau's World: Miniatures from His Journal

Edited by Charles R. Anderson

Library of Congress Catalog Card Number: 79–137899   Printed
in the United States of America T   Prentice-Hall International,
Inc., London   Prentice-Hall of Australia, Pty. Ltd., Sydney
Prentice-Hall of Canada, Ltd., Toronto   Prentice-Hall of India
Private Ltd., New Delhi   Prentice-Hall of Japan, Inc., Tokyo

Typography, binding, and jacket design by Janet Anderson

LETTERS TO THE GODS

My Journal is that of me which would else spill over and run to waste, gleanings from the field which in action I reap. I must not live for it, but in it for the gods. They are my correspondent, to whom daily I send off this sheet postpaid. I am clerk in their counting-room, and at evening transfer the account from day-book to ledger. It is as a leaf which hangs over my head in the path. I bend the twig and write my prayers on it; then letting it go, the bough springs up and shows the scrawl to heaven. As if it were not kept shut in my desk, but were as public a leaf as any in nature. It is papyrus by the riverside; it is vellum in the pastures; it is parchment on the hills. I find it everywhere as free as the leaves which troop along the lanes in autumn. The crow, the goose, the eagle carry my quill, and the wind blows the leaves as far as I go. Or, if my imagination does not soar, but gropes in slime and mud, then I write with a reed.

THOREAU'S JOURNAL   8 FEBRUARY 1841

PREFACE

The *Journal* of Henry Thoreau is too voluminous to be read by any but specialists. Although on rare occasions one of them may read it all the way through, more normally it is only thumbed, with the aid of a index, to run down particular facts or ideas. Yet as a whole it is such a great achievement there have been several attempts to make its riches more accessible to readers, by compiling a volume of representative selections. This method of presentation, by reducing the fifteen volumes to one, provides a usable sample of Thoreau's extraordinary *Journal:* his observations on the world around him, his meditations on the inner life, first drafts of essays and passages later used in books, bird and flower lists, random jottings of a miscellaneous sort. But the emphasis in these compilations has usually been on the variety of Thoreau's subject matter rather than on his distinction as a literary artist. And the endless series of short entries, arranged in the rather meaningless chronological or "diary" order of the *Journal* itself, does not make for sustained reader interest.

Buried in the *Journal* and less well known, there are compositions of a very different kind from those listed above, pieces which for lack of a better term I shall call "miniatures." Ranging from a single paragraph to several pages, these brief essays usually appear in the *Journal* as finished creations, unified wholes intended to stand alone. Yet for the most part these remarkable miniatures have been neglected by readers of Thoreau, though he practiced the form assiduously and brought it to a high degree of perfection. Scattered through the fifteen volumes are nearly a thousand of them, from which I have chosen two hundred and fifty for *Thoreau's World* by a rigorous process of selection.

My only criterion has been literary excellence, distinction of manner rather than variety or representativeness of matter. Even so, happily enough, they are written on a wide range of themes and in several styles, surprisingly attuned to the modern ear. The groupings have been supplied editorially ("People," "Places," "Wildlife," etc.) and also titles for the miniatures, using Thoreau's own words when possible, in order to make the selections more readily available to readers. Finally, my ordering within the groups makes for cumulative interest, as can be illustrated by a sequence of titles such as Lightning, Thunder, Wind, Echoes, etc. (from "Events"). Still, my emphasis is on the unity and finish of the individual miniatures. And since nothing has been included that was used in his books and essays, *Thoreau's World,* culled from the vast and generally unread *Journal,* constitutes a new addition to his shelf. Second only to *Walden,* it represents his highest achievement as a writer.

The present volume, though assembled by me, was written by Thoreau—all except two essays, "The Journal" and "'The Writer's Art," which precede and follow the miniatures themselves. For critical aid in preparing the manuscript I would like to thank two colleagues and friends, Ron Paulson (Johns Hopkins) and Maynard Mack (Yale).

C.R.A.

The text here followed is that of *The Writings of Henry David Thoreau* (Boston, 1906), twenty volumes. At the end of each miniature there are citations of date and of volume and page (using the separate numbering series for the *Journal*).

The miniatures are reproduced exactly as they are in the *Journal*, with the following exceptions: a few proper names have been added in brackets after an initial in the text; in a very few instances the parts of a miniature have been brought together from two or three places in the *Journal*, because though scattered they were clearly returns to the same topic. A final editorial policy needs explanation. Since Thoreau considered his *Journal* to be a writer's workbook and since he was unwilling to waste paper, he did not hesitate to intrude into the middle of a passage any idea or observation that occurred to him at the moment, regardless of its relevance to the topic already in hand; similarly, he often went on to a new topic without bothering to begin a new paragraph. This being so, I have felt justified in deleting what was irrelevant to the miniatures selected, the ellipses being indicated (. . .) so that skeptical readers can check the validity of my judgments.

Footnotes have been kept to a minimum by limiting them to matters important to an understanding of the text but not available in standard desk reference works. Local places and people named in the text are not further identified if their roles are clear from the context.

CONTENTS

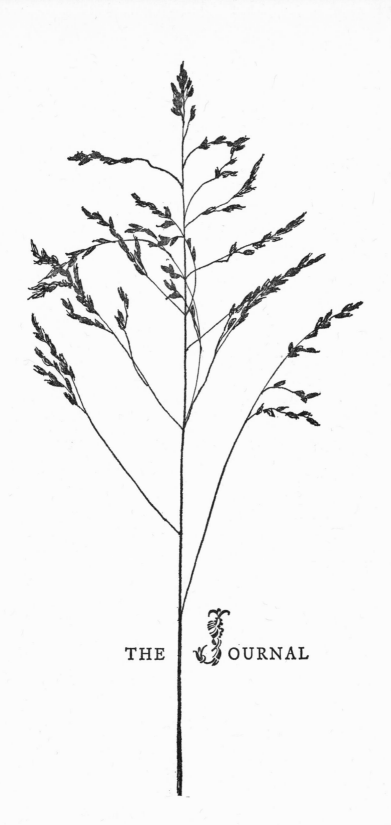

THE JOURNAL

THE JOURNAL

" 'What are you doing now?' he asked. 'Do you keep a jour-
nal?' So I make my first entry today."

With these words, in response to a prodding from Emerson,
Henry David Thoreau embarked on a writing enterprise—his *Jour-*
nal—that occupied him continuously over the entire period of his
literary career, from 1837 to 1862. Beginning a few months after
his graduation from Harvard and ending only a few months before
his death, this extraordinary creation runs to more than seven thousand pages. In one sense Thoreau's *Journal* is his greatest achievement
as a writer, the remarkable record of a remarkable man's view of the
world. Yet one would have a hard time proving it a unified whole,
harder still fitting it into any traditional genre of literature. One way
to explore for a definition is to start by indicating what it is not.

It is neither diary nor autobiography in the usual meaning of
these terms, because the daily chronicle and the narrative of outward events are minor aspects of this voluminous work. The entries
are usually dated, it is true, but this is significant only for a fraction
of them—mostly for seasonal passages such as the blossoming of
flowers, the breakup of ice on the ponds, meadow-haying, the October leaf fall. Furthermore, days at a time are skipped, occasionally
weeks, without comment. The *Journal* is clearly not the work of a
diarist, but the notebook of a writer dedicated to the continuous practice of composition. As for the autobiographical aspect, in an 1855
entry Thoreau himself remarks: "In a true history or biography, of
how little consequence those events of which so much is commonly
made! . . . I find in my Journal that the most important events
in my life, if recorded at all, are not dated." (VIII, 64)[1] Two years
later he seems to be contradicting himself when he queries: "Is not
the poet bound to write his own biography? Is there any other work

---

[1] All references in parentheses are to *The Writings of Henry David
Thoreau* (Boston, 1906), twenty vols.—to the *Journal* by volume
and page only, to the works by short title and page. In addition to the
fourteen vols. of the *Journal* in this edition, there is the "lost journal"
published by Perry Miller in *Consciousness in Concord* (1958), here
cited as LJ.

for him but a good journal? We do not wish to know how his imaginary hero, but how he, the actual hero, lived from day to day." (x, 115) That Thoreau is speaking figuratively here can be easily demonstrated by reference to such a book as *Leaves of Grass.* Though the persona there is specifically named "Walt Whitman" he is clearly a mask for the author; the personality and spiritual "self" are only projections of his potentialities; the experiences described are symbolic ones rather than transcriptions from the poet's actual life. So in the works of Thoreau.

Indeed, this pretense that all writing is autobiographical is a favorite paradox with him. It is used at the very beginning of *Walden,* in a mock apology for retaining the "I" in his book: "I should not talk so much about myself if there were anybody else whom I knew as well. Unfortunately I am confined to this theme by the narrowness of my experience." All he requires of any writer, he concludes, is "a simple and sincere account of his own life." (ii, 4) Having delivered himself of this wry dictum, he proceeds to ignore it. What he gives instead in that famous book is the merest thread of autobiographical story on which to hang his images; *Walden* is essentially an exploration of his inner world as mirrored in the outer one.

A similar discrimination must be made in regard to the *Journal.* If biographers had to depend upon it as the main source for facts— the actual people, places, events in Thoreau's life—they would fare poorly indeed. For example, his first vocation was teaching school, 1838–1840, but this part of his life receives no mention whatsoever in the *Journal.* Again, the single great influence on him as a literary man was Emerson, especially during the two years Thoreau lived at his house, but the only reference to that episode is on the date of going there in 1841: "*April 26 Monday. At R. W. E.'s*"— that's all. (i, 253) One might try to explain the omission by noting that only a small part of the early *Journal* has survived. But such an explanation can be countered by quoting the entire entry for one of the climactic days in Thoreau's life at a period when the *Journal* is at its fullest, running to more than five hundred pages a year: "*Aug. 9, 1854 Wednesday.*—To Boston. 'Walden' published. Elderberries. Waxwork yellowing." (vi, 429) This and four equally laconic entries are all that relate to his masterpiece. The *Journal* is scarcely "his own biography," the account of how he "lived from day to day."

If autobiography is not the correct word to define Thoreau's *Journal*, neither is the commonly held opinion exactly right: that it was just a storehouse of random observations and ideas, brightened with an occasional aphorism, which he "mined" for his published writings. It was indeed levied upon for books and essays—including the posthumous volumes put together by his literary executors—though in ways too complex to be described here.[2] But all told these uses do not account for more than one-third of the *Journal*, perhaps only a fourth.

What then of the remaining five thousand pages? The answer is not simple, since Thoreau used them for a wide variety of purposes. A large number of passages beginning about 1850, for example, are devoted to his obsessive effort to construct a calendar that would chronicle the phenomena of the seasons in the order of their occurrence, hoping to recover the rapport with nature instinctive to plants and animals but lost to civilized man. Notations of several lines each—on the arrival of a spotted warbler, the unfolding of woolly ferns, and so on—are often strung out over a dozen or more pages. Dull as this kind of writing is, one might call it highly readable in comparison with the stark lists of birds, flowers, trees, and shrubs that clog the later volumes of the *Journal*. Thoreau's "scientific" study of nature did not produce any first-rate compositions, nor is it even of much interest to the biologist today.

There are several other categories of *Journal* writing that for present purposes can be excluded from serious consideration. One of these is the occasional attempt at a long narrative. For example, in 1852 there is a ten-page account of a day's boating on Concord River, and in 1858 a continuous sixty-page account of an excursion to the White Mountains of New Hampshire. But narrative was not Thoreau's forte. His most successful efforts in this line were pulled out of the *Journal* after his death and published as *The Maine Woods* and *Cape Cod*, but even these volumes fall far below his best work.

At the opposite pole from discursive narratives are the apho-

---

[2] See "The Writer's Art," pp. 356–364, below.

risms Thoreau frequently indulged in. For a typical sample: "The youth gets together his materials to build a bridge to the moon, or perchance a palace or temple on earth, and at length the middle-aged man concludes to build a woodshed with them." (IV, 227) Somewhat better are those that take the form of a proverb: "Murder will out. I find, in the dry excrement of a fox left on a rock, the vertebrae and talons of a partridge which he has consumed. They are *mémoires pour servir*." (V, 242) Best of all are the terse epigrams, such as those that found their way into *Walden*, to clinch a point by witty antithesis: "As if you could kill time without injuring eternity." (II, 8) At worst these aphorisms are merely clever or sententious in the bad sense; at their most successful they sparkle with ingenuity. But Thoreau was no master of the *pensée*, being a poet and a wit rather than a profound moralist. To search through the *Journal* for aphorisms is like hunting for seashells or bright colored pebbles during a walk; there is some pleasure in the discovery, but what to do with them when found? Such collections have been made—"gems from Thoreau"—but they do not sustain the reader's interest.

Even more typical are the long random series of short paragraphs that make up such a large part of the *Journal*. Sometimes they are ideas loosely linked by association. Sometimes they are a mere sequence of observations whose only unifying thread is the walk that produced them, as in the following spring pictures from a hillside:

> It is pleasant when the road winds along the side of a hill with a thin fringe of wood through which to look into the low land. It furnishes both shade and frame for your pictures,—as this Corner road. . . . See now the woodchuck rollicking across a field toward his hole and tumbling into it. See where he has just dug a new hole. Their long claws are rather weak-looking for digging. The woodpeckers tapping. The first columbine (Aquilegia Canadensis) to-day, on Conantum. Shade is grateful, and the walker feels a desire to bathe in some pond or stream for coolness and invigoration.
>
> Cowslips show at a distance in the meadows (Miles's). The new butter is white still, but with these cows' lips in the grass it will soon be yellow, I trust. This yellowness in the spring, derived from the sun, affects even the cream in the cow's bag,

and flowers in yellow butter at last. Who has not turned pale at the sight of hay butter? These are the cows' lips.

The music of all creatures has to do with their loves, even of toads and frogs. Is it not the same with man?

There are odors enough in nature to remind you of everything, if you had lost every sense but smell. The fever-bush is an apothecary's shop.

The farmers are very busily harrowing and rolling in their grain. The dust flies from their harrows across the field. The tearing, toothed harrow and the ponderous cylinder, which goes creaking and rumbling over the surface, heard afar, and vying with the sphere. The cylinder is a simple machine, and must go into the new symbols. It is an interesting object, seen drawn across a grain-field. The willows are now suddenly of a light, fresh, tender yellowish-green. A green bittern, a gawky bird. As I return over the bridge, shadflies very numerous. Many insects now in the evening sunshine, especially over the water. (IV, 26–28)

It was undoubtedly passages like this one that Thoreau had in mind when he commented: "I do not know but thoughts written down thus in a journal might be printed in the same form with greater advantage than if the related ones were brought together into separate essays. . . . It is more simple, less artful." After trying at some length to convince himself of the validity of this "natural" form, however, he was forced to conclude: "Yet Plutarch did not so; Montaigne did not so. Men have written travels in this form, but perhaps no man's daily life has been rich enough to be journalized." (III, 239–240) Such writing is lacking in both the distinction and the unity required for inclusion in *Thoreau's World*. Yet most of the pages in previous volumes of "representative selections" that have been made from Thoreau's *Journal* are taken up with just such random sequences as the long one quoted above— supplemented by flower and bird lists, narratives, and aphorisms.

There is one final category of compositions in the *Journal*— most interesting of all—the "miniatures" which make up the present volume. Ranging from a single paragraph to four or five pages, these very brief "essays" seem to have been created as unified wholes. They show a keenness of observation and a precision of statement that only a poet's sensitivity to the world around him can attain, yet the factual content is always transformed by wit, symbol, or myth. Second only to *Walden*, they represent Thoreau's highest achievement as a writer— masterpieces in miniature.

In an earlier period such as the seventeenth century the best of these would have found their way into print, but in nineteenth-century America there was no market for pieces of such brevity. This did not keep Thoreau from persevering in his favorite genre. For one thing, any practice in writing would increase his skills for longer and more publishable compositions. For another, almost from the beginning he had resigned himself to having only a small audience, if any at all. Even *The Dial*, a little magazine edited by Transcendentalist friends, had rejected his first long and ambitious essay (see p. 356, below).

How seriously this affected him is shown by a *Journal* entry six weeks after the rejection, 15 January 1841, suggesting a substitute audience:

We should offer up our perfect thoughts to the gods daily—our writing should be hymns and psalms. Who keeps a journal is purveyor for the Gods. There are two sides to every sentence; the one is contiguous to me, but the other faces the gods, and no man ever fronted it. When I utter a thought I launch a vessel which never sails in my haven more, but goes sheer off into the deep. Consequently it demands a godlike insight—a fronting view, to read what was greatly written. (LJ, 212)

This was followed 8 February 1841 by the extraordinary passage chosen as the epigraph for the present volume:

My Journal is that of me which would else spill over and run to waste, gleanings from the field which in action I reap. I must not live for it, but in it for the gods. They are my correspondent, to whom daily I send off this sheet postpaid. I am clerk in their counting-room, and at evening transfer the account from day-book to ledger. It is as a leaf which hangs over my head in the path. I bend the twig and write my prayers on it; then letting it go, the bough springs up and shows the scrawl to heaven. As if it were not kept shut in my desk, but were as public a

leaf as any in nature. It is papyrus by the riverside; it is vellum in the pastures; it is parchment on the hills. I find it everywhere as free as the leaves which troop along the lanes in autumn. The crow, the goose, the eagle carry my quill, and the wind blows the leaves as far as I go. Or, if my imagination does not soar, but gropes in slime and mud, then I write with a reed.
(I, 206–207)

The title given to this epigraph, "Letters to the Gods," describes so perfectly the poetic aspect of these miniatures it could have been adopted for the whole volume— except for the danger of leading read-ers to expect a series of discourses on religion!

Both passages quoted above are concerned with the ambition to write perfectly. But the actual experience that touched them off gives a practical basis for the idealism: if you do not have any audi-ence at all, any public to write *down* to, you can afford to write *up* toward heaven. All during the 1840's Thoreau's effort to get his writings published met with little success. Yet his dedication to ex-pression was such that he continued to write with unabated zeal. Meantime, in 1845 he took up residence at Walden Pond for the purpose, on the practical side, of solving a problem in economics: how to be a non-selling author and survive. The first product of this experiment, *A Week*, after being turned down by several publishers, was printed at his own expense in 1849 but it sold only two hundred copies in four years. His reaction to the disastrous failure of this his first book may be found in the witty essay reproduced below, p. 237. In spite of all frustrations in his efforts to get essays and books pub-lished, his daily private writing continued but now under a new defi-nition: "'Says I to myself' should be the motto of my journal." (III, 107) Letters to the gods or letters to himself, it amounts to the same thing as far as audience is concerned; and in either case the "correspondent" is one who demands perfection.

The most satisfactory definition of Thoreau's *Journal*, therefore, is that it was a writer's workbook, serving all the purposes included in that comprehensive term. Besides being a mill for grinding much of the raw material that went into his finished essays and books— with the inevitable chaff left over—it was a workshop where these extraordinary "miniatures," now first collected in *Thoreau's World*, were created. The best are a fusion of two kinds of writing: the observation recorded today, the memory of it tomorrow. Thoreau discusses them in connection with the two kinds of themes proper for a writer: the factual and homely (for the daily record), the poetic and transcendent (for what is remembered). Passages from the *Journal* dealing with these two kinds of writing, and their relevant themes, will now be presented for consideration.

Thoreau once queried: "Might not my Journal be called 'Field Notes?'" (v, 32) Certainly much of the fifteen volumes could be gathered under that rubric, for "Field Notes" offers a wide spectrum if we take it to include all observations of the actual world. Thoreau so expands it:

> It is wise to write on many subjects, to try many themes, that so you may find the right and inspiring one. Be greedy of occasions to express your thought. . . . Probe the universe in a myriad points. . . . You must try a thousand themes before you find the right one, as nature makes a thousand acorns to get one oak. He is a wise man and experienced who has taken many views; to whom stones and plants and animals and a myriad objects have each suggested something, contributed something. (11, 457)

Though there are some hints of going beyond the factual here, the focus is on writing about things. Similarly when he chooses the homely as his subject matter. "I omit the unusual—the hurricanes and earthquakes—and describe the common," he says in a *Journal* entry of 1851: "You may have the extraordinary for your province, if you will let me have the ordinary. Give me the obscure life, the cottage of the poor and humble, the workdays of the world, the barren fields, the smallest share of all things but poetic perception." (11, 428–429) Again, in the last two words, there is a suggestion that the facts may be looked at in a special way, but his emphasis is still on the external world.

Finally, in a long passage near the end of his career, he spells out this aspect of his writing in great detail, tying it to the local scene:

> My themes shall not be far-fetched. I will tell of homely everyday phenomena and adventures. Friends! Society! It seems to me that I have an abundance of it, there is so much that I re-

joice and sympathize with, and men, too, that I never speak to but only know and think of. What you call bareness and poverty is to me simplicity. I love the winter, with its imprisonment and cold, for it compels the prisoner to try new fields and resources. I love to have the river closed up for a season and put a pause to my boating, to be obliged to get my boat in. I shall launch it again in the spring with so much more pleasure. . . . I love best to have each thing in its season only, and enjoy doing without it at all other times. . . . I have never got over my surprise that I should have been born into the most estimable place in the world, and in the very nick of time, too. (IX, 160)

There is enough material of this kind in the later volumes of the *Journal* to support the thesis that he was planning a picture-book-in-words of his native region. At the very beginning of his career he had suggested such a project, though it was never carried out:

I think I could write a poem to be called "Concord." For argument I should have the River, the Woods, the Ponds, the Hills, the Fields, the Swamps and Meadows, the Streets and Buildings, and the Villagers. Then the Morning, Noon, and Evening, Spring, Summer, Autumn, and Winter, Night and Indian summer, and the Mountains in the Horizon (I, 282)

This is an apt description of much of what appears in the selections that follow in the present volume—that is, what appears on the surface. But what lifts them up into distinction is something quite different.

Thoreau was not simply an observer and recorder of the world around him, remarkable as his skills were in that kind of writing— the kind for which he is best known. In the last analysis external reality interested him only as analogy for spirit, and it was through inward exploration that he sought for meanings. A number of *Journal* entries discuss various aspects of this very different kind of writing. "The poet deals with his privatest experience," Thoreau declares. He makes his books out of this rather than out of other books, "stands bodily behind his words with his own experience." (III, 276; VI, 188) Then in a late *Journal* passage he drives home his point:

My work is writing, and I do not hesitate, though I know that no subject is too trivial for me, tried by ordinary standards; for,

*ye fools, the theme is nothing, the life is everything. All that
interests the reader is the depth and intensity of the life excited.
We touch our subject but by a point which has no breadth, but
the pyramid of our experience, or our interest in it, rests on us
by a broader or narrower base. That is, man is all in all, Nature
nothing, but as she draws him out and reflects him. Give me
simple, cheap, and homely themes.* (IX, 121)

"Homely" is used here in the sense of unpretentious, natural rather
than literary or philosophical.

Almost the same language he had used to describe themes drawn
from the outer world is now used for those drawn from the inner:
"The forcible writer does not go far for his themes. His ideas are not
far-fetched. He derives inspiration from his chagrins and his satisfac-
tions." (III, 246) The writer must speak out of a genuine and contented life, however limited in range, if he would interest readers:
"They must have the essence or oil of himself, tried out in the fat of
his experience and joy." (IX, 195) Again, "Pay for your victuals,
then, with poetry; give back life for life." (XI, 457) It is the intensity of the felt life that counts, rather than the subject matter that
embodies it:

*It is in vain to write on chosen themes. We must wait till they
have kindled a flame in our minds. There must be the copu-
lating and generating force of love behind every effort destined
to be successful. The cold resolve gives birth to, begets, nothing.
The theme that seeks me, not I it. The poet's relation to his
theme is the relation of lovers.* (III, 253)

Thoreau's emphasis on the inner life of feeling as a source for
themes, in these passages, does not mean that he excluded the inner
world of ideas from his writing. The two play a balanced role in his
published books and in the present volume. The *Journal* itself bears
eloquent testimony to his commitment to mind. In a long passage,
calling for original thinking, he sets forth much that is central to his
own "way" as a self-reliant author:

*. . . We seek too soon to ally the perceptions of the mind to
the experience of the hand, to prove our gossamer truths practical, to show their connection with our every-day life (better
show their distance from our every-day life), and to relate them*

*to the cider-mill and the banking institution. Ah, give me pure
mind, pure thought!*

*. . . Though you should only speak to one kindred mind in
all time, though you should not speak to one, but only utter
aloud, that you may the more completely realize and live in the
idea which contains the reason for your life, that you may build
yourself up to the height of your conceptions, that you may remember your Creator in the days of your youth and justify His
ways to man, that the end of life may not be its amusement,
speak—though your thought presupposes the non-existence of
your hearers—thoughts that transcend life and death.* (111,
156–158)

A second passage gives a new dimension to this same kind of writing
by putting his advocacy in terms of an elaborate conceit, which links
intellect to spiritual insight:

*The poet must be continually watching the moods of his mind,
as the astronomer watches the aspects of the heavens. What
might we not expect from a long life faithfully spent in this wise?
The humblest observer would see some stars shoot. A faithful
description as by a disinterested person of the thoughts which
visited a certain mind in threescore years and ten. . . . As
travellers go round the world and report natural objects and
phenomena, so faithfully let another stay at home and report the
phenomena of his own life,—catalogue stars, those thoughts
whose orbits are as rarely calculated as comets. It matters not
whether they visit my mind or yours,—whether the meteor falls
in my field or in yours,—only that it come from heaven. . . .
A meteorological journal of the mind.* (11, 403)

This describes some of the miniatures in *Thoreau's World*. Others fit more nearly with the suggested title of 'Field Notes.' The best
are a fusion of the two kinds of writing, as described in the *Journal*
for 1852, at the height of his creativity:

*I have a commonplace book for facts and another for poetry,
but I find it difficult always to preserve the vague distinction
which I had in my mind, for the most interesting and beautiful
facts are so much the more poetry and that is their success. They
are translated from earth to heaven. I see that if my facts were*

sufficiently vital and significant,—perhaps transmuted into the substance of the human mind—I should need but one book of poetry to contain them all. (111, 311)

Walden was the only such book Thoreau published during his life-time. The present volume is submitted as another, though somewhat lesser, of the same sort.

A close reading of one miniature will illustrate the quality of the writing in *Thoreau's World*. Anyone who cares for nature or litera-ture, for the American past in general or Thoreau in particular, will find "Fox Chase" (p. 146) remarkably interesting:

Suddenly, looking down the river, I saw a fox some sixty rods off, making across to the hills on my left. As the snow lay five inches deep, he made but slow progress, but it was no impedi-ment to me. So, yielding to the instinct of the chase, I tossed my head aloft and bounded away, snuffing the air like a fox-hound, and spurning the world and the Humane Society at each bound. It seemed the woods rang with the hunter's horn, and Diana and all the satyrs joined in the chase and cheered me on. Olympian and Elean youths were waving palms on the hills. In the mean-while I gained rapidly on the fox; but he showed a remarkable presence of mind, for, instead of keeping up the face of the hill, which was steep and unwooded in that part, he kept along the slope in the direction of the forest, though he lost ground by it. Notwithstanding his fright, he took no step which was not beautiful. The course on his part was a series of most graceful curves. It was a sort of leopard canter, I should say, as if he were nowise impeded by the snow, but were husbanding his strength all the while. When he doubled I wheeled and cut him off, bounding with fresh vigor, and Antaeus-like, recover-ing my strength each time I touched the snow. Having got near enough for a fair view, just as he was slipping into the wood, I gracefully yielded him the palm. He ran as though there were not a bone in his back, occasionally dropping his muzzle to the snow for a rod or two, and then tossing his head aloft when satisfied of his course. When he came to a declivity he put his fore feet together and slid down it like a cat. He trod so softly

*that you could not have heard it from any nearness, and yet
with such expression that it would not have been quite inaudible
at any distance. So, hoping this experience would prove a useful lesson to him, I returned to the village by the highway of
the river.*

The precision of detail here—setting, flight, pursuit— reflects
the careful observations of one who has kept 'Field Notes' for many
years on the woods, the streams, the wildlife of Concord township.
But the naturalist's facts are quickly transformed into poetry by language and structure. Similes at the beginning and end compare the
pursuer to a fox-hound, as he snuffs the air, and the pursued to a cat,
as it slides down a snowy declivity. A metaphor at the center turns
the fox's graceful bounds into a "leopard canter." And the whole
event is framed by the river, in opening and closing sentences. All
this, and more, the reader can see for himself. Like all poetic writing,
however, the more one brings to it the richer his reward. References
to Greek myths lift the meaning to another plane. Most readers will
see the appropriateness of alluding to Diana and Antaeus, goddess of
the chase and strong son of Earth in narrating such an incident. But
it is more important still to remember that one function of classical
mythology was to remind man—whose civilization seemed to set him
so apart—of his essential kinship with the earth and all its creatures.
In this connection it should be added that Thoreau was well acquainted with the teachings of Pythagoras, the precursor of Socrates
who, according to his biographer, "possessed the same dominion as
Orpheus over savage animals." Thoreau even playfully claimed the
same magic power when he charmed the perch with his flute, in
Walden.[3]

There are many other examples in his books and in the *Journal*
of this rapport with nature and its wildlife. The very context in which
"Fox Chase" is set in the present volume will furnish illustrations
enough. It is preceded by "Capturing an Owl" and "Taming a
Woodchuck." It is followed by the "Origin of Aesop" and several
short pieces in the manner of these Greek fables and the equally
famous Hindu ones (both classics being cited by Thoreau), which

[3]   See my book *The Magic Circle of Walden* (1968), pp. 176,
185, 153–155, citing Thoreau's use of Iamblicus, *Life of Pythagoras*.

bear out the thesis of man's kinship with the animals. None of this is specifically in the text of "Fox Chase," to be sure. But the conclud-ing phrase, "hoping this experience would prove a useful lesson to him," implies that the fabulist could have drawn a moral if he wished. And the use of echo language proves the success of this chase on a mythical level, pursuer and pursued becoming virtually identified. As it begins, the human fox-hound exclaims: "I tossed my head aloft and bounded away," cheered on by "Elean youths waving palms on the hills." As it ends, the narrator relents: "I gracefully yielded him the palm," and the fox escaped "tossing *his* head aloft." One refer-ence in this miniature seemed too recondite to go without a footnote; it reads, "Elea was the seat of a Greek school of philosophy teaching the universal unity of Being: that the All is One." "Fox Chase" is a long remove from the well-known English sport, in which the hunter is separated as far as possible from the hunted— by his hounds, his mount, and his pink-coated habit (which separates him from nature as well); even strikingly different from the rustic New England version, in which the hunter has dismounted and unfrocked himself. Both leave the hunting to the hounds, man having resigned himself to the role of spectator or being largely concerned with mastery of his horse. Thoreau's version goes behind all this to recapture the Greek ideal of man at home in the natural world. His hunter merges first with the tamed hound, then with the wild fox.

So "Fox Chase" offers a good example of the fusion of two kinds of writing. On the surface it seems like one of Thoreau's "Field Notes," at least on first reading; then by subtle stages it is lifted up into symbol and myth. As he declared in the *Journal* passage quoted a few pages above: "The most interesting and beautiful facts are so much the more poetry and that is their success. They are translated from earth to heaven." The miniatures in *Thoreau's World*, read singly or in sequence, can indeed be rich and rewarding.

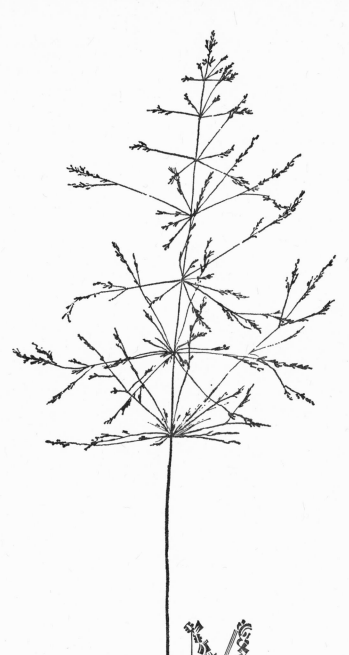

THE **M**INIATURES

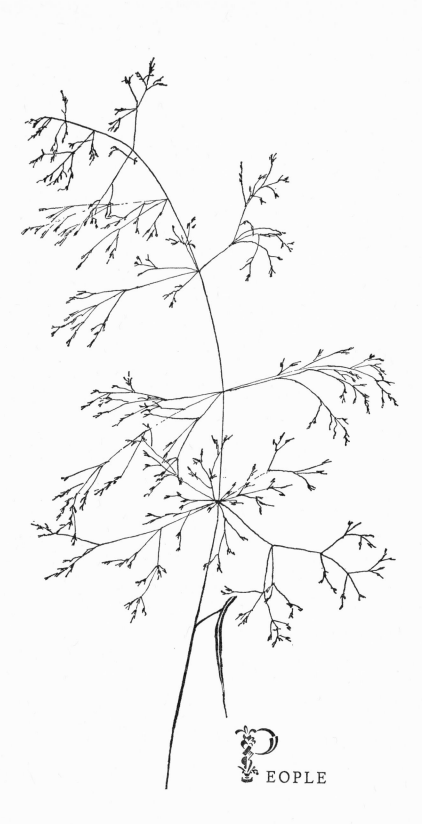

EOPLE

EMERSON AND ALCOTT *

The way to compare men is to compare their respective ideals.
The actual man is too complex to deal with. . . .

Emerson . . . is a critic, poet, philosopher, with talent not so
conspicuous, not so adequate to his task; but his field is still higher, his
task more arduous. Lives a far more intense life; seeks to realize a
divine life; his affections and intellect equally developed. Has advanced farther, and a new heaven opens to him. Love and Friendship, Religion, Poetry, the Holy are familiar to him. The life of an
Artist; more variegated, more observing, finer perception; not so
robust, elastic; practical enough in his own field; faithful, a judge
of men. There is no such general critic of men and things, no such
trustworthy and faithful man. More of the divine realized in him
than in any. A poetic critic, reserving the unqualified nouns for the
gods.

Alcott is a geometer, a visionary, the Laplace of ethics, more
intellect, less of the affections, sight beyond talents, a substratum of
practical skill and knowledge unquestionable, but overlaid and concealed by a faith in the unseen and impracticable. Seeks to realize an
entire life; a catholic observer; habitually takes in the farthest star and
nebula into his scheme. Will be the last man to be disappointed as the
ages revolve. His attitude is one of greater faith and expectation than
that of any man I know; with little to show; with undue share, for a
philosopher, of the weaknesses of humanity. The most hospitable intellect, embracing high and low. For children how much that means,
for the insane and vagabond, for the poet and scholar!

Emerson has special talents unequalled. The divine in man has
had no more easy, methodically distinct expression. His personal in-

---

* Thoreau's friendship with R. W. Emerson (1803–1882) began
soon after his graduation from Harvard in 1838. He lived for two years
as a member of Emerson's household, 1841–1843, and again for another year in 1847. This character sketch was written in the period between. The friendship with Bronson Alcott (1799–1888) ripened
during the winter of 1847 at Walden Pond.

fluence upon young persons greater than any man's. In his world every man would be a poet, Love would reign, Beauty would take place, Man and Nature would harmonize.

When Alcott's day comes, laws unsuspected by most will take effect, the system will crystallize according to them, all seals and falsehood will slough off, everything will be in its place.

1, 431-433   1845-1847

ALCOTT

Alcott spent the day with me yesterday. He spent the day before with Emerson. He observed that he had got his wine and now he had come after his venison. Such was the compliment he paid me. The question of a livelihood was troubling him. He knew of nothing which he could do for which men would pay him. He could not compete with the Irish in cradling grain. His early education had not fitted him for a clerkship. He had offered his services to the Abolition Society, to go about the country and speak for freedom as their agent, but they declined him. This is very much to their discredit; they should have been forward to secure him. Such a connection with him would confer unexpected dignity on their enterprise. But they cannot tolerate a man who stands by a head above them. They are as bad—Garrison and Phillips,* etc.—as the overseers and faculty of Harvard College. They require a man who will train well *under* them. Consequently they have not in their employ any but small men,—trainers. . . .

I have devoted most of my day to Mr. Alcott. He is broad and genial, but indefinite; some would say feeble; forever feeling vainly in his speech and touching nothing. But this is a very negative account of him, for he thus suggests far more than the sharp and definite practical mind. The feelers of his thought diverge,—such is the breadth of their grasp,—not converge; and in his society almost alone I can

* William Lloyd Garrison (1805–1879) and Wendell Phillips (1811–1884) were leading Abolitionists, noted for their uncompromising radicalism and violence.

express at my leisure, with more or less success, my vaguest but most cherished fancy or thought. There are never any obstacles in the way of our meeting. He has no creed. He is not pledged to any institution. The sanest man I ever knew; the fewest crotchets, after all, has he.

It has occurred to me, while I am thinking with pleasure of our day's intercourse, "Why should I not think aloud to you?" Having each some shingles of thought well dried, we walk and whittle them, trying our knives, and admiring the clear yellowish grain of the pump-kin pine. We wade so gently and reverently, or we pull together so smoothly, that the fishes of thought are not scared from the stream, but come and go grandly, like yonder clouds that float peacefully through the western sky. When we walk it seems as if the heavens—whose mother-o'-pearl and rainbow tints come and go, form and dis-solve—and the earth had met together, and righteousness and peace had kissed each other. I have an ally against the arch-enemy. A blue-robed man dwells under the blue concave. The blue sky is a distant reflection of the azure serenity that looks out from under a human brow. We walk together like the most innocent children, going after wild pinks with case-knives. Most with whom I endeavor to talk soon fetch up against some institution or particular way of viewing things, theirs not being a universal view. They will continually bring their own roofs or—what is not much better—their own narrow skylights between us and the sky, when it is the unobstructed heavens I would view.*

v, 130-131, 365   9 May, 9 Aug. 1853

*   About one fourth of this sketch was used in *Walden*, pp. 296–297 (Ch. 14, "Winter Visitors"), the meeting on 9 May 1853 being treated as if it had occurred in the winter of 1847.

MARY MOODY EMERSON*

Just spent a couple of hours (eight to ten) with Miss Mary Emerson at Holbrook's. The wittiest and most vivacious woman that I know, certainly that woman among my acquaintance whom it is most profitable to meet, the least frivolous, who will most surely provoke to good conversation and the expression of what is in you. She is singular, among women at least, in being really and perseveringly interested to know what thinkers think. She relates herself surely to the intellectual where she goes. It is perhaps her greatest praise and peculiarity that she, more surely than any other woman, gives her companion occasion to utter his best thought. In spite of her own biases, she can entertain a large thought with hospitality, and is not prevented by any intellectuality in it, as women commonly are. In short, she is a genius, as woman seldom is, reminding you less often of her sex than any woman whom I know. In that sense she is capable of a masculine appreciation of poetry and philosophy. I never talked with any other woman who I thought accompanied me so far in describing a poetic experience. Miss Fuller is the only woman I think of in this connection, and of her rather from her fame than from any knowledge of her. Miss Emerson expressed to-night a singular want of respect for her own sex, saying that they were frivolous almost without exception, that woman was the weaker vessel, etc.; that into whatever family she might go, she depended more upon the "clown" for society than upon the lady of the house. Men are more likely to have opinions of their own.

III, 113-114   13 Nov. 1851

---

*   R. W. Emerson's eccentric but learned aunt, one of the most important mentors of his youth. Thoreau enjoyed a notable friendship with her.

   Margaret Fuller (1810–1850), mentioned near the end, was a well-known feminist and Transcendental author. Thoreau's relations with her were never cordial.

CHANNING AS LECTURER

Heard C.* lecture to-night. It was a bushel of nuts. Perhaps the most original lecture I ever heard. Ever so unexpected, not to be foretold, and so sententious that you could not look at him and take his thought at the same time. You had to give your undivided attention to the thoughts, for you were not assisted by set phrases or modes of speech intervening. There was no sloping up or down to or from his points. It was all genius, no talent. It required more close attention, more abstraction from surrounding circumstances, than any lecture I have heard. For, well as I know C., he more than any man disappoints my expectation. When I see him in the desk, hear him, I cannot realize that I ever saw him before. He will be strange, unexpected, to his best acquaintance. I cannot associate the lecturer with the companion of my walks. It was from so original and peculiar a point of view, yet just to himself in the main, that I doubt if three in the audience apprehended a tithe that he said. It was so hard to hear that doubtless few made the exertion. A thick succession of mountain passes and no intermediate slopes and plains. Other lectures, even the best, in which so much space is given to the elaborate development of a few ideas, seemed somewhat meagre in comparison. Yet it would be how much more glorious if talent were added to genius, if there [were] a just arrangement and development of the thoughts, and each step were not a leap, but he ran a space to take a yet higher leap!

Most of the spectators sat in front of the performer, but here was one who, by accident, sat all the while on one side, and his report was peculiar and startling. . . .

Channing's lecture was full of wise, acute, and witty observations, yet most of the audience did not know but it was mere incoherent and reckless verbiage and nonsense. I lose my respect for people who do not know what is good and true. I know full well that readers and hearers, with the fewest exceptions, ask me for my second best.

III, 249-250   29-30 Jan. 1852

* William Ellery Channing (1818–1901), Transcendental poet, one of Thoreau's closest friends and a constant walking companion.

UNCLE CHARLES*

Charles grew up to be a remarkably eccentric man. He was of large frame, athletic, and celebrated for his feats of strength. [He could jump over a yoke of oxen.] His lungs were proportionately strong. There was a man who heard him named once, and asked if it was the same Charles Dunbar whom he remembered when he was a little boy walking on the coast of Maine. A man came down to the shore [he recalled] and hailed a vessel that was sailing by. He should never forget that man's name. . . .

E. Hosmer says that a man told him that he had seen my uncle Charles take a twelve-foot ladder, set it up straight, and then run up and down the other side, kicking it from behind him as he went down. . . .

People are talking about my Uncle Charles. Minott tells how he heard Tilly Brown once asking him to show him a peculiar (inside?) lock in wrestling. "Now, don't hurt me, don't throw me hard." He struck his antagonist inside his knees with his feet, and so deprived him of his legs. Hosmer remembers his tricks in the barroom, shuffling cards, etc. He could do anything with cards, yet he did not gamble. He would toss up his hat, twirling it over and over, and catch it on his head invariably. Once wanted to live at Hosmer's, but the latter was afraid of him. "Can't we study up something?" he asked. He asked him into the house and brought out apples and cider, and Charles talked. "You!" said he, "I burst the bully of Lowell" (or Haverhill?). He wanted to wrestle; would not be put off. "Well, we won't wrestle in the house." So they went out to the yard, and a crowd got round. "Come spread some straw here," said C. "I don't want to hurt him." He threw him at once. They tried again. He told them to spread more straw and he "burst" him.

---

*   Charles Dunbar was Thoreau's uncle on the maternal side. His death in 1856 at the age of seventy-six triggered a number of anecdotes, including the long one printed here. It is prefaced by two others from the *Journal* of 1850 and 1859 to round out the portrait.

He had a strong head and never got drunk; would drink gin sometimes, but not to excess. Did not use tobacco, except snuff out of another's box sometimes. Was very neat in his person. Was not profane, though vulgar.

Uncle Charles used to say that he hadn't a single tooth in his head. The fact was they were all double, and I have heard that he lost about all of them by the time he was twenty-one. Ever since I knew him he could swallow his nose.

    VIII, 245-246; II, 65;   13 Apr. 1856; Sept. 1850;
    XII, 38   7 Mar. 1859

REFORMERS

Here have been three ultra-reformers, lecturers on Slavery, Temperance, the Church, etc., in and about our house and Mrs. Brooks's* the last three or four days.—A. D. Foss, once a Baptist minister in Hopkinton, N. H.; Loring Moody, a sort of travelling pattern-working chaplain; and H. C. Wright, who shocks all the old women with his infidel writings. Though Foss was a stranger to the others, you would have thought them old and familiar cronies. (They happened here together by accident.) They addressed each other constantly by their Christian names, and rubbed you continually with the greasy cheeks of their kindness. They would not keep their distance, but cuddle up and lie spoon-fashion with you, no matter how hot the weather nor how narrow the bed . . . I was awfully pestered with [Foss's] benignity; feared I should get greased all over with it past restoration; tried to keep some starch in my clothes. He wrote a book called "A Kiss for a Blow," and he behaved as if there were no alternative between these, or as if I had given him a blow. I would have preferred the blow, but he was bent on giving me the kiss, when there was neither quarrel nor agreement between us. I wanted that he

---

    * Mary Merrick Brooks, a friend of the Thoreau family and an ardent member of the Anti-Slavery Society. The three reformers, mentioned following, have not been further identified.

should straighten his back, smooth out those ogling wrinkles of benignity about his eyes, and, with a healthy reserve, pronounce something in a downright manner. It was difficult to keep clear of his slimy
benignity, with which he sought to cover you before he swallowed you
and took you fairly into his bowels. It would have been far worse than
the fate of Jonah. I do not wish to get any nearer to a man's bowels
than usual. They lick you as a cow her calf. They would fain wrap
you about with their bowels. —— addressed me as "Henry" within
one minute from the time I first laid eyes on him, and when I spoke,
he said with drawling, sultry sympathy, "Henry, I know all you
would say; I understand you perfectly; you need not explain anything to me;" and to another, "I am going to dive into Henry's inmost
depths." I said, "I trust you will not strike your head against the bottom." He could tell in a dark room, with his eyes blinded and in perfect stillness, if there was one there whom he loved. One of the most
attractive things about the flowers is their beautiful reserve. The
truly beautiful and noble puts its lover, as it were, at an infinite distance, while it attracts him more strongly than ever. I do not like the
men who come so near me with their bowels. It is the most disagreeable kind of snare to be caught in. Men's bowels are far more slimy
than their brains. They must be ascetics indeed who approach you by
this side. What a relief to have heard the ring of one healthy reserved
tone! With such a forgiving disposition, as if he were all the while
forgiving you for existing. Considering our condition or *habit* of soul,
—maybe corpulent and asthmatic,—maybe dying of atrophy, with
all our bones sticking out,—is it kindness to embrace a man? They
lay their sweaty hand on your shoulder, or your knee, to magnetize
you.

v, 263-265   17 June 1853

YOUNG WOMEN AT PARTIES

In the evening went to a party. It is a bad place to go to,—
thirty or forty persons, mostly young women, in a small room, warm

and noisy. Was introduced to two young women. The first one was as lively and loquacious as a chickadee; had been accustomed to the society of watering-places, and therefore could get no refreshment out of such a dry fellow as I. The other was said to be pretty-looking, but I rarely look people in their faces, and, moreover, I could not hear what she said, there was such a clacking,—could only see the motion of her lips when I looked that way. I could imagine better places for conversation, where there should be a certain degree of silence sur-rounding you, and less than forty talking at once. Why, this after-noon, even, I did better. There was old Mr. Joseph Hosmer and I ate our luncheon of cracker and cheese together in the woods. I heard all he said, though it was not much, to be sure, and he could hear me. And then he talked out of such a glorious repose, taking a leisurely bite at the cracker and cheese between his words; and so some of him was communicated to me, and some of me to him, I trust.

These parties, I think, are a part of the machinery of modern society, that young people may be brought together to form marriage connections.

III, 115   14 Nov. 1851

BATHERS

Boys are bathing at Hubbard's Bend, playing with a boat (I at the willows). The color of their bodies in the sun at a distance is pleas-ing, the not often seen flesh-color. I hear the sound of their sport borne over the water. As yet we have not man in nature. What a singular fact for an angel visitant to this earth to carry back in his note-book, that men were forbidden to expose their bodies under the severest penalties! A pale pink, which the sun would soon tan. White men! There are no white men to contrast with the red and the black; they are of such colors as the weaver gives them. I wonder that the dog knows his master when he goes in to bathe and does not stay by his clothes.

IV, 92   12 June 1852

KNOWING YOUR NEIGHBOR IN THE DARK

Coming home last night in the twilight, I recognized a neighbor a dozen rods off by his walk or carriage, though it was so dark that I could not see a single feature of his person. Indeed, his person was all covered up excepting his face and hands, and I could not possibly have distinguished these at this distance from another man's. Nor was it owing to any peculiarity in his dress, for I should have known him though he had had on a perfectly new suit. It was because the man within the clothes moved them in a peculiar manner that I knew him thus at once at a distance and in the twilight. He made a certain figure in any clothes he might wear, and moved in it in a peculiar manner. Indeed, we have a very intimate knowledge of one another; we see through thick and thin; spirit meets spirit. A man hangs out innumerable signs by which we may know him. So, last summer, I knew another neighbor half a mile off up the river, though I did not see him, by the manner in which the breath from his lungs and mouth, *i. e.* his voice, made the air strike my ear. In that manner he communicated himself to all his acquaintance within a diameter of one mile (if it were all up and down the river). So I remember to have been sure once in a very dark night who was preceding me on the sidewalk,—though I could not see him,—by the sound of his tread. I was surprised to find that I knew it.

And to-day, seeing a peculiar very long track of a man in the snow, who has been along up the river this morning, I guessed that it was George Melvin, because it was accompanied by a hound's track. There was a thin snow on the ice, and I observed that he not only furrowed the snow for a foot before he completed his step, but that the (toe) of his track was always indefinite, as if his boot had been worn out and prolonged at the toe. I noticed that I and my companion made a clear and distinct track at the toe, but when I experimented, and tried to make a track like this by not lifting my feet but gliding and partly scuffing along, I found myself walking just like Melvin, and that perfectly convinced me that it was he.

We have no occasion to wonder at the instinct of a dog. In these last two instances I surpassed the instinct of the dog.

XIII, 127-128   5 Feb. 1860

MINOTT, THE POETICAL FARMER

Minott * was telling me to-day that he used to know a man in Lincoln who had no floor to his barn, but waited till the ground froze, then swept it clean in his barn and threshed his grain on it. He also used to see men threshing their buckwheat in the field where it grew, having just taken off the surface down to a hardpan.

Minott used the word "gavel" to describe a parcel of stalks cast on the ground to dry. His are good old English words, and I am always sure to find them in the dictionary, though I never heard them before in my life.

I was admiring his corn-stalks disposed about the barn to dry, over or astride the braces and the timbers of such a fresh, clean, and handsome green, retaining their strength and nutritive properties so, unlike the gross and careless husbandry of speculating, money-making farmers, who suffer their stalks to remain out till they are dry and dingy and black as chips.

Minott is, perhaps, the most poetical farmer—who most realizes to me the poetry of the farmer's life—that I know. He does nothing with haste and drudgery, but as if he loved it. He makes the most of his labor, and takes infinite satisfaction in every part of it. He is not looking forward to the sale of his crops or any pecuniary profit, but he is paid by the constant satisfaction which his labor yields him. He has not too much land to trouble him,—too much work to do,—no hired man nor boy,—but simply to amuse himself and live. He cares not so much to raise a large crop as to do his work well. He knows every pin and nail in his barn. If another linter is to be floored, he lets no hired

---

*   George Minott, Thoreau's close friend, who fulfilled Emerson's ideal of "man on the farm" as opposed to a mere farmer (see "The American Scholar").

man rob him of that amusement, but he goes slowly to the woods and, at his leisure, selects a pitch pine tree, cuts it, and hauls it or gets it hauled to the mill; and so he knows the history of his barn floor.

Farming is an amusement which has lasted him longer than gun-ning or fishing. He is never in a hurry to get his garden planted and yet [it] is always planted soon enough, and none in the town is kept so beautifully clean.

He always prophesies a failure of the crops, and yet is satisfied with what he gets. His barn floor is fastened down with oak pins, and he prefers them to iron spikes, which he says will rust and give way. He handles and amuses himself with every ear of his corn crop as much as a child with its playthings, and so his small crop goes a great way. He might well cry if it were carried to market. The seed of weeds is no longer in his soil.

He loves to walk in a swamp in windy weather and hear the wind groan through the pines. He keeps a cat in his barn to catch the mice. He indulges in no luxury of food or dress or furniture, yet he is not penurious but merely simple. If his sister dies before him, he may have to go to the almshouse in his old age; yet he is not poor, for he does not want riches. He gets out of each manipulation in the farmers' operations a fund of entertainment which the speculating drudge hardly knows. With never-failing rheumatism and trembling hands, he seems yet to enjoy a perennial health. Though he never reads a book,—since he has finished the "Naval Monument,"—he speaks the best of English.

Minott adorns whatever part of nature he touches; whichever way he walks he transfigures the earth for me. If a common man speaks of Walden Pond to me, I see only a shallow, dull-colored body of water without reflections or peculiar color, but if Minott speaks of it, I see the green water and reflected hills at once, for he *has been* there. I hear the rustle of the leaves from woods which he goes through.

III, 41-43; X, 168   4 Oct. 1851; 6 Nov. 1857

FARMER HUBBARD, THE NATURAL MAN

I see the old pale-faced farmer out again on his sled now for the five-thousandth time,—Cyrus Hubbard, a man of a certain New England probity and worth, immortal and natural, like a natural product, like the sweetness of a nut, like the toughness of hickory. He, too, is a redeemer for me. How superior actually to the faith he professes! He is not an office-seeker. What an institution, what a revelation is a man! We are wont foolishly to think that the creed which a man professes is more significant than the fact he is. It matters not how hard the conditions seemed, how mean the world, for a man is a prevalent force and a new law himself. He is a system whose law is to be observed. The old farmer condescends to countenance still this nature and order of things. It is a great encouragement that an honest man makes this world his abode. He rides on the sled drawn by oxen, world-wise, yet comparatively so young, as if they had seen scores of winters. The farmer spoke to me, I can swear, clean, cold, moderate as the snow. He does not melt the snow where he treads. Yet what a faint impression that encounter may make on me after all! Moderate, natural, true, as if he were made of earth, stone, wood, snow. I thus meet in this universe kindred of mine, composed of these elements. I see men like frogs; their peeping I partially understand.

IX, 144-145   11 Dec. 1856

NATURE'S PENSIONER

I had gone but little way on the old Carlisle road when I saw Brooks Clark, who is now about eighty and bent like a bow, hastening along the road, bare-footed, as usual, with an axe in his hand; was in haste perhaps on account of the cold wind on his bare feet. It is he who took the *Centinel* so long. When he got up to me, I saw that besides the axe in one hand, he had his shoes in the other, filled with knurly apples and a dead robin. He stopped and talked with me a few moments; said that we had had a noble autumn and might now expect some cold weather. I asked if he had found the robin dead. No, he said, he found it with its wing broken and killed it. He also added that he had found some apples in the woods, and as he hadn't anything to carry them in, he put 'em in his shoes. They were queer-looking trays to carry fruit in. How many he got in along toward the toes, I don't know. I noticed, too, that his pockets were stuffed with them. His old tattered frock coat was hanging in strips about the skirts, as were his pantaloons about his naked feet. He appeared to have been out on a scout this gusty afternoon, to see what he could find, as the youngest boy might. It pleased me to see this cheery old man, with such a feeble hold on life, bent almost double, thus enjoying the evening of his days. Far be it from me to call it avarice or penury, this childlike delight in finding something in the woods or fields and carrying it home in the October evening, as a trophy to be added to his winter's store. Oh, no; he was happy to be Nature's pensioner still, and bird-like to pick up his living. Better his robin than your turkey, his shoes full of apples than your barrels full; they will be sweeter and suggest a better tale. He can afford to tell how he got them, and we to listen. There is an old wife, too, at home, to share them and hear how they were obtained. Like an old squirrel shuffling to his hole with a nut. Far less pleasing to me the loaded wain, more suggestive of avarice and of spiritual penury.

This old man's cheeriness was worth a thousand of the church's sacraments and *memento mori*'s. It was better than a prayerful mood. It proves to me old age as tolerable, as happy, as infancy. I was glad of an occasion to suspect that this afternoon he had not been at "work" but living somewhat after my own fashion (though he did not explain the axe),—had been out to see what nature had for him, and now was hastening home to a burrow he knew, where he could warm his old feet. If he had been a young man, he would probably have thrown away his apples and put on his shoes when he saw me coming, for shame. But old age is manlier; it has learned to live, makes fewer apologies, like infancy. This seems a very manly man. I have known him within a few years building [a] stone wall by himself, barefooted. I keep along the old Carlisle road. The leaves having mostly fallen, the country now seems deserted, and you feel further from home and more lonely.

x, 109-110   19 Oct. 1857

UP-COUNTRY MEN

The retirement in which Green has lived for nearly eighty years in Carlisle * is a retirement very different from and much greater than that in which the pioneer dwells at the West; for the latter dwells within sound of the surf of those billows of migration which are breaking on the shores around him, or near him, of the West, but those billows have long since swept over the spot which Green inhabits, and left him in the calm sea. There is somewhat exceedingly pathetic to think of in such a life as he must have lived,—with no more to redeem it,—such a life as an average Carlisle man may be supposed to live drawn out to eighty years. And he has died, perchance, and there is nothing but the mark of his cider-mill left. Here was the cider-mill, and there the orchard, and there the hog-pasture; and so men lived, and ate, and drank, and passed away,—like vermin. Their long life was mere duration. As respectable is the life of the woodchucks, which perpetuate their race in the orchard still. That is the life of these *select-men* (!) spun out. They will be forgotten in a few years, even by such as themselves, like vermin. They will be known only like Kibbe, who is said to have been a large man who weighed two hundred and fifty, who had five or six heavy daughters who rode to Concord meeting-house on horseback, taking turns,—they were so heavy that only one could ride at once. What, then, would redeem such a life? We only know that they ate, and drank, and built barns, and died and were buried, and still, perchance, their tombstones cumber the ground. But if I could know that there was ever entertained over their cellar-hole some divine thought, which came as a messenger of the gods, that he who resided here acted once in his life from a noble impulse, rising superior to his grovelling and penurious life, if only a single

---

* A neighboring town, which to Thoreau was the epitome of a benighted, run-down, and deservedly abandoned place.

verse of poetry or of poetic prose had ever been written or spoken or conceived here beyond a doubt, I should not think it in vain that man had lived here. It would to some extent be true then that God had lived here. That all his life he lived only as a farmer—as the most valuable stock only on a farm—and in no moments as a man!

III, 9-11   21 Sept. 1851

VETERAN OF WATERLOO*

I had one neighbor within half a mile for a short time when I first went to the woods, Hugh Quoil, an Irishman who had been a soldier at Waterloo, Colonel Quoil, as he was called,—I believe that he had killed a colonel and ridden off his horse,—who lived from hand—sometimes to mouth,—though it was commonly a glass of rum that the hand carried. He and his wife awaited their fate together in an old ruin in Walden woods. What life he got—or what means of death—he got by ditching.

I never was much acquainted with Hugh Quoil, though sometimes I met him in the path, and now do believe that a solid shank-bone, and skull which no longer aches, lie somewhere, and can still be produced, which once with garment of flesh and broadcloth were called and hired to do work as Hugh Quoil. He was a man of manners and gentlemanlike, as one who had seen the world, and was capable of more civil speech than you could well attend to. At a distance he had seemingly a ruddy face as of biting January, but nearer at hand it was bright carmine. It would have burnt your finger to touch his cheek. He wore a straight-bodied snuff-colored coat which had long been familiar with him, and carried a turf-knife in his hand— instead of a sword. He had fought on the English side before, but he

---

* About one fourth of this was used in *Walden*, pp. 288–289. Most of it was taken from the last paragraph, with one interesting addition: "His pipe lay broken on the hearth, instead of a bowl broken at the fountain. The last could never have been the symbol of his death, for he confessed to me that, though he had heard of Brister's Spring, he had never seen it."

fought on the Napoleon side now. Napoleon went to St. Helena; Hugh Quoil came to Walden Pond. I heard that he used to tell travellers who inquired about myself that [Emerson?] and Thoreau owned the *farm* together, but Thoreau lived on the *place* and carried it on.

He was thirstier than I, and drank more, probably, but not out of the pond. That was never the lower for him. Perhaps I ate more than he. The last time I met him, the only time I spoke with him, was at the foot of the hill on the highway as I was crossing to the spring one summer afternoon, the pond water being too warm for me. I was crossing the road with a pail in my hand, when Quoil came down the hill, wearing his snuff-colored coat, as if it were winter, and shaking with delirium tremens. I hailed him and told him that my errand was to get water at a spring close by, only at the foot of the hill over the fence. He answered, with stuttering and parched lips, bloodshot eye, and staggering gesture, he'd like to see it. "Follow me there, then." But I had got my pail full and back before he scaled the fence. And he, drawing his coat about him, to warm him, or to cool him, answered in delirium-tremens, hydrophobia dialect, which is not easy to be written here, he'd heard of it, but had never seen it; and so shivered his way along to town,—to liquor and to oblivion.

On Sundays, brother Irishmen and others, who had gone far astray from steady habits and the village, crossed my bean-field with empty jugs toward Quoil's. But what for? Did they sell rum there? I asked. "Respectable people they," "Know no harm of them," "Never heard that they drank too much," was the answer of all wayfarers. They went by sober, stealthy, silent, skulking (no harm to get elm bark Sundays); returned loquacious, sociable, having long intended to call on you.

At length one afternoon Hugh Quoil, feeling better, perchance, with snuff-colored coat, as usual, paced solitary and soldier-like, thinking [of] Waterloo, along the woodland road to the foot of the hill by the spring; and there the Fates met him, and threw him down in his snuff-colored coat on the gravel, and got ready to cut his thread; but not till travellers passed, who would raise him up, get him perpendicular, then settle, settle quick; but legs, what are they? "Lay me down," says Hugh hoarsely. "House locked up—key—in pocket—wife in town." And the Fates cut, and there he lay by the wayside, five feet ten, and looking taller than in life.

He has gone away; his house here "all tore to pieces." What kind of fighting or ditching work he finds to do now, how it fares with him, whether his thirst is quenched, whether there is still some semblance of that carmine cheek, struggles still with some liquid demon— perchance on more equal terms—till he swallow him completely, I cannot by any means learn. What his salutation is now, what his January-morning face, what he thinks of Waterloo, what start he has gained or lost, what work still for the ditcher and forester and soldier now, there is no evidence. He was here, the likes of him, for a season, standing light in his shoes like a faded gentleman, with gesture almost learned in drawing-rooms; wore clothes, hat, shoes, cut ditches, felled wood, did farm work for various people, kindled fires, worked enough, ate enough, drank too much. He was one of those unnamed, countless sects of philosophers who founded no school.

Now that he was gone, and his wife was gone too,—for she could not support the solitude,—before it was too late and the house was torn down, I went over to make a call. Now that Irishmen with jugs avoided the old house, I visited it,—an "unlucky castle now," said they. There lay his old clothes curled up by habit, as if it were himself, upon his raised plank bed. His pipe lay broken on the hearth; and scattered about were soiled cards—king of diamonds, hearts, spades—on the floor. One black chicken, which they could not catch, still went to roost in the next apartment, stepping silent over the floor, frightened by the sound of its own wings, black as night and as silent, too, not even croaking; awaiting Reynard, its god actually dead. There was the dim outline of a garden which had been planted, but had never received its first hoeing, now overrun with weeds, with burs and cockles, which stick to your clothes; as if in the spring he had contemplated a harvest of corn and beans before that strange trembling of the limbs overtook him. Skin of woodchuck fresh-stretched, never to be cured, met once in bean-field by the Waterloo man with uplifted hoe; no cap, no mittens wanted. Pipe on hearth no more to be lighted, best buried with him.

No thirst for glory, only for strong drink.

I, 414-415   1845-1847

A RETIRED SEA CAPTAIN

Talked with Webster's * nearest neighbor, Captain Hewit, whose small farm he surrounds and endeavors in vain to buy. A fair specimen of a retired Yankee sea-captain turned farmer. Proud of the quantity of carrots he had raised on a small patch. It was better husbandry than Webster's. . . . These men are not so remarkable for anything as the quality of hardness. The very fixedness and rigidity of their jaws and necks express a sort of adamantine hardness. This is what they have learned by contact with the elements. The man who does not grow rigid with years and experience! Where is he? What avails it to grow hard merely? The harder you are, the more brittle really, like the bones of the old. How much rarer and better to grow mellow! A sort of stone fruit the man bears commonly; a bare stone it is, without any sweet and mellow pericarp around it. It is like the peach which has dried to the stone as the season advanced; it is dwindled to a dry stone with its almond. In presence of one of these hard men I think: "How brittle! How easily you would crack! What a poor and lame conclusion!" I can think of nothing but a stone in his head. Truly genial men do not grow [hard]. It is the result of despair, this attitude of resistance. They behave like men already driven to the wall. Notwithstanding that the speaker trembles with infirmity while he speaks,—his hand on the spade,—it is such a trembling as betrays a stony nature. His hand trembles so that the full glass of cider which he prizes to a drop will have lost half its contents before it reaches his lips, as if a tempest had arisen in it. Hopelessly hard. But there is another view of him. He is somebody. He has an opinion to express, if you will wait to hear him. A certain manliness and refreshing resistance is in him. He generally makes Webster a call, but Webster does not want to see you more than twenty minutes. It does not take him long to say all he has got to say. He had not seen him to speak to him since he had come home this time. He had sent

---

*   Daniel Webster, statesman (1782–1852), spent the last years of his life at Marshfield, Mass., south of Boston.

him over a couple of fine cod the night before. Such a man as Hewit
sees not finely but coarsely.

11, 361·362   30 July 1851

THE TOWN DRUNKARD

Bill Wheeler had two clumps for feet and progressed slowly, by
short steps, having frozen his feet once, as I understood. Him I have
been sure to meet once in five years, progressing into the town on his
stubs, holding the middle of the road as if he drove an invisible herd
before him, especially on a military day,—out of what confines, whose
hired man having been, I never knew,—in what remote barn having quartered all these years. He seemed to belong to a different caste
from other men, and reminded me of both the Indian Pariah and
martyr. I understood that somebody was found to give him his drink
for the few chores he could do. His meat was never referred to, he
had so sublimed his life. One day since this, not long ago, I saw in
my walk a kind of shelter such as woodmen might use, in the woods
by the Great Meadows, made of meadow-hay cast over a rude frame.
Thrusting my head in at a hole, as I am wont to do in such cases, I
found Bill Wheeler there curled up asleep on the hay, who, being
suddenly wakened from a sound sleep, rubbed his eyes and inquired
if I found any game, thinking I was sporting. I came away reflecting
much on that man's life,—how he communicated with none; how
now, perchance, he did chores for none; how low he lived, perhaps
from a deep principle, that he might be some mighty philosopher,
greater than Socrates or Diogenes, simplifying life, returning to nature, having turned his back on towns; how many things he had put
off,—luxuries, comforts, human society, even his feet,—wrestling
with his thoughts. I felt even as Diogenes when he saw the boy drinking out of his hands, and threw away his cup. Here was one who went
alone, did no work, and had no relatives that I knew of, was not ambitious that I could see, did not depend on the good opinion of men.
Must he not see things with an impartial eye, disinterested, as a toad
observes the gardener? Perchance here is one of a sect of philos-

ophers, the only one, so simple, so abstracted in thought and life from his contemporaries, that his wisdom is indeed foolishness to them. Who knows but in his solitary meadow-hay bunk he indulges, in thought, only in triumphant satires on men? Who knows but here is a superiority to literature and such things, unexpressed and inexpressible? Who has resolved to humble and mortify himself as never man was humbled and mortified. Whose very vividness of perception, clear knowledge, and insight have made him dumb, leaving no common consciousness and ground of parlance with his kind,—or, rather, his unlike kindred! Whose news plainly is not my news nor yours. I was not sure for a moment but here was a philosopher who had left far behind him the philosophers of Greece and India, and I envied him his advantageous point of view. I was not to be deceived by a few stupid words, of course, and apparent besottedness. It was his position and career that I contemplated.

But to return to Bill. I would have liked to know what view he took on life. A month or two after this, as I heard, he was found dead among the brush over back of the hill,—so far decomposed that his coffin was carried to his body and it was put into it with pitchforks. I have my misgivings still that he may have died a Brahmin's death, dwelling at the roots of trees at last, and been absorbed into the spirit of Brahm; though I have since been assured that he suffered from disappointed love,—was what is called love-cracked,—than which can there be any nobler suffering, any fairer death, for a human creature? —that that made him to drink, froze his feet, and did all the rest for him. Why have not the world the benefit of his long trial?

III, 195-197 16 Jan. 1852

HE STONE–MASON

Every artisan learns positively something by his trade. Each craft is familiar with a few simple, well-known, well-established facts, not requiring any genius to discover, but mere use and familiarity. You may go by the man at his work in the street every day of your life, and though he is there before you, carrying into practice certain essential information, you shall never be the wiser. Each trade is in fact a craft, a cunning, a covering an ability; and its methods are the result of a long experience. There sits a stone-mason, splitting Westford granite for fence-posts. Egypt has perchance taught New England something in this matter. His hammer, his chisels, his wedges, his shims or half-rounds, his iron spoon,—I suspect that these tools are hoary with age as with granite dust. He learns as easily where the best granite comes from as he learns how to erect that screen to keep off the sun. He knows that he can drill faster into a large stone than a small one, because there is less jar and yielding. He deals in stone as the carpenter in lumber. In many of his operations only the materials are different. His work is slow and expensive. Nature is here hard to be overcome. He wears up one or two drills in splitting a single stone. He must sharpen his tools oftener than the carpenter. He fights with granite. He knows the temper of the rocks. He grows stony himself. His tread is ponderous and steady like the fall of a rock. And yet by patience and art he splits a stone as surely as the carpenter or wood-cutter a log. So much time and perseverance will accomplish. One would say that mankind had much less moral than physical energy, that any day you see men following the trade of splitting rocks, who yet shrink from undertaking apparently less arduous moral labors, the solving of moral problems. See how surely he proceeds. He does not hesitate to drill a dozen holes, each one the labor of a day or two for a savage; he carefully takes out the dust with his iron spoon; he inserts his wedges, one in each hole, and protects the sides of the holes and gives resistance to his wedges by thin pieces of half-round iron (or shims); he marks the red line which he has drawn, with his chisel, carefully cutting it straight; and then how carefully he drives each wedge in succession, fearful lest he should not have a good split!

The habit of looking at men in the gross makes their lives have less of human interest for us. But though there are crowds of laborers before us, yet each one leads his little epic life each day. There is the stone-mason, who, methought, was simply a stony man that hammered stone from breakfast to dinner, and dinner to supper, and then went to his slumbers. But he, I find, is even a man like myself, for he feels the heat of the sun and has raised some boards on a frame to protect him. And now, at mid-forenoon, I see his wife and child have come and brought him drink and meat for his lunch and to assuage the stoniness of his labor, and sit to chat with him.

There are many rocks lying there for him to split from end to end, and he will surely do it. This only at the command of luxury, since stone posts are preferred to wood. But how many moral blocks are lying there in every man's yard, which he surely will not split nor earnestly endeavor to split. There lie the blocks which will surely get split, but here lie the blocks which will surely not get split. Do we say it is too hard for human faculties? But does not the mason dull a basketfull of steel chisels in a day, and yet, by sharpening them again and tempering them aright, succeed? Moral effort! Difficulty to be overcome!!! Why, men work in stone, and sharpen their drills when they go home to dinner!

II, 490-493   11 Sept. 1851

HE GIANT

Saw a teamster coming up the Boston road this afternoon, sitting on his load, which was bags of corn or salt, apparently, behind two horses and beating his hands for warmth. He finally got off and walked behind, to make his blood circulate faster, and I saw that he was a large man. But when I came near him, I found that he was a monstrous man and dwarfed all whom he stood by, so that I did not know whether he was large or they were small. Yet, though he stood so high, he stooped considerably, more than anybody I think of, and he wore a flat glazed cap to conceal his height, and when he got into the village he sat down on his bags again. I heard him remark to a boy that it was a cold day, and it was; but I wondered that he should feel the cold so sensibly, for I thought it must take a long time to cool so large a body. . . .

I felt a little wonder the other night that the large man went so as a matter of course with the human race, that he did not suspect that he belonged to some other genus, that he did not go off with some menagerie, with the elephant or the camelopard. You do not have to go far, to grow much, to get beyond the sphere of humanity. Why

he should exist as a sort of attaché to the human race. Where was the
rest of his family? He was, as it were, astray. There is something
comically pathetic about it. What made him think that he belonged
to the human race? Did he gradually grow up to that faith? His was a
vegetable growth. His face lacked expression. When his large features were done, his face still bulged out and grew this way and that,
just like a mammoth squash which magnifies all its warts. Great growth
of a body suggests the vegetable. He was pumpkin pine, sycamore.
The extra growth was squash and pumpkin all. It was more flesh than
his soul could animate. There is something monstrous even about his
thoughts.

III, 202, 205-206   17, 19 Jan. 1852

INDIANS

The names of those who bought these fields of the red men,
the wild men of the woods, are Buttrick, Davis, Barrett, Bulkley,
etc., etc. . . . Here and there still you will find a man with Indian
blood in his veins, an eccentric farmer descended from an Indian chief;
or you will see a solitary pure-blooded Indian, looking as wild as ever
among the pines, one of the last of the Massachusetts tribes, stepping
into a railroad car with his gun.

Still here and there an Indian squaw with her dog, her only
companion, lives in some lone house, insulted by school-children,
making baskets and picking berries her employment. You will meet
her on the highway, with few children or none, with melancholy face,
history, destiny; stepping after her race; who had stayed to tuck them
up in their long sleep. For whom berries condescend to grow. I have
not seen one on the Musketaquid for many a year, and some who came
up in their canoes and camped on its banks a dozen years ago had to
ask me where it came from. A lone Indian woman without children,
accompanied by her dog, wearing the shroud of her race, performing
the last offices for her departed race. Not yet absorbed into the elements again; a daughter of the soil; one of the nobility of the land.

The white man an imported weed,—burdock and mullein, which displace the ground-nut.

II, 42   1850

HE FISHERMAN

Met Sudbury Haines on the river before the Cliffs, come a-fishing. Wearing an old coat, much patched, with many colors. He represents the Indian still. The very patches in his coat and his improvident life do so. I feel that he is as essential a part, nevertheless, of our community as the lawyer in the village. He tells me that he caught three pickerel here the other day that weighed seven pounds all together. It is the old story. The fisherman is a natural story-teller. No man's imagination plays more pranks than his, while he is tending his reels and trotting from one to another, or watching his cork in summer. He is ever waiting for the sky to fall. He has sent out a venture. He has a ticket in the lottery of fate, and who knows what it may draw? He ever expects to catch a bigger fish yet. He is the most patient and believing of men. Who else will stand so long in wet places? When the haymaker runs to shelter, he takes down his pole and bends his steps to the river, glad to have a leisure day. He is more like an inhabitant of nature. The weather concerns him. He is an observer of her phenomena.

III, 290   9 Feb. 1852

HE HUNTER

Saw Melvin's lank bluish-white black-spotted hound, and Melvin * with his gun near, going home at eve. He follows hunting, praise be to him, as regularly in our tame fields as the farmers follow farm-

---

* George Melvin, who appears frequently in the *Journal*, was an ardent sportsman and well versed in country things. Thoreau greatly enjoyed talking with him.

ing. Persistent Genius! How I respect him and thank him for him! I trust the Lord will provide us with another Melvin when he is gone. How good in him to follow his own bent, and not continue at the Sabbath-school all his days! What a wealth he thus becomes in the neighborhood! Few know how to take the census. I thank my stars for Melvin. I think of him with gratitude when I am going to sleep, grateful that he exists,—that Melvin who is such a trial to his mother. Yet he is agreeable to me as a tinge of russet on the hillside. I would fain give thanks morning and evening for my blessings. Awkward, gawky, loose-hung, dragging his legs after him. He is my contemporary and neighbor. He is one tribe, I am another, and we are not at war.

    IX, 148   1 Dec. 1856

GOODWIN, THE ONE-EYED AJAX

Yesterday, toward night, . . . a sail as far as the Battle-Ground. One-eyed John Goodwin,* the fisherman, was loading into a hand-cart and conveying home the piles of driftwood which of late he had collected with his boat. It was a beautiful evening, and a clear amber sunset lit up all the eastern shores; and that man's employment, so simple and direct,—though he is regarded by most as a vicious character,—whose whole motive was so easy to fathom,—thus to obtain his winter's wood,—charmed me unspeakably. So much do we love actions that are simple. They are all poetic. We, too, would fain be so employed. So unlike the pursuits of most men, so artificial or complicated. . . . This simplicity it is, and the vigor it imparts, that enables the simple vagabond, though he does get drunk and is sent to the house of correction so often, to hold up his head among men.

"If I go to Boston every day and sell tape from morning till night," says the merchant (which we will admit is not a beautiful action), "some time or other I shall be able to buy the best of fuel

* Though considered disreputable by his fellow townsmen, Goodwin interested Thoreau because he spent most of his life in nature, like an Indian.

without stint." Yes, but not the pleasure of picking it up by the river-side, which, I may say, is of more value than the warmth it yields, for it but keeps the vital heat in us that we may repeat such pleasing ex-ercises. It warms us twice, and the first warmth is the most wholesome and memorable, compared with which the other is mere coke. It is to give no account of my employment to say that I cut wood to keep me from freezing, or cultivate beans to keep me from starving. Oh, no, the greatest value of these labors is received before the wood is teamed home, or the beans are harvested (or winnowed from it). Goodwin stands on the solid earth. The earth looks solider under him, and for such as he no *political* economies, with *their* profit and loss, supply and demand, need ever be written, for they will need to use no policy. As for the complex ways of living, I love them not, however much I practice them. In as many places as possible, I will get my feet down to the earth. There is no secret in his trade, more than in the sun's. It is no mystery how he gets his living; no, not even when he steals it. But there is less double-dealing in his living than in your trade.

Goodwin is a most constant fisherman. He must well know the taste of pickerel by this time. He will fish, I would not venture to say how many days in succession. When I can remember to have seen him fishing almost daily for some time, if it rains, I am surprised on looking out to see him slowly wending his way to the river in his oil-cloth coat, with his basket and pole. I saw him the other day fishing in the middle of the stream, the day after I had seen him fishing on the shore, while by a kind of magic I sailed by him; and he said he was catching minnow for bait in the winter. When I was twenty rods off, he held up a pickerel that weighed two and a half pounds, which he had forgot to show me before, and the next morning, as he after-ward told me, he caught one that weighed three pounds. If it is ever necessary to appoint a committee on fish-ponds and pickerel, let him be one of them. Surely he is tenacious of life, hard to scale. . . .

On the 1st, when I stood on Poplar Hill, I saw a man, far off by the edge of the river, splitting billets off a stump. Suspecting who it was, I took out my glass, and beheld Goodwin, the one-eyed Ajax, in his short blue frock, short and square-bodied, as broad as for his height he can afford to be, getting his winter's wood; for this is one of

the phenomena of the season. As surely as the ants which he disturbs
go into winter quarters in the stump when the weather becomes cool,
so does G. revisit the stumpy shores with his axe. As usual, his powder-
flask peeped out from a pocket on his breast, his gun was slanted over
a stump near by, and his boat lay a little further along. He had been
at work laying wall still further off, and now, near the end of the day,
betook himself to those pursuits which he loved better still. . . . I
helped him tip over a stump or two. He said that the owner of the
land had given him leave to get them out, but it seemed to me a con-
descension for him to ask any man's leave to grub up these stumps.
The stumps to those who can use them, I say,—to those who will
split them. He might as well ask leave of the farmer to shoot the
musquash and the meadow-hen, or I might as well ask leave to look
at the landscape. Near by were large hollows in the ground, now
grassed over, where he had got out white oak stumps in previous
years. But, strange to say, the town does not like to have him get his
fuel in this way. They would rather the stumps would rot in the
ground, or be floated down-stream to the sea. They have almost without dissent agreed on a different mode of living, with their division of
labor. They would have him stick to laying wall, and buy corded
wood for his fuel, as they do. He has drawn up an old bridge sleeper
and cut his name in it for security, and now he gets into his boat and
pushes off in the twilight, saying he will go and see what Mr. Musquash is about.

     v, 444-447; xi, 283-284   22 Oct. 1853; 4 Nov. 1858

HE MUSQUASH–HUNTERS

Many are out in boats, steering outside the ice of the river over
the newly flooded meadows, shooting musquash. Cocks crow as in
spring.

    The energy and excitement of the musquash-hunter even, not
despairing of life, but keeping the same rank and savage hold on it
that his predecessors have for so many generations, while so many are

sick and despairing, even this is inspiriting to me. Even these deeds of death are interesting as evidences of life, for life will still prevail in spite of all accidents. I have a certain faith that even musquash are immortal and not born to be killed by Melvin's double-B (?) shot. . . .

The musquash-hunter (last night), with his increased supply of powder and shot and boat turned up somewhere on the bank, now that the river is rapidly rising, dreaming of his exploits to-day in shoot-ing musquash, of the great pile of dead rats that will weigh down his boat before night, when he will return wet and weary and weather-beaten to his hut with an appetite for his supper and for much slug-gish (punky) social intercourse with his fellows,—even he, dark, dull, and battered flint as he is, is an inspired man to his extent now, perhaps the most inspired by this freshet of any, and the Musketaquid Meadows cannot spare him. There are poets of all kinds and degrees, little known to each other. The Lake School * is not the only or the principal one. They love various things. Some love beauty, and some love rum. Some go to Rome, and some go a-fishing, and are sent to the house of correction once a month. They keep up their fires by means unknown to me. I know not their comings and goings. How can I tell what violets they watch for? I know them wild and ready to risk all when their muse invites. The most sluggish will be up early enough then, and face any amount of wet and cold. I meet these gods of the river and woods with sparkling faces (like Apollo's) late from the house of correction, it may be carrying whatever mystic and for-bidden bottles or other vessels concealed, while the dull regular priests are steering their parish rafts in a prose mood. What care I to see galleries full of representatives of heathen gods, when I can see nat-ural living ones by an infinitely superior artist, without perspective tube? . . .

I hear these guns going to-day, and I must confess they are to me a springlike and exhilarating sound, like the cock-crowing, though each one may report the death of a musquash. This, methinks, or the like of this, with whatever mixture of dross, is the real morning or eve-ning hymn that goes up from these vales to-day, and which the stars

* The English Romantic poets, Wordsworth being the acknowledged founder of their "school."

echo. This is the best sort of glorifying of God and enjoying him that at all prevails here to-day, without any clarified butter or sacred ladles.

As a mother loves to see her child imbibe nourishment and ex-pand, so God loves to see his children thrive on the nutriment he has furnished them. In the musquash-hunters I see the Almouchicois still pushing swiftly over the dark stream in their canoes. These aboriginal men cannot be repressed, but under some guise or other they survive and reappear continually. Just as simply as the crow picks up the worms which all over the fields have been washed out by the thaw, these men pick up the musquash that have been washed out the banks. And to serve such ends men plow and sail, and power and shot are made, and the grocer exists to retail them, though he may think him-self much more the deacon of some church.

XI, 422-425   22 Jan. 1858

WOODCHOPPER AND SCIENTIST

The chopper who works in the woods all day for many weeks or months at a time becomes intimately acquainted with them in his way. He is more open in some respects to the impressions they are fitted to make than the naturalist who goes to see them. He is not liable to exaggerate insignificant features. He really forgets himself, forgets to observe, and at night he *dreams* of the swamp, its phe-nomena and events. Not so the naturalist; enough of his unconscious life does not pass there.

A man can hardly be said to be *there* if he *knows* that he is there, or to go there if he knows where he is going. The man who is bent upon his work is frequently in the best attitude to observe what is irrelevant to his work. (*Mem.* Wordsworth's observations on relaxed attention.)* You must be conversant with things for a long time to know much about them, like the moss which has hung from the

---

* A reference to the Wordsworthian doctrine of "wise passiveness," one of the starting points for Thoreau's theory of the poet's proper re-lation to nature (see *The Magic Circle of Walden,* 113 ff.).

spruce, and as the partridge and the rabbit are acquainted with the thickets and at length have acquired the color of the places they fre-quent. If the man of science can put all his knowledge into proposi-tions, the woodman has a great deal of incommunicable knowledge.

III, 123·124   18 Nov. 1851

WOODCHOPPER AND POET

These warmer days the woodchopper finds that the wood cuts easier than when it had the frost in its sapwood, though it does not split so readily. Thus every change in the weather has its influence on him, and is appreciated by him in a peculiar way. The woodcutter and his practices and experiences are more to be attended to; his accidents, perhaps more than any other's, should mark the epochs in the winter day. Now that the Indian is gone, he stands nearest to nature. Who has written the history of his day? How far still is the writer of books from the man, his old playmate it may be, who chops in the woods! There are ages between them. Homer refers to the progress of the woodcutter's work, to mark the time of day on the plains of Troy,* and the inference from such passages commonly is that he lived in a more primitive state of society than the present. But I think that this is a mistake. Like proves like in all ages, and the fact that I myself should take pleasure in referring to just such simple and peaceful labors which are always proceeding, that the contrast itself always attracts the civilized poet to what is rudest and most primitive in his contempo-raries, all this rather proves a certain interval between the poet and the chopper whose labor he refers to, than an unusual nearness to him, on the principle that familiarity breeds contempt. Homer is to be subjected to a very different kind of criticism from any he has received.

III, 244·245   28 Jan. 1852

* *Iliad*, XI, 86·91.

PLACES

LIBRARIES

When looking over the dry and dusty volumes of the English poets, I cannot believe that those fresh and fair creations I had imagined are contained in them. English poetry from Gower down, collected into one alcove, and so from the library window compared with the commonest nature, seems very mean. Poetry cannot breathe in the scholar's atmosphere. The Aubreys and Hickeses,* with all their learning, prophane it yet indirectly by their zeal. You need not envy his feelings who for the first time has cornered up poetry in an alcove. I can hardly be serious with myself when I remember that I have come to Cambridge after poetry; and while I am running over the catalogue and collating and selecting, I think if it would not be a shorter way to a complete volume to step at once into the field or wood, with a very low reverence to students and librarians. Milton did not forsee what company he was to fall into. On running over the titles of these books, looking from time to time at their first pages or farther, I am oppressed by an inevitable sadness. One must have come into a library by an oriel window, as softly and undisturbed as the light which falls on the books through a stained window, and not by the librarian's door, else all his dreams will vanish. Can the Valhalla be warmed by steam and go by clock and bell?

Good poetry seems so simple and natural a thing that when we meet it we wonder that all men are not always poets. Poetry is nothing but healthy speech. Though the speech of the poet goes to the heart of things, yet he is that one especially who speaks civilly to Nature as a second person and in some sense is the patron of the world. Though more than any he stands in the midst of Nature, yet more than any he can stand aloof from her. The best lines, perhaps, only suggest to me that that man simply saw or heard or felt what seems the commonest fact in my experience.

I, 288-289   30 Nov. 1841

* Probably John Aubrey (1626–1697), author of learned works on natural history, and George Hickes (1642–1715), a theologian and Anglo-Saxon scholar.

USEUMS

I hate museums; there is nothing so weighs upon my spirits. They are the catacombs of nature. One green bud of spring, one willow catkin, one faint trill from a migrating sparrow would set the world on its legs again. The life that is in a single green weed is of more worth than all this death. They are dead nature collected by dead men. I know not whether I muse most at the bodies stuffed with cotton and sawdust or those stuffed with bowels and fleshy fibre out-side the cases.

Where is the proper herbarium, the true cabinet of shells, and museum of skeletons, but in the meadow where the flower bloomed, by the seaside where the tide cast up the fish, and on the hills and in the valleys where the beast laid down its life and the skeleton of the traveller reposes on the grass? What right have mortals to parade these things on their legs again, with their wires, and, when heaven has decreed that they shall return to dust again, to return them to sawdust? Would you have a dried specimen of a world, or a pickled one?

Embalming is a sin against heaven and earth,—against heaven, who has recalled the soul and set free the servile elements, and against the earth, which is thus robbed of her dust. I have had my right-perceiving senses so disturbed in these haunts as to mistake a veritable living man for a stuffed specimen, and surveyed him with dumb won-der as the strangest of the whole collection.

1, 464-465   1837-1847

MINOTT'S HOUSE*

Minott's is a small, square, one-storied and unpainted house, with a hipped roof and at least one dormer-window, a third the way

* This is the house of George Minott, Thoreau's close friend (see "Minott, the Poetical Farmer," p. 31).

up the south side of a long hill which is some fifty feet high and ex-
tends east and west. A traveller of taste may go straight through the
village without being detained a moment by any dwelling, either the
form or surroundings being objectionable, but very few go by this
house without being agreeably impressed, and many are therefore
led to inquire who lives in it. Not that its form is so incomparable,
nor even its weather-stained color, but chiefly, I think, because of its
snug and picturesque position on the hillside, fairly lodged there,
where all children like to be, and its perfect harmony with its surroundings and position. For if, preserving this form and color, it
should be transplanted to the meadow below, nobody would notice it
more than a schoolhouse which was lately of the same form. It is
there because somebody was independent or bold enough to carry out
the happy thought of placing it high on the hillside. It is the locality,
not the architecture, that takes us captive. There is exactly such a site,
only of course less room on either side, between this house and the
next westward, but few if any, even of the admiring travellers, have
thought of this as a house-lot, or would be bold enough to place a
cottage there.

Without side fences or gravelled walks or flower-plats, that
simple sloping bank before it is pleasanter than any front yard, though
many a visitor—and many times the master—has slipped and fallen
on the steep path. From its position and exposure, it has shelter and
warmth and dryness and prospect. He overlooks the road, the meadow
and brook, and houses beyond, to the distant woods. The spring
comes earlier to that dooryard than to any, and summer lingers longest
there.

x, 207-208   26 Nov. 1857

A REAL ESTATE

A fine, freshening air, a little hazy, that bathes and washes
everything, saving the day from extreme heat. Walked to the hills
south of Wayland by the road by Deacon Farrar's. First vista just
beyond Merron's, looking west down a valley, with a verdant-

columned elm at the extremity of the vale and the blue hills and horizon beyond. These are the resting-places in a walk. We love to see
any part of the earth tinged with blue, cerulean, the color of the sky,
the celestial color. I wonder that houses are not oftener located mainly
that they may command particular rare prospects, every convenience
yielding to this. The farmer would never suspect what it was you were
buying, and such sites would be the cheapest of any. A site where
you might avail yourself of the art of Nature for three thousand years,
which could never be materially changed or taken from you, a noble
inheritance for your children. The true sites for human dwellings are
unimproved. They command no price in the market. Men will pay
something to look into a travelling showman's box,* but not to look
upon the fairest prospects on the earth. A vista where you have the
near green horizon contrasted with the distant blue one, terrestrial with
celestial earth. The prospect of a vast horizon must be accessible in
our neighborhood. Where men of enlarged views may be educated.
An unchangeable kind of wealth, a *real* estate.

II, 215-216   25 May 1851

GONE–TO–SEED COUNTRY

As I stand under the hill beyond J. Hosmer's and look over the
plains westward toward Acton and see the farmhouses nearly half a
mile apart, few and solitary, in these great fields between these stretching woods, out of the world, where the children have to go far to
school; the still, stagnant, heart-eating, life-everlasting, and gone-to-
seed country, so far from the post-office where the weekly paper
comes, wherein the new-married wife cannot live for loneliness, and
the young man has to depend upon his horse for society; see young
J. Hosmer's house, whither he returns with his wife in despair after
living in the city,—I standing in Tarbell's road, which he alone cannot break out,—the world in winter for most walkers reduced to a

* Diorama: a miniature scene, painted on a set of transparent cloth
curtains so as to give a three-dimensional effect, looked at through a
small opening in the box.

sled track winding far through the drifts, all springs sealed up and no digressions; where the old man thinks he may possibly afford to rust it out, not having long to live, but the young man pines to get nearer the post-office and the Lyceum, is restless and resolves to go to California, because the depot is a mile off (he hears the rattle of the cars at a distance and thinks the world is going by and leaving him); where rabbits and partridges multiply, and muskrats are more numerous than ever, and none of the farmer's sons are willing to be farmers, and the apple trees are decayed, and the cellar-holes are more numerous than the houses, and the rails are covered with lichens, and the old maids wish to sell out and move into the village, and have waited twenty years in vain for this purpose and never finished but one room in the house, never plastered nor painted, inside or out, lands which the Indian was long since dispossessed [of], and now the farms are run out, and what were forests are grain-fields, what were grain-fields, pastures; dwellings which only those Arnolds of the wilderness,* those *coureurs de bois*, the baker and the butcher visit, to which at least the latter penetrates for the annual calf,—and as he returns the cow lows after;—whither the villager never penetrates, but in huckleberry time, perchance, and if he does not, who does?—where some men's breaths smell of rum, having smuggled in a jugful to alleviate their misery and solitude; where the owls give a regular serenade;—I say, standing there and seeing these things, I cannot realize that this is that hopeful young America which is famous throughout the world for its activity and enterprise, and this is the most thickly settled and Yankee part of it. What must be the condition of the *old* world! The *sphagnum* must by this time have concealed it from the eye.

In new countries men are scattered broadcast; they do not wait for roads to place their houses on, but roads seek out the houses, and each man is a prince in his principality and depends on himself. Perchance when the virgin soil is exhausted, a reaction takes place, and men concentrate in villages again, become social and commercial, and leave the steady and moderate few to work the country's mines.

III, 237-238   27 Jan. 1852

* Benedict Arnold (1741–1801); the well-known Revolutionary patriot and traitor, took part in numerous wilderness campaigns in upper New York and Maine before betraying the cause of the American colonies.

AN OLD CELLAR

I observed yesterday, in the cellar of the old Conantum house, a regular frame or "horse" to rest barrels (of cider, vinegar, etc.) on. It was probably made before the house was built, being exactly the length of the cellar,—two pieces of timber framed together, that is, connected by crosspieces and lying on the cellar-bottom against one side, the whole length, with concavities cut in them to receive the barrels and prevent their rolling. There were places for eight barrels. It suggests how much more preparation was made in those days for the storing of liquors. We have at most one keg in our cellar for which such a horse would be a convenient place; yet in this now remote and uncovered cellar-hole lies a horse with places for eight barrels of liquor. It would make a toper's mouth water to behold it. You wonder how they got apples and cider-mills a-going so early, say a hundred and fifty years ago. No doubt they worked hard and sweated a good deal, and perhaps they required, or could bear, more strong drink than the present generation. This horse is a fixture, framed with the house, or rather with the cellar; a first thought it must have been, perchance made by a separate contract, since it comes below the sills. The barrels and their contents, and they who emptied them, and the house above, are all gone, and still the scalloped logs remain now in broad daylight to testify to the exact number of barrels of liquor which the former occupant expected to, and probably did, lay in. His gravestone somewhere tells one sober story no doubt, and this his barrel-horse tells another,—and the only one that I hear. For twenty and odd years only the woodchucks and wild mice to my knowledge have occupied this cellar. Such is the lowest stick of timber in an old New England man's house. He dug a hole six feet into the earth and laid down a timber to hold his cider-barrel. Then he proceeded to build a house over it, with kitchen and sitting and sleeping rooms. It reminds me of travellers' stories of the London docks, of rows of hogsheads, of bonded liquors. Every New England cellar was once something like it. It is a relic of old England with her ale. The first settlers made preparations to drink a good deal, and they did not disappoint themselves.

XIII, 247·249   16 Apr. 1860

INDIAN LAND

When I walk in the fields of Concord and meditate on the destiny of this prosperous slip of the Saxon family, the unexhausted energies of this new country, I forget that this which is now Concord was once Musketaquid, and that the *American race* has had its destiny also. Everywhere in the fields, in the corn and grain land, the earth is strewn with the relics of a race which has vanished as completely as if trodden in with the earth. I find it good to remember the eternity behind me as well as the eternity before. Wherever I go, I tread in the tracks of the Indian. I pick up the bolt which he has but just dropped at my feet. And if I consider destiny I am on his trail. I scatter his hearthstones with my feet, and pick out of the embers of his fire the simple but enduring implements of the wigwam and the chase. In planting my corn in the same furrow which yielded its increase to his support so long, I displace some memorial of him.

I have been walking this afternoon over a pleasant field planted with winter rye, near the house, where this strange people once had their dwelling-place. Another species of mortal men, but little less wild to me than the musquash they hunted. Strange spirits, dæmons, whose eyes could never meet mine; with another nature and another fate than mine. The crows flew over the edge of the woods, and, wheeling over my head, seemed to rebuke, as dark-winged spirits more akin to the Indian than I. Perhaps only the present disguise of the Indian. If the new has a meaning, so has the old. . . .

The pines and the crows are not changed, but instead that Philip and Paugus stand on the plain, here are Webster and Crockett.*

* Daniel Webster and David Crockett, the statesman and the frontiersman, symbols of American civilization. Philip and Paugus were Indian Sachems of the seventeenth century, the former being the famous

Instead of the council-house is the legislature. What a new aspect have new eyes given to the land! Where is this country but in the hearts of its inhabitants? Why, there is only so much of Indian America left as there is of the American Indian in the character of this generation.

I, 337-338   19 Mar. 1842

 FOREST SCENE: LOGGING

Though they are cutting off the woods at Walden, it is not all loss. It makes some new and unexpected prospects. We read books about logging in the Maine woods as if it were wholly strange to these parts. But I here witness almost exactly the same things, scenes that might be witnessed in Maine or New Hampshire: the logger's team, his oxen on the ice chewing the cud, the long pine tree, stripped of its branches, chained upon his sled, resting on a stout cross-bar or log and trailing behind, the smoke of his fire curling up blue amid the trees, the sound of the axe and of the teamsters' voices. A pretty forest scene, seeing oxen, so patient and stationary, good for pictures, standing on the ice,—a piece of still life. Oh, it is refreshing to see, to think of, these things after hearing of the discussions and politics of the day! The smoke I saw was quite blue. As I stood on the partially cleared bank at the east end of the pond, I looked south over the side of the hill into a deep dell still wooded, and I saw, not more than thirty rods off, a chopper at his work. I was half a dozen rods distant from the standing wood, and I saw him through a vista between two trees (it was now mainly an oak wood, the pine having been cut), and he appeared to me apparently half a mile distant, yet charmingly distinct, as in a pic-ture of which the two trees were the frame. He was seen against the snow on the hillside beyond. I could distinguish each part of his dress perfectly, and the axe with distinct outline as he raised it above his head, the black iron against the snow, and could hear every stroke

leader of King Philip's War, which was brought to an end only with his death, in 1676.

distinctly. Yet I should have deemed it ridiculous to have called to him, he appeared so distant. He appeared with the same distinctness as objects seen through a pinhole in a card. This was the effect rather than by comparison of him, his size, with the nearer trees, between which I saw him and which made the canopied roof of the grove far above his head. It was, perhaps, one of those coincidences and effects which have made men painters. I could not behold him as an actual man; he was more ideal than in any picture I have seen. He refused to be seen as actual. Far in the hollow, yet somewhat enlightened, aisles of this wooded dell. Some scenes will thus present themselves as picture. Those scenes which are picture, subjects for the pencil, are distinctly marked; they do not require the aid of genius to idealize them. They must be seen as ideal.

III, 253-254   30 Jan. 1852

MOUNT MONADNOCK*

They who simply climb to the peak of Monadnock have seen but little of the mountain. I came not to look *off from* it, but to look *at* it. The view of the pinnacle itself from the plateau below surpasses any view which you get from the summit. It is indispensable to see the top itself and the sierra of its outline from one side. The great charm is not to look off from a height but to walk over this novel and wonderful rocky surface. Moreover, if you would enjoy the prospect, it is, methinks, most interesting when you look from the edge of the plateau immediately down into the valleys, or where the edge of the lichen-clad rocks, only two or three rods from you, is seen as the lower frame of a picture of green fields, lakes, and woods, suggesting a more stupendous precipice than exists. There are much more surprising effects of this nature along the edge of the plateau than on the summit. It is remarkable what haste the visitors make to get to the top of the mountain and then look away from it. . . .

* One of Thoreau's favorite mountains, located in the southwest corner of New Hampshire. He made excursions there in 1844, 1852, 1858, and 1860. Emerson celebrated it in a poem.

There were a great many visitors to the summit, both by the south and north, *i. e.* the Jaffrey and Dublin paths, but they did not turn off from the beaten track. One noon, when I was on the top, I counted forty men, women, and children around me, and more were constantly arriving while others were going. Certainly more than one hundred ascended in a day. When you got within thirty rods you saw them seated in a row along the gray parapets, like the inhabitants of a castle on a gala-day; and when you behold Monadnock's blue summit fifty miles off in the horizon, you may imagine it covered with men, women, and children in dresses of all colors, like an observatory on a muster-field. They appeared to be chiefly mechanics and farmers' boys and girls from the neighboring towns. The young men sat in rows with their legs dangling over the precipice, squinting through spy-glasses and shouting and hallooing to each new party that issued from the woods below. Some were playing cards; others were trying to see their house or their neighbor's. Children were running about and playing as usual. Indeed, this peak in pleasant weather is the most trivial place in New England. There are probably more arrivals daily than at any of the White Mountain houses. Several were busily en-graving their names on the rocks with cold-chisels, whose incessant clink you heard, and they had but little leisure to look off. The moun-tain was not free of them from sunrise to sunset, though most of them left about 5 P.M. At almost any hour of the day they were seen wend-ing their way single file in various garb up or down the shelving rocks of the peak. These figures on the summit, seen in relief against the sky (from our camp), looked taller than life. I saw some that camped there, by moonlight, one night. On Sunday, twenty or thirty, at least, in addition to the visitors to the peak, came up to pick blueberries, and we heard on all sides the rattling of dishes and their frequent calls to each other.

XIV, 36-37, 39-40   9 Aug. 1860

CONCORD RIVER

I think that I speak impartially when I say that I have never met with a stream so suitable for boating and botanizing as the Concord, and fortunately nobody knows it. I know of reaches which a single country-seat would spoil beyond remedy, but there has not been any important change here since I can remember. The willows slumber along its shore, piled in light but low masses, even like the cumuli clouds above. We pass haymakers in every meadow, who may think that we are idlers. But Nature takes care that every nook and crevice is explored by some one. While they look after the open meadows, we farm the tract between the river's brinks and behold the shores from that side. We, too, are harvesting an annual crop with our eyes, and think you Nature is not glad to display her beauty to us?

XI, 77   6 Aug. 1858

THE RIVER AT NIGHT

The sun sets when we are off Israel Rice's. A few golden coppery clouds, intensely glowing, like fishes in some molten metal of the sky, and then the small scattered clouds grow blue-black above, or one half, and reddish or pink the other half, and after a short twilight the night sets in. We think it is pleasantest to be on the water at this hour. We row across Fair Haven in the thickening twilight and far below it, steadily and without speaking. As the night draws on her veil, the shores retreat; we only keep in the middle of this low stream of light; we know not whether we float in the air or in the lower regions. We seem to recede from the trees on shore or the island very slowly, and yet a few reaches make all our voyage. Nature has divided it agreeably into reaches. The reflections of the stars in the water are dim and elongated like the zodiacal light straight down into the depths, but no mist rises to-night. It is pleasant not to get home till after dark,—to steer by the lights of the villagers. The lamps in the houses twinkle now like stars; they shine doubly bright.

III, 78   15 Oct. 1851

THE RIVER BY MOONLIGHT

To Fair Haven Pond by boat, the moon four-fifths full, not a cloud in the sky; paddling all the way.

The water perfectly still, and the air almost, the former gleaming like oil in the moonlight, with the moon's disk reflected in it.

When we started, saw some fishermen kindling their fire for spearing by the riverside. It was a lurid, reddish blaze, contrasting with the white light of the moon, with dense volumes of black smoke from the burning pitch pine roots rolling upward in the form of an inverted pyramid. The blaze reflected in the water, almost as distinct as the substance. It looked like tarring a ship on the shore of the Styx or Cocytus. For it is still and dark, notwithstanding the moon, and no sound but the crackling of the fire. The fishermen can be seen only near at hand, though their fire is visible far away; and then they appear as dusky, fuliginous figures, half enveloped in smoke, seen only by their enlightened sides. Like devils they look, clad in old coats to defend themselves from the fogs, one standing up forward holding the spear ready to dart, while the smoke and flames are blown in his face, the other paddling the boat slowly and silently along close to the shore with almost imperceptible motion.

The river appears indefinitely wide; there is a mist rising from the water, which increases the indefiniteness. A high bank or moonlit hill rises at a distance over the meadow on the bank, with its sandy gullies and clamshells exposed where the Indians feasted. The shore line, though close, is removed by the eye to the side of the hill. It is at high-water mark. It is continued till it meets the hill. Now the fisherman's fire, left behind, acquires some thick rays in the distance and becomes a star. As surely as sunlight falling through an irregular chink makes a round figure on the opposite wall, so the blaze at a distance appears a star. Such is the effect of the atmosphere. The bright sheen of the moon is constantly travelling with us, and is seen at the same angle in front on the surface of the pads; and the reflection of its disk in the rippled water by our boat-side appears like bright gold pieces falling on the river's counter. This coin is incessantly poured forth as from some unseen horn of plenty at our side.

II, 48-50   6 Oct. 1851

LANDSCAPE BY MOONLIGHT

Moon not quite full. Going across Depot Field. The western sky is now a crescent of saffron inclining to salmon, a little dunnish, perhaps. The grass is wet with dew. The evening star has come out, but no other. There is no wind. I see a nighthawk in the twilight, flitting near the ground. I hear the hum of a beetle going by. The greenish fires of lightning-bugs are already seen in the meadow. I almost lay my hand on one amid the leaves as I get over the fence at the brook. I pass through Hubbardston along the side of a field of oats, which wet one leg. I perceive the smell of a burning far off by the river, which I saw smoking two days ago. The moon is laboring in a mackerel cloud, and my hopes are with her. Why do I hear no bull-frogs yet? Do they ever trump as early and as universally as on that their first evening? I hear the whip-poor-wills on different sides. White flowers alone show much at night,—white clover and white-weed. It is commonly still at night, as now. The day has gone by with its wind like the wind of a cannon-ball, and now far in the west it blows. By that dun-colored sky you may track it. There is no motion nor sound in the woods (Hubbard's Grove) along which I am walk-ing. The trees stand like great screens against the sky. The distant village sounds are the barking of dogs, that animal with which man has allied himself, and the rattling of wagons, for the farmers have gone into town a-shopping this Saturday night. The dog is the tamed wolf, as the villager is the tamed savage. But near, the crickets are heard in the grass, chirping from everlasting to everlasting, a mosquito sings near my ear, and the humming of a dor-bug drowns all the noise of the village, so roomy is the universe. The moon comes out of the mackerel cloud, and the traveller rejoices. How can a man write the same thoughts by the light of the moon, resting his book on a rail by the side of a remote potato-field, that he does by the light of the sun, on his study table? The light is but a luminousness. My pencil seems to move through a creamy, mystic medium. The moonlight is rich and somewhat opaque, like cream, but the daylight is thin and blue, like skimmed milk. I am less conscious than in the presence of the sun; my instincts have more influence.

v, 277   18 June 1852

RIVER VALLEY IN AUTUMN

When I turn round half-way up Fair Haven Hill, by the orchard wall, and look northwest, I am surprised for the thousandth time at the beauty of the landscape, and I sit down to behold it at my leisure. I think that Concord affords no better view. It is always incredibly fair, but ordinarily we are mere objects in it, and not witnesses of it. I see, through the bright October air, a valley extending southwest and northeast and some two miles across,—so far I can see distinctly, —with a broad, yellow meadow tinged with brown at the bottom, and a blue river winding slowly through it northward, with a regular edging of low bushes on the brink, of the same color with the meadow. Skirting the meadow are straggling lines, and occasionally large masses a quarter of a mile wide, of brilliant scarlet and yellow and crimson trees, backed by and mingled with green forests and green and hoary russet fields and hills; and on the hills around shoot up a million scarlet and orange and yellow and crimson fires amid the green; and here and there amid the trees, often beneath the largest and more graceful of those which have brown-yellow dome-like tops, are bright white or gray houses; and beyond stretches a forest, wreath upon wreath, and between each two wreaths I know lies a similar vale; and far beyond all, on the verge of the horizon, are half a dozen dark-blue mountain-summits. Large birds of a brilliant blue and white plumage are darting and screaming amid the glowing foliage a quarter of a mile below, while smaller blue birds warble faintly but sweetly around me.

Such is the dwelling-place of man; but go to a caucus in the village to-night or to a church to-morrow, and see if there is anything said to suggest that the inhabitants of those houses know what kind of world they live in. But hark! I hear the tolling of a distant funeral bell, and they are conveying a corpse to the churchyard from one of the houses that I see, and its serious sound is more in harmony with this scenery than any ordinary bustle could be. It suggests that a man must die to his present life before he can appreciate his opportunities and the beauty of the abode that is appointed him.

x, 72-73   7 Oct. 1857

MAPLE SWAMP IN AUTUMN

I go across Bartonia Meadow direct to Bear Garden Hill-side. Approaching the sand-slide, I see, some fifty rods off, looking toward the sun, the top of the maple swamp just appearing over the sheeny russet edge of the hill,—a strip, apparently twenty rods long and ten feet deep, of the most intensely brilliant scarlet, orange, and yellow, equal to any flowers or fruits or any tints ever painted. As I advance, lowering the edge of the hill, which makes the firm foreground or lower frame to the picture, the depth of this brilliant grove revealed steadily increases, suggesting that the whole of the concealed valley is filled with such color. As usual, there is one tree-top of an especially brilliant scarlet, with which the others contrast.

One wonders that the tithing-men and fathers of the town are not out to see what the trees mean by their high colors and exuberance of spirits, fearing that some mischief is brewing. I do not see what the Puritans did at that season when the maples blazed out in scarlet. They certainly could not have worshipped in groves then. Perhaps that is what they built meeting-houses and surrounded them with horse-sheds for.

No wonder we must have our annual cattle-show and fall training and perhaps Cornwallis,* our September courts, etc. Nature holds her annual fair and gala-days in October in every hollow and on every hillside.

* A military muster in masquerade, commemorating the surrender of Lord Cornwallis at Yorktown, 19 October 1781.

Look into that hollow all aglow, where the trees are clothed in their vestures of most dazzling tints. Does it not suggest a thousand gypsies beneath, rows of booths, and that man's spirits should rise as high, that the routine of his life should be interrupted by an analogous festivity and rejoicing?

X, 71·72   7 Oct. 1857

HE GLOBE IS A RIPE FRUIT

The brilliant autumnal colors are red and yellow and the various tints, hues, and shades of these. Blue is reserved to be the color of the sky, but yellow and red are the colors of the earth flower. Every fruit, on ripening, and just before its fall, acquires a bright tint. So do the leaves; so the sky before the end of the day, and the year near its setting. October is the red sunset sky, November the later twilight. Color stands for all ripeness and success. We have dreamed that the hero should carry his color aloft, as a symbol of the ripeness of his virtue. The noblest feature, the eye, is the fairest-colored, the jewel of the body. The warrior's flag is the flower which precedes his fruit. He unfurls his flag to the breeze with such confidence and brag as the flower its petals. Now we shall see what kind of fruit will succeed.

The very forest and herbage, the pellicle of the earth as it were, must acquire a bright color, an evidence of its ripeness, as if the globe itself were a fruit on its stem, with ever one cheek toward the sun.

Our appetites have commonly confined our views of ripeness and its phenomena—color and mellowness and perfectness—to the fruits which we eat, and we are wont to forget that an immense harvest which we do not eat, hardly use at all, is annually ripened by nature. At our annual cattle-shows and horticultural exhibitions we make, as we think, a great show of fair fruits, destined, however, to a rather ignoble fate, fruits not worshipped for this chiefly; but round about and within our towns there is annually another show of fruits, on an infinitely grander scale, fruits which address our taste for beauty alone.

XI, 243·244   24 Oct. 1858

THE WILDERNESS TAMED

I have lately been surveying the Walden woods so extensively and minutely that I now see it mapped in my mind's eye—as, indeed, on paper—as so many men's wood-lots, and am aware when I walk there that I am at a given moment passing from such a one's wood-lot to such another's. I fear this particular dry knowledge may affect my imagination and fancy, that it will not be easy to see so much wildness and native vigor there as formerly. No thicket will seem so unexplored now that I know that a stake and stones may be found in it. In these respects those Maine woods differed essentially from ours. There you are never reminded that the wilderness which you are threading is, after all, some villager's familiar wood-lot from which his ancestors have sledded their fuel for generations, or some widow's thirds, minutely described in some old deed, which is recorded, of which the owner has got a plan, too, and old bound marks may be found every forty rods if you will search. What a history this Concord wilderness which I affect so much may have had! How many old deeds describe it,—some particular wild spot,—how it passed from Cole to Robinson, and Robinson to Jones, and Jones finally to Smith, in course of years! Some have cut it over three times during their lives, and some burned it and sowed it with rye, and built walls and made a pasture of it, perchance. All have renewed the bounds and reblazed the trees many times. Here you are not reminded of these things. 'T is true the map informs you that you stand on land granted by the State to such an academy, or on Bingham's Purchase, but these names do not impose on you, for you see nothing to remind you of the academy or of Bingham.

x, 233-234   1 Jan. 1858

THE RAILROAD CUT

The railroad men have now their hands full. I hear and see bluebirds, come with the warm wind. The sand is flowing in the Deep Cut. I am affected by the sight of the moist red sand or subsoil under the edge of the sandy bank, under the pitch pines. The railroad is perhaps our pleasantest and wildest road. It only makes deep cuts into and through the hills. On it are no houses nor foot-travellers. The travel on it does not disturb me. The woods are left to hang over it. Though straight, is wild in its accompaniments. All is raw edges. Even the laborers on it are not like other laborers. Its houses, if any, are shanties, and its ruins the ruins of shanties, shells where the race that built the railroad dwelt, and the bones they gnawed lie about. I am cheered by the sound of running water now down the wooden troughs on each side the cut. Then it is the driest walking in wet weather, and the easiest in snowy. This road breaks the surface of the earth.

III, 342   9 Mar. 1852

FOOTPATHS AND CART-PATHS

To have a hut here, and a footpath to the brook! For roads, I think that a poet cannot tolerate more than a footpath through the fields; that is wide enough, and for purposes of winged poesy suffices. It is not for the muse to speak of cart-paths. I would fain travel by a footpath round the world. I do not ask the railroads of commerce, not even the cart-paths of the farmer. Pray, what other path would you have than a footpath? What else should wear a path? This is the track of man alone. What more suggestive to the pensive walker? One walks in a wheel-track with less emotion; he is at a greater distance from man; but this footpath was, perchance, worn by the bare feet of human beings, and he cannot but think with interest of them. . . .

And now, methinks, this wider wood-path is not bad, for it

admits of society more conveniently. Two can walk side by side in it in the ruts, aye, and one more in the horse-track. The Indian walked in single file more solitary,—not side by side, chatting as he went. The woodman's cart and sled make just the path two walkers want through the wood.

    II, 455-475   4 Sept. 1851

WILD WALKS NEAR CONCORD

I can easily walk ten, fifteen, twenty, any number of miles, commencing at my own door, without going by any house, without crossing a road except where the fox and the mink do. Concord is the oldest inland town in New England, perhaps in the States, and the walker is peculiarly favored here. There are square miles in my vicinity which have no inhabitant. First along by the river, and then the brook, and then the meadow and the woodside. Such solitude! From a hundred hills I can see civilization and abodes of man afar. These farmers and their works are scarcely more obvious than woodchucks.

    I, 52   1850

RIVER TOWNS ARE WINGED TOWNS

What a relief and expansion of my thoughts when I come out from that inland position by the graveyard to this broad river's shore! This vista was incredible there. Suddenly I see a broad reach of blue beneath, with its curves and headlands, liberating me from the more terrene earth. What a difference it makes whether I spend my four hours' nooning between the hills by yonder roadside, or on the brink of this fair river, within a quarter of a mile of that! Here the earth is fluid to my thought, the sky is reflected from beneath, and around yonder cape is the highway to other continents. This current allies me to all the world. Be careful to sit in an elevating and inspiring place. There my thoughts were confined and trivial, and I hid myself from the gaze of travellers. Here they are expanded and elevated, and I am charmed by the beautiful river-reach. It is equal to a different season and country and creates a different mood. As you travel northward from Concord, probably the reaches of the Merrimack River, looking up or down them from the bank, will be the first inspiring sight. There is something in the scenery of a broad river equivalent to culture and civilization. Its channel conducts our thoughts as well as bodies to classic and famous ports, and allies us to all that is fair and great. I like to remember that at the end of half a day's walk I can stand on the bank of the Merrimack. It is just wide enough to interrupt the land and lead my eye and thoughts down its channel to the sea. A river is superior to a lake in its liberating influence. It has motion and indefinite length. A river touching the back of a town is like a wing, it may be unused as yet, but ready to waft it over the world. With its rapid current it is a slightly fluttering wing. River towns are winged towns.

XI, 4·5   2 July 1858

LAND AND WATER

How charming the contrast of land and water, especially a temporary island in the flood, with its new and tender shores of waving outline, so withdrawn yet habitable, above all if it rises into a hill high above the water and contrasting with it the more, and if that hill is wooded, suggesting wildness! Our vernal lakes have a beauty to my mind which they would not possess if they were more permanent. Everything is in rapid flux here, suggesting that Nature is alive to her extremities and superficies. To-day we sail swiftly on dark rolling waves or paddle over a sea as smooth as a mirror, unable to touch the bottom, where mowers* work and hide their jugs in August; coasting the edge of maple swamps, where alder tassels and white maple flowers are kissing the tide that has risen to meet them. But this particular phase of beauty is fleeting. Nature has so many shows for us she cannot afford to give much time to this. In a few days, perchance, these lakes

* The banks of Concord River are so low that when it overflows at spring floodtime, the Great Meadows are turned into a lake.

will have all run away to the sea. Such are the pictures which she paints. When we look at our masterpieces we see only dead paint and its vehicle, which suggests no liquid life rapidly flowing off from beneath. In the former case—in Nature—it is constant surprise and novelty. In many arrangements there is a wearisome monotony. We know too well what [we] shall have for our Saturday's dinner, but each day's feast in Nature's year is a surprise to us and adapted to our appetite and spirits. She has arranged such an order of feasts as never tires. Her motive is not economy but satisfaction.

XII, 95-96   28 Mar. 1859

THE MEADOWS FLOODED IN SPRING

The water on the meadows is now quite high on account of the melting snow and the rain. It makes a lively prospect when the wind blows, where our summer meads spread,—a tumultuous sea, a myriad waves breaking with whitecaps, like gambolling sheep, for want of other comparison in the country. Far and wide a sea of motion, schools of porpoises, lines of Virgil * realized. One would think it a novel sight for inland meadows. Where the cranberry and andromeda and swamp white oak and maple grow, here is a mimic sea, with its gulls. At the bottom of the sea, cranberries. . . .

The two states of the meadow are to be remembered: first in a March or April wind, as I have described it; second in a perfectly calm and beautiful mild morning or evening or midday, as lately, at the same season, such as I have also partially described, when there are no gulls circling over it. What different thoughts it suggests! Would it not be worth the while to describe the different states of our meadows which cover so large a portion of the town? It is not as if we had a few acres only of water surface. From every side the milkman rides over long causeways into the village, and carries the vision of much meadow's surface with him into his dreams. They answer to moods of

* Probably an allusion to the *Aeneid*, VIII, 671–674, where Vergil describes the dolphins on Aeneas' shield.

the Concord mind. There might be a chapter: The Sudbury Meadows, the Humors of the Town. . . .

I think our overflowing river far handsomer and more abounding
in soft and beautiful contrasts than a merely broad river would be. A
succession of bays it is, a chain of lakes, an endlessly scalloped shore,
rounding wood and field. Cultivated field and wood and pasture and
house are brought into ever new and unexpected positions and relations to the water. There is just stream enough for a flow of thought;
that is all. Many a foreigner who has come to this town has worked
for years on its banks without discovering which way the river runs.

III, 424-426   16 Apr. 1852

FAIR HAVEN: LANDSCAPE

In all my rambles I have seen no landscape which can make me
forget Fair Haven. I still sit on its Cliff in a new spring day, and look
over the awakening woods and the river, and hear the new birds sing,
with the same delight as ever. It is as sweet a mystery to me as ever,
what this world is. Fair Haven Lake in the south, with its pine-
covered island and its meadows, the hickories putting out fresh young
yellowish leaves, and the oaks light-grayish ones, while the oven-bird
thrums his sawyer-like strain, and the chewink rustles through the dry
leaves or repeats his jingle on a tree-top, and the wood thrush, the
genius of the wood, whistles for the first time his clear and thrilling
strain,—it sounds as it did the first time I heard it. The sight of these
budding woods intoxicates me,—this diet drink.

The strong-colored pine, the grass of trees, in the midst of which
other trees are but as weeds or flowers,—a little exotic.

II, 9-10   1850

AIR HAVEN: ENIGMA

I saw Fair Haven Pond with its island, and meadow between the island and the shore, and a strip of perfectly still and smooth water in the lee of the island, and two hawks, fish hawks perhaps, sailing over it. I did not see how it could be improved. Yet I do not see what these things can be. I begin to see such an object when I cease to *understand* it and see that I did not realize or appreciate it before, but I get no further than this. How adapted these forms and colors to my eye! A meadow and an island! What are these things? Yet the hawks and the ducks keep so aloof! and Nature is so reserved! I am made to love the pond and the meadow, as the wind is made to ripple the water.

II, 107   21 Nov. 1850

SUNLIGHT AFTER STORM

As I sat at the wall-corner, high on Conantum, the sky generally covered with continuous cheerless-looking slate-colored clouds, except in the west, I saw, through the hollows of the clouds, here and there the blue appearing. All at once a low-slanted glade of sunlight from one of heaven's west windows behind me fell on the bare gray maples, lighting them up with an incredibly intense and pure white light; then, going out there, it lit up some white birch stems south of the pond, then the gray rocks and the pale reddish young oaks of the lower cliffs, and then the very pale brown meadow-grass, and at last the brilliant white breasts of two ducks, tossing on the agitated surface far off on the pond, which I had not detected before. It was but a transient ray, and there was no sunshine afterward, but the intensity of the light was surprising and impressive, like a halo, a glory in which only the just deserved to live.

It was if the air, purified by the long storm, reflected these few rays from side to side with a complete illumination, like a perfectly polished mirror, while the effect was greatly enhanced by the contrast with the dull dark clouds and sombre earth. As if Nature did not dare at once to let in the full blaze of the sun to this combustible atmosphere. It was a serene, elysian light, in which the deeds I have dreamed of but not realized might have been performed. At the eleventh hour, late in the year, we have visions of the life we might have lived. No perfectly fair weather ever offered such an arena for noble acts. It was such a light as we behold but dwell not in! In each case, every recess was filled and lit up with this pure white light. The maples were Potter's, far down stream, but I dreamed I walked like a liberated spirit in their maze. The withered meadow-grass was as soft and glorious as paradise. And then it was remarkable that the light-giver should have revealed to me, for all life, the heaving white breasts of those two ducks within this glade of light. It was extinguished and relit as it travelled.

Tell me precisely the value and significance of these transient gleams which come sometimes at the end of the day, before the close of the storm, final dispersion of the clouds, too late to be of any service to the works of man for the day, and notwithstanding the whole night after may be overcast! Is not this a language to be heard and understood? There is, in the brown and gray earth and rocks, and the withered leaves and bare twigs at this season, a purity more correspondent to the light itself than summer offers.

x, 132-134   27 Oct. 1857

THE OUTSIDE TO THE GLOBE

Now I sit on the Cliffs and look abroad over the river and Conantum hills. I live so much in my habitual thoughts, a routine of thought, that I forget there is any outside to the globe, and am surprised when I behold it as now,—yonder hills and river in the moonlight, the monsters. Yet it is salutary to deal with the surface of things. What are these rivers and hills, these hieroglyphics which my eyes behold? There is something invigorating in this air, which I am peculiarly sensible is a real wind, blowing from over the surface of a planet. I look out at my eyes, I come to my window, and I feel and breathe the fresh air. It is a fact equally glorious with the most inward experience. Why have we ever slandered the outward? The perception of surfaces will always have the effect of miracle to a sane sense. I can see Nobscot* faintly.

IV, 312–313   23 Aug. 1852

MILES'S BLUEBERRY SWAMP

There is a pond-hole there perfectly covered with the leaves of the floating-heart and whiter than ever with its small white flowers, as if a slight large-flaked snow had fallen on it. The ground rises gently on every side, and first by the edge grow a few gratiolas, then the *Lysimachia stricta*, with a few blossoms left, then, a rod or two distant, in the higher rows of this natural coliseum, the red-panicled racemes of the hardhack rise. That is a glorious swamp of Miles's,— the more open parts, where the dwarf andromeda prevails. Now perhaps, an olivaceous green is the tint, not at all reddish, the lambkill and the bluish or glaucous rhodora and the pyrus intermixed making an extensive rich moss-like bed, in which you sink three feet to a dry bottom of moss or dead twigs, or, if peaty ground, it is covered with cup lichens; surrounded all by wild-looking woods, with the wild white spruce advancing into it and the pitch pine here and there, and high blueberry and tall pyrus and holly and other bushes under their countenance and protection. These are the wildest and richest gardens that we have. Such a depth of verdure into which you sink. They were never cultivated by any. Descending wooded hills, you come suddenly to this beautifully level pasture, comparatively open, with a close border of high blueberry bushes. You cannot believe that this can possibly abut on any cultivated field. Some wood or pasture, at least, must intervene. Here is a place, at last, which no woodchopper nor farmer frequents and to which no cows stray, perfectly wild, where the bittern and the hawk are undisturbed. The men, women, and children who perchance come hither blueberrying in their season get

* A hill ten miles southwest of Concord.

more than the value of the berries in the influences of the scene. How wildly rich and beautiful hang on high there the blueberries which might so easily be poisonous, the cool blue clusters high in air. Choke-berries, fair to the eye but scarcely palatable, hang far above your head, weighing down the bushes. The wild holly berry, perhaps the most beautiful of berries, hanging by slender threads from its more light and open bushes and more delicate leaves. The bushes, eight feet high, are black with choke-berries, and there are no wild animals to eat them.

IV, 280-281   4 Aug. 1852

BECK STOW'S SWAMP

I seemed to have reached a new world, so wild a place that the very huckleberries grew hairy and were inedible. I feel as if I were in Rupert's Land,* and a slight cool but agreeable shudder comes over me, as if equally far away from human society. What's the need of visiting far-off mountains and bogs, if a half-hour's walk will carry me into such wildness and novelty? But why should not as wild plants grow here as in Berkshire, as in Labrador? Is Nature so easily tamed? Is she not as primitive and vigorous here as anywhere? How does this particular acre of secluded, unfrequented, useless (?) quaking bog differ from an acre in Labrador? Has any white man ever settled on it? Does any now frequent it? Not even the Indian comes here now. I see that there are some square rods within twenty miles of Boston just as wild and primitive and unfrequented as a square rod in Lab-rador, as unaltered by man. Here grows the hairy huckleberry as it did in Squaw Sachem's day and a thousand years before, and concerns me perchance more than it did her. I have no doubt that for a mo-ment I experience exactly the same sensations as if I were alone in a bog in Rupert's Land, and it saves me the trouble of going there; for what in any case makes the difference between being here and being there but many such little differences of flavor and roughness put to-

* The Indian territories in eastern Canada held by the Hudson's Bay Company, synonymous in Thoreau's day with the idea of wild country.

gether? Rupert's Land is recognized as much by one sense as another. I felt a shock, a thrill, an agreeable surprise in one instant, for, no doubt, all the possible inferences were at once drawn, with a rush, in my mind,—I could be in Rupert's Land and supping at home within the hour! This beat the railroad. I recovered from my surprise without danger to my sanity, and permanently annexed Rupert's Land. That wild hairy huckleberry, inedible as it was, was equal to a domain secured to me and reaching to the South Sea. That was an unexpected harvest. I hope you have gathered as much, neighbor, from your corn and potato fields. I have got in my huckleberries. I shall be ready for Thanksgiving. It is in vain to dream of a wildness distant from ourselves. There is none such. It is the bog in our brain and bowels, the primitive vigor of Nature in us, that inspires that dream. I shall never find in the wilds of Labrador any greater wildness than in some recess in Concord, *i. e.* than I import into it. A little more manhood or virtue will make the surface of the globe anywhere thrillingly novel and wild. That alone will provide and pay the fiddler; it will convert the district road into an untrodden cranberry bog, for it restores all things to their original primitive flourishing and promising state.

A cold white horizon sky in the north, forerunner of the fall of the year. I go to bed and dream of cranberry-pickers far in the cold north. With windows partly closed, with continent concentrated thoughts, I dream. I get my new experiences still, not at the opera listening to the Swedish Nightingale, but at Beck Stow's Swamp listening to the native wood thrush.

IX, 42-44   30 Aug. 1856

WILD ROAD

Going along this old Carlisle road,—road for walkers, for berry-pickers, and no more worldly travellers; road for Melvin and Clark,*

---

* George Melvin, "The Hunter," and Brooks Clark, "Nature's Pensioner" (see pp. 45, 33). Carlisle was an all but deserted town near Concord. Flying Childers (five lines below) was a famous English racehorse of the eighteenth century.

not for the sheriff nor butcher nor the baker's jingling cart; road where all wild things and fruits abound, where there are countless rocks to jar those who venture there in wagons; which no jockey, no wheel-wright in his right mind, drives over, no little spidery gigs and Flying Childers; road which leads to and through a great but not famous garden, zoölogical and botanical garden, at whose *gate* you never ar-rive,—as I was going along there, I perceived the grateful scent of the dicksonia fern, now partly decayed, and it reminds me of all up-country with its springy mountainsides and unexhausted vigor. Is there any essence of dicksonia fern, I wonder? Surely that giant who, my neighbor expects, is to bound up the Alleghanies will have his hand-kerchief scented with that. In the lowest part of the road the dicksonia by the wall-sides is more than half frost-bitten and withered,—a sober Quaker-color, brown crape!—though not so tender or early [?] as the cinnamon fern; but soon I rise to where they are more yellow and green, and so my route is varied. On the higher places there are very handsome tufts of it, all yellowish outside and green within. The sweet fragrance of decay! When I wade through by narrow cow-paths, it is as if I had strayed into an ancient and decayed herb-garden. Proper for old ladies to scent their handkerchiefs with. Nature per-fumes her garments with this essence now especially. She gives it to those who go a-barberrying and on dank autumnal walks. The essence of this as well as of new-mown hay, surely! The very scent of it, if you have a decayed frond in your chamber, will take you far up coun-try in a twinkling. You would think you had gone after the cows there, or were lost on the mountains. It will make you as cool and well as a frog,—a wood frog, *Rana sylvatica*. It is the scent the earth yielded in the saurian period, before man was created and fell, before milk and water were invented, and the mints. Far wilder than they. . . .

Road—that old Carlisle one—that leaves towns behind; where you put off worldly thoughts; where you do not carry a watch, nor remember the proprietor; where the proprietor is the only trespasser, —looking after *his* apples!—the only one who mistakes his calling there, whose title is not good; where fifty may be a-berrying and you do not see one. It is an endless succession of glades where the bar-berries grow thickest, successive yards amid the barberry bushes where you do not see out. There I see Melvin and the robins. . . . The lonely horse in its pasture is glad to see company, comes forward to be noticed and takes an apple from your hand. Others are called *great* roads, but this is greater than [them] all. The road is only laid out, offered to walkers, not *accepted* by the town and the travelling world. To be represented by a dotted line on charts, or drawn in lime-juice, undiscoverable to the uninitiated, to be held to a warm imagination. No guide-boards indicate it. No odometer would indicate the miles a wagon had run there. Rocks which the druids *might* have raised—if they could. There I go searching for malic acid of the right quality, with my tests. The process is simple. Place the fruit * between your jaws and then endeavor to make your teeth meet. The very earth contains it. The Easterbrooks Country contains malic acid.

To my senses the dicksonia fern has the most wild and primitive fragrance, quite unalloyed and untamable, such as no human institutions give out,—the early morning fragrance of the world, antediluvian, strength and hope imparting. They who scent it can never faint. It is ever a new and untried field where it grows, and only when we think original thoughts can we perceive it. If we keep that [in] our boudoir we shall be healthy and evergreen as hemlocks. Older than, but related to, strawberries. Before strawberries were, it was, and it will outlast them. Good for the trilobite and saurian in us; death to dandies. It yields its scent most morning and evening. Growing without manure; older than man, refreshing him; preserving his original strength and innocence. When the New Hampshire farmer, far from travelled roads, has cleared a space for his mountain home and conducted the springs of the mountain to his yard, already it grows about the sources of that spring, before any mint is planted in his garden. There his sheep and oxen and he too scent it, and he realizes that the world is new to him. There the pastures are rich, the cattle do not die of disease, and the men are strong and free.

XII, 345-350   24 Sept. 1859

* The tang of wild apples is caused by an extra amount of malic acid.

WILDLIFE

OTANIZING

My first botany, as I remember, was Bigelow's "Plants of Bos-ton and Vicinity," * which I began to use about twenty years ago, looking chiefly for the popular names and the short references to the localities of plants, even without any regard to the plant. I also learned the names of many, but without using any system, and forgot them soon. I was not inclined to pluck flowers; preferred to leave them where they were, liked them best there. I was never in the least in-terested in plants in the house. But from year to year we look at Na-ture with new eyes. About half a dozen years ago I found myself again attending to plants with more method, looking out the name of each one and remembering it. I began to bring them home in my hat, a straw one with a scaffold lining to it, which I called my botany-box. I never used any other, and when some whom I visited were evidently surprised at its dilapidated look, as I deposited it on their front entry table, I assured them it was not so much my hat as my botany-box. I remember gazing with interest at the swamps about those days and wondering if I could ever attain to such familiarity with plants that I should know the species of every twig and leaf in them, that I should be acquainted with every plant (excepting grasses and cryptogamous ones), summer and winter, that I saw. Though I knew most of the flowers, and there were not in any particular swamp more than half a dozen shrubs that I did not know, yet these made it seem like a maze to me, of a thousand strange species, and I even thought of commenc-ing at one end and looking it faithfully and laboriously through till I knew it all. I little thought that in a year or two I should have at-tained to that knowledge without all that labor. Still I never studied botany, and do not to-day systematically, the most natural system is still so artificial. I wanted to know my neighbors, if possible,—to get a

* Jacob Bigelow (1787–1879), botanist. His *Florula Bostoniensis*, when first published in 1814, dealt only with the flora within a ten-mile radius of Boston; it was later enlarged so as to be useful for all New England and remained the standard treatise until Gray's *Manual* (1848).

little nearer to them. I soon found myself observing when plants first blossomed and leafed, and I followed it up early and late, far and near, several years in succession, running to different sides of the town and into the neighboring towns, often between twenty and thirty miles in a day. I often visited a particular plant four or five miles distant, half a dozen times within a fortnight, that I might know exactly when it opened, beside attending to a great many others in different direc‑ tions and some of them equally distant, at the same time. At the same time I had an eye for birds and whatever else might offer.

IX, 156‑158   9 Dec. 1856

ANDROMEDA

Observed in the second of the chain of ponds between Fair Haven and Walden a large (for the pond) island patch of the dwarf andromeda, I sitting on the east bank; its fine brownish‑red color very agreeable and memorable to behold. In the last long pond, looking at it from the south, I saw it filled with a slightly grayish shrub which I took for the sweet‑gale, but when I had got round to the east side, chancing to turn round, I was surprised to see that all this pond‑hole also was filled with the same warm brownish‑red‑colored andromeda. The fact was I was opposite to the sun, but from every other position I saw only the sun reflected from the surface of the andromeda leaves, which gave the whole a grayish‑brown hue tinged with red; but from this position alone I saw, as it were, through the leaves which the opposite sun lit up, giving to the whole this charming warm, what I call *Indian*, red color,—the mellowest, the ripest, red imbrowned color; but when I looked to the right or left, *i. e.* north or south, the more the swamp had the mottled light or grayish aspect where the light was reflected from the surfaces of the leaves. And afterward, when I had risen higher up the hill, though still opposite the sun, the light came reflected upward from the surfaces, and I lost that warm, rich red tinge, surpassing cathedral windows. Let me look again at a different hour of the day, and see if it is really so. It is a very interesting piece of magic. It is the autumnal tints in spring, only more subdued and mellow. . . .

How sweet is the perception of a new natural fact! suggesting what worlds remain to be unveiled. That phenomenon of the andromeda seen against the sun cheers me exceedingly. When the phenomenon was not observed, it was not at all. I think that no man ever takes an original [*sic*], or detects a principle, without experiencing an inexpressible, as quite infinite and sane, pleasure, which advertises him of the dignity of that truth he has perceived. The thing that pleases me most within these three days is the discovery of the andromeda phenomenon. It makes all those parts of the country where it grows more attractive and elysian to me. It is a natural magic. These little leaves are the stained windows in the cathedral of my world. At sight of any redness I am excited like a cow.

III, 430-431, 441-442   17, 19 Apr. 1852

WATER LILIES

The *Nymphœa odorata,* water nymph, sweet water-lily, pond-lily, in bloom. A superb flower, our lotus, queen of the waters. Now is the solstice in still waters. How sweet, innocent, wholesome its fragrance! How pure its white petals, though its root is in the mud! It must answer in my mind for what the Orientals say of the lotus flower. Probably the first a day or two since. To-morrow, then, will be the first Sabbath when the young men, having bathed, will walk slowly and soberly to church in their best clothes, each with a lily in his hand or bosom,—with as long a stem as he could get. At least I used to see them go by and come into church smelling a pond-lily, when I used to go myself. So that the flower is to some extent associated with bathing in Sabbath mornings and going to church, its odor contrasting and atoning for that of the sermon. . . . The water-lily floats on the smooth surface of slow waters, amid rounded shields of leaves, bucklers, red beneath, which simulate a green field, perfuming the air. Each instantly the prey of the spoiler,—the rose-bug and water-insects. How transitory the perfect beauty of the rose and lily! The highest, intensest color belongs to the land, the purest, perchance, to the water. The lily is perhaps the only flower which all are eager to pluck; it may be partly because of its inaccessibility to most. The farmers' sons will frequently collect every bud that shows itself above the surface within half a mile. They are so infested by insects, and it is so rare you get a perfect one which has opened itself,—though these only are perfect,—that the buds are commonly plucked and opened by hand. I have a faint recollection of pleasure derived from smoking dried lily stems before I was a man. I had commonly a sup' ply of these. I have never smoked anything more noxious. I used to amuse myself with making the yellow drooping stamens rise and fall by blowing through the pores of the long stem.

IV, 147·149   26 June 1852

CARRION–FLOWER

Under the cool, glossy green leaves of small swamp white oaks, and leaning against their scaly bark near the water, you see the wild roses, five or six feet high, looking forth from the shade; but almost every bush or copse near the river or in low land which you approach these days emits the noisome odor of the carrion-flower, so that you would think that all the dead dogs had drifted to that shore. All things, both beautiful and ugly, agreeable and offensive, are expressed in flowers,—all kinds and degrees of beauty and all kinds of foulness. For what purpose has nature made a flower to fill the lowlands with the odor of carrion? Just so much beauty and virtue as there is in the world, and just so much ugliness and vice, you see expressed in flow' ers. Each human being has his flower, which expresses his character. In them nothing is concealed, but everything published. Many a vil' lager whose garden bounds on the river, when he approaches the willows and cornels by the river's edge, thinks that some carrion has lodged on his shore, when it is only the carrion-flower he smells.

IV, 149·150   26 June 1852

ITCH-HAZEL

The witch-hazel here is in full blossom on this magical hillside, while its broad yellow leaves are falling. Some bushes are completely bare of leaves, and leather-colored they strew the ground. It is an extremely interesting plant,—October and November's child, and yet reminds me of the very earliest spring. Its blossoms smell like the spring, like the willow catkins; by their color as well as fragrance they belong to the saffron dawn of the year, suggesting amid all these signs of autumn, falling leaves and frost, that the life of Nature, by which she eternally flourishes, is untouched. It stands here in the shadow on the side of the hill, while the sunlight from over the top of the hill lights up its top-most sprays and yellow blossoms. Its spray, so jointed and angular, is not to be mistaken for any other. I lie on my back with joy under its boughs. While its leaves fall, its blossoms spring. The autumn, then, is indeed a spring. All the year is a spring. I see two blackbirds high overhead, going south, but I am going north in my thought with these hazel blossoms. It is a faery place. This is a part of the immortality of the soul. When I was thinking that it bloomed too late for bees or other insects to extract honey from its flowers,—that perchance they yielded no honey,—I saw a bee upon it. How important, then, to the bees this late-blossoming plant!

III, 59-60

8-9 Oct. 1851

HRUB OAK

A ridge of earth, with the red cockscomb lichen on it, peeps out still at the rut's edge. The dear wholesome color of shrub oak leaves, so clean and firm, not decaying, but which have put on a kind of immortality, not wrinkled and thin like the white oak leaves, but full-veined and plump, as nearer earth. Well-tanned leather on the one side, sun-tanned, color of colors, color of the cow and the deer, silver-downy beneath, turned toward the late bleached and russet fields.

What are acanthus leaves and the rest to this? Emblem of my winter
condition. I love and could embrace the shrub oak *with its scanty
garment of leaves rising above the snow, lowly whispering to me,
akin to winter thoughts, and sunsets, and to all virtue. Covert which
the hare and the partridge seek, and I too seek. What cousin of mine
is the shrub oak? How can any man suffer long? For a sense of want
is a prayer, and all prayers are answered. Rigid as iron, clean as the
atmosphere, hardy as virtue, innocent and sweet as a maiden is the
shrub oak. In proportion as I know and love it, I am natural and
sound as a partridge. I felt a positive yearning toward one bush this
afternoon. There was a match found for me at last. I fell in love with a
shrub oak. Tenacious of its leaves, which shrivel not but retain a certain wintry life in them, firm shields, painted in fast colors a rich
brown. The deer mouse, too, knows the shrub oak and has its hole in
the snow by the shrub oak's stem.

IX, 145-146   1 Dec. 1856

WILD FRUITS

I have carried an apple in my pocket to-night—a sopsivine, they
call it—till, now that I take my handkerchief out, it has got so fine a
fragrance that it really seems like a friendly trick of some pleasant
dæmon to entertain me with. It is redolent of sweet-scented orchards,
of innocent, teeming harvests. I realize the existence of a goddess
Pomona, and that the gods have really intended that men should feed
divinely, like themselves, on their own nectar and ambrosia. They
have so painted this fruit, and freighted it with such a fragrance, that
it satisfies much more than an animal appetite. Grapes, peaches, berries, nuts, etc., are likewise provided for those who will sit at their
sideboard. I have felt, when partaking of this inspiring diet, that my
appetite was an indifferent consideration; that eating became a sacrament, a method of communion, and ecstatic exercise, a mingling of

* What follows is an inverted version of the myth of Apollo pursuing
the chaste Daphne, only to find her transformed into a laurel tree to
escape his ravishing embrace.

bloods, and [a] sitting at the communion table of the world; and so have not only quenched my thirst at the spring but the health of the universe.

The indecent haste and grossness with which our food is swallowed have cast a disgrace on the very act of eating itself. But I do believe that, if this process were rightly conducted, its aspects and effects would be wholly changed, and we should receive our daily life and health, Antæus-like, with an ecstatic delight, and, with upright front, an innocent and graceful behavior, take our strength from day to day. This fragrance of the apple in my pocket has, I confess, deterred me from eating of it. I am more effectually fed by it another way.

It is, indeed, the common notion that this fragrance is the only food of the gods, and inasmuch as we are partially divine we are compelled to respect it.

1, 371-373   1845

BERRIES, SYMBOL OF COMMMUNION

The berries of the *Vaccinium vacillans* are very abundant and large this year on Fair Haven, where I am now. Indeed these and huckleberries and blackberries are very abundant in this part of the town. Nature does her best to feed man. The traveller need not go out of the road to get as many as he wants; every bush and vine teems with palatable fruit. Man for once stands in such relation to Nature as the animals that pluck and eat as they go. The fields and hills are a table constantly spread. Wines of all kinds and qualities, of noblest vintage, are bottled up in the skins of countless berries, for the taste of men and animals. To men they seem offered not so much for food as for sociality, that they may picnic with Nature,—diet drinks, cordials, wines. We pluck and eat in remembrance of Her. It is a sacrament, a communion. The not-forbidden fruits, which no serpent tempts us to taste. Slight and innocent savors, which relate us to Nature, make us her guests and entitle us to her regard and protection. It is a Saturnalia, and we quaff her wines at every turn. This season of

berrying is so far respected that the children have a vacation to pick
berries, and women and children who never visit distant hills and
fields and swamps on any other errand are seen making haste thither
now, with half their domestic utensils in their hands. The woodchopper goes into the swamp for fuel in the winter; his wife and children
for berries in the summer.

v, 330-331   24 July 1853

ACORNS: NUTS OF THE GODS

How handsome the great red oak acorns now! I stand under the
tree on [R. W.] Emerson's lot. They are still falling. I heard one fall
into the water as I approached, and thought that a musquash had
plunged. They strew the ground and the bottom of the river thickly,
and while I stand here I hear one strike the boughs with force as it
comes down, and drop into the water. The part that was covered by
the cup is whitish-woolly. How munificent is Nature to create this
profusion of wild fruit, as it were merely to gratify our eyes! Though
inedible they are more wholesome to my immortal part, and stand by
me longer, than the fruits which I eat. If they had been plums or
chestnuts I should have eaten them on the spot and probably forgotten
them. They would have afforded only a momentary gratification, but
being acorns, I remember, and as it were *feed* on, them still. They are
untasted fruits forever in store for me. I know not of their flavor as
yet. That is postponed to some still unimagined winter evening. These
which we admire but do not eat are nuts of the gods. When time is
no more we shall crack them. I cannot help liking them better than
horse-chestnuts, which are of a similar color, not only because they
are of a much handsomer form, but because they are indigenous. What
hale, plump fellows they are! They can afford not to be useful to me,
nor to know me or be known by me. They go their way, I go mine,
and it turns out that sometimes I go *after* them.

xi, 257   27 Oct. 1858

LICHENS, MOSSES, AND GRASS

As we sweep [in our boat] past the north end of Poplar Hill, with a sand-hole in it, its now dryish, pale-brown mottled sward clothing its rounded slope, which was lately saturated with moisture, presents very agreeable hues. . . . These earth colors, methinks, are never so fair as in the spring. Now the green mosses and lichens contrast with the brown grass, but ere long the surface will be uniformly green. I suspect that we are more amused by the effects of color in the skin of the earth now than in summer. Like the skin of a python, greenish and brown, a fit coat for it to creep over the earth and be concealed in. Or like the skin of a pard, the great leopard mother that Nature is, where she lies at length, exposing her flanks to the sun. I feel as if I could land to stroke and kiss the very sward, it is so fair. It is homely and domestic to my eyes like the rug that lies before my hearth-side. Such ottomans and divans are spread for us to recline on. Nor are these colors mere thin superficial figures, vehicles for paint, but wonderful living growths,—these lichens, to the study of which learned men have devoted their lives,—and libraries have been written about them. The earth lies out now like a leopard, drying her lichen and moss spotted skin in the sun, her sleek and variegated hide. I know that the few raw spots will heal over. Brown is the color for me, the color of our coats and our daily lives, the color of the poor man's loaf. The bright tints are pies and cakes, good only for October feasts, which would make us sick if eaten every day.

XII, 96-98   28 Mar. 1859

THE LICHENIST

Going along the Nut Meadow or Jimmy Miles road, when I see the sulphur lichens on the rails brightening with the moisture I feel like studying them again as a relisher or tonic, to make life go down and digest well, as we use pepper and vinegar and salads. They are a sort of winter greens which we gather and assimilate with our eyes. That's the true use of the study of lichens. I expect that the lichenist will have the keenest relish for Nature in her every-day mood and dress. He will have the appetite of the worm that never dies, of the grub. To study lichens is to get a taste of earth and health, to go gnaw-ing the rails and rocks. This product of the bark is the essence of all times. The lichenist extracts nutriment from the very crust of the earth. A taste for this study is an evidence of titanic health, a sane earthiness. It makes not so much blood as soil of life. It fits a man to deal with the barrenest and rockiest experience. A little moisture, a fog, or rain, or melted snow makes his wilderness to blossom like the rose.* As some strong animal appetites, not satisfied with starch and muscle and fat, are fain to eat that which eats and digests,—the contents of the crop and the stomach and entrails themselves,—so the lichenist loves the tripe of the rock,—that which eats and digests the rocks. He eats the eater. "Eat-all" may be his name. A lichenist fats where others starve. His provender never fails. What is the barrenest waste to him, the barest rocks? A rail is the sleekest and fattest of coursers for him. He picks anew the bones which have been picked a generation since, for when their marrow is gone they are clothed with new flesh for him. What diet drink can be compared with a tea or soup made of the very crust of the earth? There is no such collyrium or salve for sore eyes as these brightening lichens in a moist day. Go and bathe and screen your eyes with them in the softened light of the woods.

XI, 439-441   7 Feb. 1859

GIANT FUNGUS

As I was going up the hill, I was surprised to see rising above the June-grass, near a walnut, a whitish object, like a stone with a white top, or a skunk erect, for it was black below. It was an enormous toadstool, or fungus, a sharply conical parasol in the form of a sugar loaf, slightly turned up at the edges, which were rent half an inch in every inch or two. The whole height was sixteen inches. The pileus

* Isaiah 35.1.

or cap was six inches long by seven in width at the rim, though it appeared longer than wide. There was no veil, and the stem was about one inch in diameter and naked. The top of the cap was quite white within and without, hoariest at top of the cone like a mountain-top, not smooth but with [a] stringy kind of scales turned upward at the edge, which declined downward, *i. e.* down the cap, into a coarse hoariness, as if the compact white fibres had been burst by the spreading of the gills and showed the black. As you looked up within, the light was transmitted between the trembling gills. It looked much like an old felt hat [that] is pushed up into a cone and its rim all ragged and with some meal shaken on to it; in fact, it was almost big enough for a child's head. It was so delicate and fragile that its whole cap trembled on the least touch, and, as I could not lay it down without injuring it, I was obliged to carry it home all the way in my hand and erect, while I paddled my boat with one hand. It was a wonder how its soft cone ever broke through the earth. Such growths ally our age to former periods, such as geology reveals. I wondered if it had not some relation to the skunk, though not in odor, yet in its colors and the general impression it made. It suggests a vegetative force which may almost make man tremble for his dominion. It carries me back to the era of the formation of the coal-measures—the age of the saurus and pleiosaurus and when bullfrogs were as big as bulls. Its stem had something massy about it like an oak, large in proportion to the weight it had to support (though not perhaps to the size of the cap), like the vast hollow columns under some piazzas, whose caps have hardly weight enough to hold their tops together. It made you think of parasols of Chinese mandarins; or it might have been used by the great fossil bullfrog in his walks. What part does it play in the economy of the world? . . .

I have just been out (7:30 A.M.) to show my fungus. The milkman and the butcher followed me to inquire what it was, and children and young ladies addressed me in the street who never spoke to me before. It is so fragile I was obliged to walk at a funereal pace for fear of jarring it. It is so delicately balanced on its stem that it falls to one side across it on the least inclination; falls about like an umbrella that has lost its stays. It is rapidly curling up on the edge, and the **rents** increasing, until it is completely fringed, **and is an inch wider** there. It is melting in the sun and light, and black drops and streams falling on my hand and fragments of the black fringed rim falling on the sidewalk. Evidently such a plant can only be seen in perfection in the early morning. It is a creature of the night, like the great moths. They wish me to send it to the first of a series of exhibitions of flowers and fruits to be held at the court-house this afternoon, which I promise to do if it is presentable then. Perhaps it might be placed in the court-house cellar and the company be invited at last to walk down and examine it. Think of placing this giant parasol fungus in the midst of all their roses; yet they admit that it would overshadow and eclipse them all. It is to be remarked that this grew, not in low and damp soil, but high up on the open side of a dry hill, about two rods from a walnut and one from a wall, in the midst of and rising above the thin June-grass. The last night was warm; the earth was very dry, and there was a slight sprinkling of rain. . . .

I put the parasol fungus in the cellar to preserve it, but it went on rapidly melting and wasting away from the edges upward, spreading as it dissolved, till it was shaped like a dish cover. By night, though kept in the cellar all the day, there was not more than two of the six inches of the height of the cap left, and the barrel-head beneath it and its own stem looked as if a large bottle of ink had been broken there. It defiled all it touched. The next morning the hollow stem was left perfectly bare, and only the hoary apex of the cone, spreading about two inches in diameter, lay on the ground beneath. Probably one night produced it, and in one day, with all our pains, it wasted away. Is it not a giant mildew or mould? In the warm, muggy night the surface of the earth is mildewed. The mould, which is the flower of humid darkness and ignorance. The Pyramids and other monuments of Egypt are a vast mildew or toadstools which have met with no light of day sufficient to waste them away. Slavery is such a mould, and superstition,—which are most rank in the warm and humid portions of the globe. Luxor sprang up one night out of the slime of the Nile. The humblest, puniest weed that can endure the sun is thus superior to the largest fungus, as is the peasant's cabin to those foul temples. It is a temple consecrated to Apis. All things flower, both vices and virtues, but the one is essentially foul, the other fair. In hell, toadstools should be represented as overshadowing men. The priest is the fungus of the graveyard, the mildew of the tomb. In the animal world there are toads and lizards.

v, 270-275   18 June 1853

CHANTICLEER

Let a full-grown but young cock stand near you. How full of life he is, from the tip of his bill through his trembling wattles and comb and his bright eye to the extremity of his clean toes! How alert and restless, listening to every sound and watching every motion! How various his notes, from the finest and shrillest alarum as a hawk sails over, surpassing the most accomplished violinist on the short strings, to a hoarse and terrene voice or cluck! He has a word for every occasion; for the dog that rushes past, and partlet cackling in the barn. And then how, elevating himself and flapping his wings, he gathers impetus and air and launches forth that world-renowned ear-piercing strain! not a vulgar note of defiance, but the mere effervescence of life, like the bursting of a bubble in a wine-cup. Is any gem so bright as his eye?

xi, 190-191   1 Oct. 1858

A SWALLOW'S CHICKS

Mr. [Jacob] Farmer tells me that one Sunday he went to his barn, having nothing to do, and thought he would watch the swallows, republican swallows. The old bird was feeding her young, and he sat within fifteen feet, overlooking them. There were five young, and he was curious to know how each received its share; and as often as the bird came with a fly, the one at the door (or opening) took it, and then they all hitched round one notch, so that a new one was presented at the door, who received the next fly; and this was the invariable order, the same one never receiving two flies in succession. At last the old bird brought a very small fly, and the young one that swallowed it did not desert his ground but waited to receive the next, but when the bird came with another, of the usual size, she commenced a loud and long scolding at the little one, till it resigned its place, and the next in succession received the fly.

x, 173·174 9 Nov. 1857

BLUEBIRD

The bluebird which some woodchopper or inspired walker is said to have seen in that sunny interval between the snow-storms is like a speck of clear blue sky seen near the end of a storm, reminding us of an ethereal region and a heaven which we had forgotten. Princes and magistrates are often styled serene, but what is their turbid serenity to that ethereal serenity which the bluebird embodies? His Most Serene Birdship! His soft warble melts in the ear, as the snow is melting in the valleys around. The bluebird comes and with his warble drills the ice and sets free the rivers and ponds and frozen ground. As the sand flows down the slopes a little way, assuming the forms of foliage where the frost comes out of the ground, so this little rill of melody flows a short way down the concave of the sky.

xii, 5 2 Mar. 1859

NUTHATCH

Going down-town this forenoon, I heard a white-bellied nuthatch on an elm within twenty feet, uttering peculiar notes and more like a song than I remember to have heard from it. There was a chickadee close by, to which it may have been addressed. It was something like *to-what what what what what*, rapidly repeated, and not the usual *gnah gnah;* and this instant it occurs to me that this may be that earliest spring note which I hear, and have referred to a woodpecker! (This is before *I* have chanced to see a bluebird, blackbird, or robin in Concord this year.) It is the spring note of the nuthatch. It paused in its progress about the trunk or branch and uttered this lively but peculiarly inarticulate song, an awkward attempt to warble almost in the face of the chickadee, as if it were one of its kind. It was thus giving vent to the spring within it. If I am not mistaken, it is what I have heard in former springs or winters long ago, fabulously early in the season, when we men had but just begun to anticipate the spring,—for it would seem that we, in our anticipations and sympathies, include in succession the moods and expressions of all creatures. When only the snow had begun to melt and no rill of song had broken loose, a note so dry and fettered still, so inarticulate and half thawed out, that you might (and would commonly) mistake for the tapping of a woodpecker. As if the young nuthatch in its hole had listened only to the tapping of woodpeckers and learned that music, and now, when it would sing and give vent to its spring ecstasy, it can modulate only some notes like that. That is its theme still. That is its ruling idea of song and music,—only a little clangor and liquidity added to the tapping of the woodpecker. It was the handle by which my thoughts took firmly hold on spring.

This herald of spring is commonly unseen, it sits so close to the bark.

XII, 13-15   5 Mar. 1859

TAKE DRIVER

Looking off on to the river meadow, I noticed, as I thought, a stout stake aslant in the meadow, three or more rods off, sharp at the top and rather light-colored on one side, as is often the case; yet, at the same time, it occurred to me that a stake-driver often resembled a stake very much, but I thought, nevertheless, that there was no doubt about this being a stake. I took out my glass to look for ducks, and my companion, seeing what I had, and asking if it was not a stake-driver, I suffered my glass at last to rest on it, and I was much surprised to find that it was a stake-driver after all. The bird stood in shallow water near a tussock, perfectly still, with its long bill pointed upwards in the same direction with its body and neck, so as perfectly to resemble a stake aslant. If the bill had made an angle with the neck it would have been betrayed at once. Its resource evidently was to rely on its form and color and immobility solely for its concealment. This was its instinct, whether it implies any conscious artifice or not. I watched it for fifteen minutes, and at length it relaxed its muscles and changed its attitude, and I observed a slight motion; and soon after, when I moved toward it, it flew. It resembled more a piece of a rail than anything else,—more than anything that would have been seen here before the white man came. It is a question whether the bird consciously coöperates in each instance with its Maker, who contrived this concealment. I can never believe that this resemblance is a mere coincidence, not designed to answer this very end—which it does answer so perfectly and usefully.

XIII, 250-251   17 Apr. 1860

AY–WING

While dropping beans in the garden . . . just after sundown (May 13th), I hear from across the fields the note of the bay-wing, *Come here here there there quick quick quick or I'm gone* (which I have no doubt sits on some fence-post or rail there), and it instantly translates me from the sphere of my work and repairs all the world that we jointly inhabit. It reminds me of so many country afternoons and evenings when this bird's strain was heard far over the fields, as I pursued it from field to field. The spirit of its earth-song, of its serene and true philosophy, was breathed into me, and I saw the world as through a glass, as it lies eternally. Some of its aboriginal contentment, even of its domestic felicity, possessed me. What he suggests is permanently true. As the bay-wing sang many a thousand years ago, so sang he to-night. In the beginning God heard his song and pronounced it good,* and hence it has endured. It reminded me of many a summer sunset, of many miles of gray rails, of many a rambling

---

* A paraphrase of Genesis, Ch. 1. At the end of each day of the Creation comes the refrain: "God saw that it was good."

pasture, of the farmhouse far in the fields, its milk-pans and well-sweep, and the cows coming home from pasture.

I would thus from time to time take advice of the birds, correct my human views by listening to their volucral (?). He is a brother poet, this small gray bird (or bard), whose muse inspires mine. His lay is an idyl or pastoral, older and sweeter than any that is classic. He sits on some gray perch like himself, on a stake, perchance, in the midst of the field, and you can hardly see him against the plowed ground. You advance step by step as the twilight deepens, and lo! he is gone, and in vain you strain your eyes to see whither, but anon his tinkling strain is heard from some other quarter. One with the rocks and with us.

IX, 363-364   12 May 1857

 OOD THRUSH

Some birds are poets and sing all summer. They are the true singers. Any man can write verses during the love season. I am reminded of this while we rest in the shade on the Major Heywood road and listen to a wood thrush, now just before sunset. We are most interested in those birds who sing for the love of the music and not of their mates; who meditate their strains, and *amuse* themselves with singing; the birds, the strains, of deeper sentiment; not bobolinks, that lose their plumage, their bright colors, and their song so early. . . .

The wood thrush's is no opera music; it is not so much the composition as the strain, the tone,—cool bars of melody from the atmosphere of everlasting morning or evening. It is the quality of the song, not the sequence. In the peawai's note there is some sultriness, but in the thrush's, though heard at noon, there is the liquid coolness of things that are just drawn from the bottom of springs. The thrush alone declares the immortal wealth and vigor that is in the forest. Here is a bird in whose strain the story is told, though Nature waited for the science of æsthetics to discover it to man. Whenever a man hears it, he is young, and Nature is in her spring. Wherever he hears it, it is a new world and a free country, and the gates of heaven are not shut against him. Most other birds sing from the level of my ordinary cheerful hours—a carol; but this bird never fails to speak to me out of an ether purer than that I breathe, of immortal beauty and vigor. He deepens the significance of all things seen in the light of his strain. He sings to make men take higher and truer views of things. He sings to amend their institutions; to relieve the slave on the plantation and the prisoner in his dungeon, the slave in the house of luxury and the prisoner of his own low thoughts.

IV, 190-191   5 July 1852

THRUSH AS SYMBOL

As I come over the hill, I hear the wood thrush singing his evening lay. This is the only bird whose note affects me like music, affects the flow and tenor of my thought, my fancy and imagination. . . . I long for wildness, a nature which I cannot put my foot through, woods where the wood thrush forever sings, where the hours are early morning ones, and there is dew on the grass, and the day is forever unproved, where I might have a fertile unknown for a soil about me. I would go after the cows, I would watch the flocks of Admetus* there forever, only for my board and clothes. A New Hampshire everlasting and unfallen. . . .

All that was ripest and fairest in the wilderness and the wild man is preserved and transmitted to us in the strain of the wood thrush. It is the mediator between barbarism and civilization. It is unrepentant as Greece.

V, 292-293   22 June 1853

* This allusion identifies Thoreau with Apollo, who kept the flocks of King Admetus. The next paragraph probably alludes to the religion of Orphism, which attempted to mediate between the Dionysian and the Apollonian aspects of man; Thoreau was well read on the subject.

TANAGER

At Loring's Wood heard and saw a tanager. That contrast of a *red* bird with the green pines and the blue sky! Even when I have heard his note and look for him and find the bloody fellow, sitting on a dead twig of a pine, I am always startled. (They seem to love the darkest and thickest pines.) That incredible red, with the green and blue, as if these were the trinity we wanted. Yet with his hoarse note he pays for his color. I am transported; these are not the woods I ordinarily walk in. He sunk Concord in his thought. How he enhances the wilderness and wealth of the woods! This and the emperor moth make the tropical phenomena of our zone. There is warmth in the pewee's strain, but this bird's colors and his note tell of Brazil.

v, 186-187   23 May 1853

CRIMSON REDPOLL

Standing there, though in this *bare* November landscape, I am reminded of the incredible phenomenon of small birds in winter,— that ere long, amid the cold powdery snow, as it were a fruit of the season, will come twittering a flock of delicate crimson-tinged birds, lesser redpolls, to sport and feed on the seeds and buds now just ripe for them on the sunny side of a wood, shaking down the powdery snow there in their cheerful social feeding, as if it were high midsummer to them. These crimson aerial creatures have wings which would bear them quickly to the regions of summer, but here is all the summer they want. What a rich contrast! tropical colors, crimson breasts, on cold white snow! Such etherealness, such delicacy in their forms, such ripeness in their colors, in this stern and barren season! It is as surprising as if you were to find a brilliant crimson flower which flourished amid snows. They greet the chopper and the hunter in their furs. Their Maker gave them the last touch and launched them forth the day of the Great Snow. He made this bitter imprisoning cold before which man quails, but He made at the same time these warm and glowing creatures to twitter and be at home in it. He said not only, Let there be linnets in winter, but linnets of rich plumage and pleasing twitter, bearing summer in their natures. The snow will be three feet deep, the ice will be two feet thick, and last night, perchance, the mercury sank to thirty degrees below zero. All the fountains of nature seem to be sealed up. The traveller is frozen on his way. But under the edge of yonder birch wood will be a little flock of crimson-breasted lesser redpolls, busily feeding on the seeds of the birch and shaking down the powdery snow! As if a flower were created to be now in bloom, a peach to be now first fully ripe on its stem. I am struck by the perfect confidence and success of nature. There is no question about the existence of these delicate creatures, their adaptedness to their circumstances. There is superadded superfluous paintings and adornments, a crystalline, jewel-like health and soundness, like the colors reflected from ice-crystals.

VIII, 42-43   11 Dec. 1855

AWK CIRCLING

Saw a large hawk circling over a pine wood below me, and screaming, apparently that he might discover his prey by their flight. Travelling ever by wider circles. What a symbol of the thoughts, now soaring, now descending, taking larger and larger circles, or smaller and smaller. It flies not directly whither it is bound, but advances by circles, like a courtier of the skies. No such noble progress! How it comes round, as with a wider sweep of thought! But the majesty is in the imagination of the beholder, for the bird is intent on its prey. Circling and ever circling, you cannot divine which way it will incline, till perchance it dives down straight as an arrow to its mark. It rises higher above where I stand, and I see with beautiful distinctness its wings against the sky,—primaries and secondaries, and the rich tracery of the outline of the latter (?), its inner wings, or wing-linings, within the outer,—like a great moth seen against the sky. A will-o'-the wind. Following its path, as it were through the vortices of the air. The poetry of motion. Not as preferring one place to another, but enjoying each as long as possible. Most gracefully so surveys new scenes and revisits the old. As if that hawk were made to be the symbol of my thought, how bravely he came round over those parts of the wood which he had not surveyed, taking in a new segment, annexing new territories! Without "heave-yo!" it trims its sail. It goes about without the creaking of a block. That America yacht of the air that never makes a tack, though it rounds the globe itself, takes in and shakes out its reefs without a flutter,—its sky-scrapers all under its control. Holds up one wing, as if to admire, and sweeps off this way, then holds up the other and sweeps that. If there are two concentrically circling, it is such a regatta as Southampton waters never witnessed.

Flights of imagination, Coleridgean thoughts.* So a man is said to soar in his thought, ever to fresh woods and pastures new. Rises as in thought.

III, 143-144   20 Dec. 1851

A PAIR OF HAWKS

As I stood by this pond, I heard a hawk scream, and, looking up, saw a pretty large one circling not far off and incessantly screaming, as I at first supposed to scare and so discover its prey, but its screaming was so incessant and it circled from time to time so near me, as I moved southward, that I began to think it had a nest near by and was angry at my intrusion into its domains. As I moved, the bird still followed and screamed, coming sometimes quite near or within gunshot, then circling far off or high into the sky. At length, as I was looking up at it, thinking it the only living creature within view, I was singularly startled to behold, as my eye by chance penetrated deeper into the blue,—the abyss of blue above, which I had taken for a solitude,—its mate silently soaring at an immense height and seeming indifferent to me. We are surprised to discover that there can be an eye

* Coleridge's famous distinction between imagination and fancy (*Biographia Literaria*, Ch. 13) seems implicit throughout this miniature. Milton's "Lycidas" is quoted in the next sentence.

on us on that side, and so little suspected, that the heavens are full of eyes, though they look so blue and spotless. Then I knew it was the female that circled and screamed below. At last the latter rose grad-ually to meet her mate, and they circled together there, as if they could not possibly feel any anxiety on my account. When I drew nearer to the tall trees where I suspected the nest to be, the female descended again, swept by screaming still nearer to me just over the tree-tops, and finally, while I was looking for the orchis in the swamp, alighted on a white pine twenty or thirty rods off. . . . At length I detected the nest about eighty feet from the ground, in a very large white pine by the edge of the swamp. It was about three feet in diameter, of dry sticks, and a young hawk, apparently as big as its mother, stood on the edge of the nest looking down at me, and only moving its head when I moved. In its imperfect plumage and by the slow motion of its head it reminded me strongly of a vulture, so large and gaunt. It appeared a tawny brown on its neck and breast, and dark brown or blackish on wings. The mother was light beneath, and apparently lighter still on rump. . . .

I have come with a spy-glass to look at the hawks. They have detected me and are already screaming over my head more than half a mile from the nest. I find no difficulty in looking at the young hawk (there appears to be one only, standing on the edge of the nest), resting the glass in the crotch of a young oak. I can see every wink and the color of its iris. It watches me more steadily than I it, now looking straight down at me with both eyes and outstreched neck, now turning its head and looking with one eye. How its eye and its whole head express anger! Its anger is more in its eye than in its beak. It is quite hoary over the eye and on the chin. The mother meanwhile is incessantly circling about and above its charge and me, farther or nearer, sometimes withdrawing a quarter of a mile, but occasionally coming to alight for a moment almost within gunshot, on the top of a tall white pine; but I hardly bring my glass fairly to bear on her, and get sight of her angry eye through the pine-needles, before she circles away again. Thus for an hour that I lay there, screaming every minute or oftener with open bill. Now and then pursued by a kingbird or a blackbird, who appear merely to annoy it by dashing down at its back. Meanwhile the male is soaring, apparently quite undisturbed, at a great height above, evidently not hunting, but amusing or recreating himself in the thinner and cooler air, as if pleased with his own circles, like a geometer, and enjoying the sublime scene. I doubt if he has his eye fixed on any prey, or the earth. He probably descends to hunt.

v, 231-233, 235-236   8, 9 June 1853

ESTING NIGHTHAWK

Visited my nighthawk on her nest. Could hardly believe my eyes when I stood within seven feet and beheld her sitting on her eggs, her head to me. She looked so Saturnian, so one with the earth, so sphinx-like, a relic of the reign of Saturn which Jupiter did not destroy, a riddle that might well cause a man to go dash his head against a stone. It was not an actual living creature, far less a winged creature of the air, but a figure in stone or bronze, a fanciful production of art, like the gryphon or phœnix. In fact, with its breast toward me, and owing to its color or size no bill perceptible, it looked like the end [of] a brand, such as are common in a clearing, its breast mottled or alternately waved with dark brown and gray, its flat, grayish, weather-beaten crown, its eyes nearly closed, purposely, lest those bright beads should betray it, with the stony cunning of the sphinx. A fanciful work in bronze to ornament a mantel. It was enough to fill one with awe. The sight of this creature sitting on its eggs impressed me with the venerableness of the globe. There was nothing novel about it. All the while, this seemingly sleeping bronze sphinx, as motionless as the earth, was watching me with intense anxiety through those narrow slits in its eyelids. Another step, and it fluttered down the hill close to the ground, with a wabbling motion, as if touching the ground now with the tip of one wing, now with the other, so ten rods to the water, which [it] skimmed close over a few rods, then rose and soared in the air above me. Wonderful creature, which sits motionless on its eggs on the barest, most exposed hills, through pelting storms of rain or hail, as if it were a rock or a part of the earth itself, the outside of the globe, with its eyes shut and its wings folded, and, after the two days' storm, when you think it has become a fit symbol of the rheumatism, it sud-

denly rises into the air a bird, one of the most aerial, supple, and graceful of creatures, without stiffness in its wings or joints! It was a fit
prelude to meeting Prometheus bound to his rock on Caucasus.

    v, 230-231   7 June 1853

H AWK AS SYMBOL

The hen-hawk and the pine are friends. The same thing which
keeps the hen-hawk in the woods, away from the cities, keeps me
here. That bird settles with confidence on a white pine top and not
upon your weathercock. That bird will not be poultry of yours, lays
no eggs for you, forever hides its nest. Though willed, or *wild*, it is
not willful in its wildness. The unsympathizing man regards the wildness of some animals, their strangeness to him, as a sin; as if all their
virtue consisted in their tamableness. He has always a charge in his
gun ready for their extermination. What we call wildness is a civilization other than our own. The hen-hawk shuns the farmer, but it seeks
the friendly shelter and support of the pine. It will not consent to walk
in the barn-yard, but it loves to soar above the clouds. It has its own
way and is beautiful, when we would fain subject it to our will. So
any surpassing work of art is strange and wild to the mass of men, as
is genius itself. No hawk that soars and steals our poultry is wilder
than genius, and none is more persecuted or above persecution. It
can never be poet laureate, to say "Pretty Poll" and "Polly want a
cracker."

    xi, 450-451   16 Feb. 1859

W ILD DUCKS

The ducks alight at this season on the windward side of the
river, in the smooth water, and swim about by twos and threes, pluming themselves and diving to peck at the root of the lily and the cranberries which the frost has not loosened. It is impossible to approach

them within gunshot when they are accompanied by the gull, which rises sooner and makes them restless. They fly to windward first, in order to get under weigh, and are more easily reached by the shot if approached on that side. When preparing to fly, they swim about with their heads erect, and then, gliding along a few feet with their bodies just touching the surface, rise heavily with much splashing and fly low at first, if not suddenly aroused, but otherwise rise directly to survey the danger. The cunning sportsman is not in haste to desert his position, but waits to ascertain if, having got themselves into flying trim, they will not return over the ground in their course to a new resting-place.

   I, 128-129   8 Mar. 1840

WILD GEESE AND HUNTERS

Going through Dennis's field with C. [Channing], saw a flock of geese on east side of river near willows. Twelve great birds on the troubled surface of the [flooded] meadow, delayed by the storm. We lay on the ground behind an oak and our umbrella, eighty rods off, and watched them. Soon we heard a gun go off, but could see no smoke in the mist and rain. And the whole flock rose, spreading their great wings and flew with clangor a few rods and lit in the water again, then swam swiftly toward our shore with outstretched necks. I knew them first from ducks by their long necks. Soon appeared the man, running toward the shore in vain, in his greatcoat; but he soon retired in vain. We remained close under our umbrella by the tree, ever and anon looking through a peep-hole between the umbrella and the tree at the birds. On they came, sometimes in two, sometimes in three, squads, warily, till we could see the steel-blue and green reflections from their necks. We held the dog close the while,—C., lying on his back in the rain, had him in his arms,—and thus we gradually edged round on the ground in this cold, wet, windy storm, keeping our feet to the tree, and the great wet calf of a dog with his eyes shut so meekly in our arms. We laughed well at our adventure. They swam fast and warily, seeing our umbrella. Occasionally one expanded a gray wing.

They showed white on breasts. And not till after half an hour, sitting cramped and cold and wet on the ground, did we leave them. . . .

That last flock of geese yesterday is still in my eye. After hearing their clangor, looking southwest, we saw them just appearing over a dark pine wood, in an irregular waved line, one abreast of the other, as it were breasting the air and pushing it before them. It made you think of the streams of Cayster, etc., etc.* They carry weight, such a weight of metal in the air. Their dark waved outline as they disappear. The grenadiers of the air. Man pygmifies himself at sight of these inhabitants of the air. These stormy days they do not love to fly; they alight in some retired marsh or river. From their lofty pathway they can easily spy out the most extensive and retired swamp. How many there must be, that one or more flocks are seen to go over almost every farm in New England in the spring!

III, 434-435, 439   18, 19 Apr. 1852

WILD GEESE FLYING

About 10 A.M. a long flock of geese are going over from northeast to southwest, or parallel with the general direction of the coast and great mountain-ranges. The sonorous, quavering sounds of the geese are the voice of this cloudy air,—a sound that comes from directly between us and the sky, an aerial sound, and yet so distinct, heavy, and sonorous, a clanking chain drawn through the heavy air. I saw through my window some children looking up and pointing their tiny bows into the heavens, and I knew at once that the geese were in the air. It is always an exciting event. The children, instinctively aware of its importance, rushed into the house to tell their parents. These travellers are revealed to you by the upward-turned gaze of men. And though these undulating lines are melting into the southwestern sky, the sound comes clear and distinct to you as the clank

* In the *Iliad*, II, 459 ff., Homer compares the clans of the Greeks to the birds near the streams of the Cayster, in Lydia. (This Homeric simile is imitated by Vergil in the *Georgics*, I, 383, and in the *Aeneid*, VII, 699.)

of a chain in a neighboring stithy. So they migrate, not flitting from hedge to hedge, but from latitude to latitude, from State to State, steering boldly out into the ocean of the air. It is remarkable how these large objects, so plain when your vision is rightly directed, may be lost in the sky if you look away for a moment,—as hard to hit as a star with a telescope.

It is a sort of encouraging or soothing sound to assuage their painful fears when they go over a town, as a man moans to deaden a physical pain. The direction of their flight each spring and autumn reminds us inlanders how the coast trends.

x, 169-170   6 Nov. 1857

BLUE HERONS BATHING

I discovered with my naked eye . . . a blue heron standing in very shallow water amid the weeds of the bar and pluming itself. . . . I floated to within twenty-five rods and watched it at my leisure. Standing on the shallowest part of the bar at that end, it was busily dressing its feathers, passing its bill like a comb down its feathers from base to tip. From its form and color, as well as size, it was singularly distinct. Its great spear-shaped head and bill was very conspicuous, though least so when turned toward me (whom it was eying from time to time). It coils its neck away upon its back or breast as a sailor might a rope, but occasionally stretches itself to its full height, as tall as a man, and looks around and at me. Growing shy, it begins to wade off, until its body is partly immersed amid the weeds,—potamogetons,—and then it looks more like a goose. The neck is continually varying in length, as it is doubled up or stretched out, and the legs also, as it wades in deeper or shallower water.

Suddenly comes a second, flying low, and alights on the bar yet nearer to me, almost high and dry. Then I hear a note from them, perhaps of warning,—a short, coarse, frog-like purring or eructating sound. You might easily mistake it for a frog. I heard it half a dozen times. It was not very loud. Anything but musical. The last proceeds to plume himself, looking warily at me from time to time, while the other continues to edge off through the weeds. . . . These were probably birds of this season. I saw some distinct ferruginous on the angle of the wing. There they stood in the midst of the open river, on this shallow and weedy bar in the sun, the leisurely sentries, lazily pluming themselves, as if the day were too long for them. They gave a new character to the stream. Adjutant they were to my idea of the river, these two winged men.

You have not seen our weedy river, you do not know the significance of its weedy bars, until you have seen the blue heron wading and pluming itself on it. I see that it was made for these shallows, and they for it. Now the heron is gone from the weedy shoal, the scene appears incomplete. Of course, the heron has sounded the depth of the water on every bar of the river that is fordable to it. The water there is not so many feet deep, but so many heron's tibiæ. Instead of a foot rule you should use a heron's legs for a measure. If you would know the depth of the water on these few shoalest places of Musketaquid, ask the blue heron that wades and fishes there. In some places a heron can wade across.

How long we may have gazed on a particular scenery and think that we have seen and known it, when, at length, some bird or quadruped comes and takes possession of it before our eyes, and imparts to it a wholly new character. The heron uses these shallows as I cannot. I give them up to him.

XII, 284-287   14 Aug. 1859

BLUE HERONS FLYING

Scared up three blue herons in the little pond close by, quite near us. It was a grand sight to see them rise, so slow and stately, so long and limber, with an undulating motion from head to foot, undulating also their large wings, undulating in two directions, and looking warily about them. With this graceful, limber, undulating motion they arose, as if so they got under way, their two legs trailing parallel far behind like an earthy residuum to be left behind. They are large, like birds of Syrian* lands, and seemed to oppress the earth, and hush the hillside to silence, as they winged their way over it, looking back toward us. It would affect our thoughts, deepen and perchance darken our reflections, if such huge birds flew in numbers in our sky. Have the effect of magnetic passes. They are few and rare. Among the birds of celebrated flight, storks, cranes, geese, and ducks. The legs hang down like a weight which they raise, to pump up as it were with [their] wings and convey out of danger.

To see the larger and wilder birds, you must go forth in the great storms like this. At such times they frequent our neighborhood and trust themselves in our midst. A life of fair-weather walks *might* never show you the goose sailing on our waters, or the great heron feeding here. When the storm increases, then these great birds that carry the mail of the seasons lay to. To see wild life you must go forth at a wild season. When it rains and blows, keeping men indoors, then the lover of Nature must forth. Then returns Nature to her wild estate. In pleasant sunny weather you may catch butterflies, but only when the storm rages that lays prostrate the forest and wrecks the mariner, do you come upon the feeding-grounds of wildest fowl,—of heron and geese.

III, 443-444   19 Apr. 1852

CROW AND HEN

Perhaps what most moves us in winter is some reminiscence of far-off summer. How we leap by the side of the open brooks! What beauty in the running brooks! What life! What society! The cold is merely superficial; it is summer still at the core, far, far within. It is in the cawing of the crow, the crowing of the cock, the warmth of the sun on our backs. I hear faintly the cawing of a crow far, far away, echoing from some unseen wood-side, as if deadened by the springlike vapor which the sun is drawing from the ground. It mingles with the

---

*   "Syrian Bird," epithet for the Phoenix, sacred to the Egyptian sun-god, and symbol of death and resurrection in both Christian and pagan literature.

slight murmur of the village, the sound of children at play, as one stream empties gently into another, and the wild and tame are one. What a delicious sound! It is not merely crow calling to crow, for it speaks to me too. I am part of one great creature with him; if he has voice, I have ears. I can hear when he calls, and have engaged not to shoot nor stone him if he will caw to me each spring. On the one hand, it may be, is the sound of children at school saying their a, b, ab's, on the other, far in the wood-fringed horizon, the cawing of crows from their blessed eternal vacation, out at their long recess, children who have got dismissed! While the vaporous incense goes up from all the fields of the spring—if it were spring. Ah, bless the Lord, O my soul! bless him for wildness, for crows that will not alight within gunshot! and bless him for hens, too, that croak and cackle in the yard!

VII, 112-113   12 Jan. 1855

RUTE NEIGHBORS

I spend a considerable portion of my time observing the habits of the wild animals, my brute neighbors. By their various movements and migrations they fetch the year about to me. Very significant are the flight of geese and the migration of suckers, etc., etc. But when I consider that the nobler animals have been exterminated here,—the cougar, panther, lynx, wolverene, wolf, bear, moose, deer, the beaver, the turkey, etc., etc.,—I cannot but feel as if I lived in a tamed, and, as it were, emasculated country. Would not the motions of those larger and wilder animals have been more significant still? Is it not a maimed and imperfect nature that I am conversant with? As if I were to study a tribe of Indians that had lost all its warriors. Do not the forest and the meadow now lack expression, now that I never see nor think of the moose with a lesser forest on his head in the one, nor of the beaver in the other? When I think what were the various sounds and notes, the migrations and works, and changes of fur and plumage which ushered in the spring and marked the other seasons of the year, I am reminded that this my life in nature, this particular round of natural phenomena which I call a year, is lamentably incomplete. I listen to [a] concert in which so many parts are wanting. The whole civilized country is to some extent turned into a city, and I am that citizen whom I pity. Many of those animal migrations and other phenomena by which the Indians marked the season are no longer to be observed. I seek acquaintance with Nature,—to know her moods and manners. Primitive Nature is the most interesting to me. I take infinite pains to know all the phenomena of the spring, for instance, thinking that I have here the entire poem, and then, to my chagrin, I hear that it is but an imperfect copy that I possess and have read, that my ancestors have torn out many of the first leaves and grandest passages, and mutilated it in many places. I should not like to think that some demigod had come before me and picked out some of the best of the stars. I wish to know an entire heaven and an entire earth. All the great trees and beasts, fishes and fowl are gone.

VIII, 220-221   23 Mar. 1856

 ILD BEASTS

Visited a menagerie this afternoon. I am always surprised to see the same spots and stripes on wild beasts from Africa and Asia and also from South America,—on the Brazilian tiger and the African leopard,—and their general similarity. All these wild animals—lions, tigers, chetas, leopards, etc.—have one hue,—tawny and commonly spotted or striped,—what you may call pard-color, a color and marking which I had not associated with America. These are wild beasts. What constitutes the difference between a wild beast and a tame one? How much more human the one than the other! Growling, scratching, roaring, with whatever beauty and gracefulness, still untamable, this royal Bengal tiger or this leopard. They have the character and the importance of another order of men. The majestic lion, the king of beasts,—he must retain his title.

I was struck by the gem-like, changeable, greenish reflections from the eyes of the grizzly bear, so glassy that you never saw the surface of the eye. They [were] quite demonic. Its claws, though extremely large and long, look weak and made for digging or pawing the earth and leaves. It is unavoidable, the idea of transmigration; not merely a fancy of the poets, but an instinct of the race.

II, 271   26 June 1851

BRUTE AND HUMAN

[A man's] dog sprang up, ran out, and growled at us, and in his eye I seemed to see the eye of his master. I have no doubt but that, as is the master, such in course of time tend to become his herds and flocks as well as dogs. One man's oxen will be clever and solid, another's mischievous, another's mangy,—in each case like their respective owners. No doubt man impresses his own character on the beasts which he tames and employs; they are not only humanized, but they acquire his particular human nature. How much oxen are like farmers generally, and cows like farmers' wives! and young steers and heifers like farmers' boys and girls! The farmer acts on the ox, and the ox reacts on the farmer. They do not meet half-way, it is true, but they do meet at a distance from the centre of each proportionate to each one's intellectual power. The farmer is ox-like in his thought, in his walk, in his strength, in his trustworthiness, in his taste.

II, 452-453   4 Sept. 1851

OX DOMESTICATED

The domestic ox has his horns tipped with brass. This and his shoes are the badges of servitude which he wears; as if he would soon get to jacket and trousers. I am singularly affected when I look over a herd of reclining oxen in their pasture, and find that every one has these brazen balls on his horns. They are partly humanized so. It is not pure brute; there is art added. Where are these balls sold? Who is their maker? The bull has a ring in his nose.

II, 270   22 June 1851

HORSES RUNNING WILD

Cattle and horses . . . retain many of their wild habits or instincts wonderfully. The seeds of instinct are preserved under their thick hides, like seeds in the bowels of the earth, an indefinite period. I have heard of a horse which his master could not catch in his pasture when the first snowflakes were falling, who persisted in wintering out. As he persisted in keeping out of his reach, his master finally left him. When the snow had covered the ground three or four inches deep, the horse pawed it away to come at the grass,—just as the wild horses of Michigan do, who are turned loose by their Indian masters,—and so he picked up a scanty subsistence. By the next day he had had enough of free life and pined for his stable, and so suffered himself to be caught.

A blacksmith, my neighbor, heard a great clattering noise the other day behind his shop, and on going out found that his mare and his neighbor the pumpmaker's were fighting. They would run at one another, then turn round suddenly and let their heels fly. The rattling of their hoofs one against the other was the noise he heard. They repeated this several times with intervals of grazing, until one prevailed. The next day they bore the marks of some bruises, some places where the skin was rucked up, and some swellings.

II, 37-38   20 June 1850

CATTLE MYTHOLOGIZED

It is interesting to meet an ox with handsomely spreading horns. There is a great variety of sizes and forms, though one horn commonly matches the other. I am willing to turn out for those that spread their branches wide. Large and spreading horns methinks indicate a certain vegetable force and naturalization in the wearer; it softens and eases off the distinction between the animals and vegetable, the unhorned animals and the trees. I should say that the horned animals approached nearer to the vegetable. The deer that run in the woods, as the moose for instance, carry perfect trees on their heads. The French call them *bois*. No wonder there are fables of centaurs and the like. No wonder there is a story of a hunter who, when his bullets failed, fired cherry-stones into the heads of his game and so trees sprouted out of them, and the hunter refreshed himself with the cherries. It is a perfect piece of mythology which belongs to these days.

III, 305-307   16 Feb. 1852

HE HEIFER *

To-day I climbed a handsome rounded hill
Covered with hickory trees, wishing to see
The country from its top, for low hills
Show unexpected prospects. I looked
Many miles over a woody lowland
Toward Marlborough, Framingham, and Sudbury;
And as I sat amid the hickory trees

And the young sumachs, enjoying the prospect, a neat herd of cows approached, of unusually fair proportions and smooth, clean skins, evidently petted by their owner, who must have carefully selected them. One more confiding heifer, the fairest of the herd, did by degrees approach as if to take some morsel from our hands, while our hearts leaped to our mouths with expectation and delight. She by degrees drew near with her fair limbs progressive, making pretense of browsing; nearer and nearer, till there was wafted toward us the bovine fragrance,—cream of all the dairies that ever were or will be,— and then she raised her gentle muzzle toward us, and snuffed an honest recognition within hand's reach. I saw 't was possible for this herd to inspire with love the herdsman. She was as delicately featured as a hind. Her hide was mingled white and fawn-color, and on her muz-

---

* When Hera became jealous of Io, beloved by Zeus, he turned her into a heifer to disguise her.

zle's tip there was a white spot not bigger than a daisy, and on her side toward me the map of Asia plain to see.

Farewell, dear heifer! Though thou forgettest me, my prayer to heaven shall be that thou may'st not forget thyself. There was a whole bucolic in her snuff. I saw her name was Sumach. And by the kindred spots I knew her mother, more sedate and matronly, with full-grown bag; and on her sides was Asia, great and small, the plains of Tartary, even to the pole, while on her daughter it was Asia Minor. She not disposed to wanton with the herdsman.

And as I walked, she followed me, and took an apple from my hand, and seemed to care more for the hand than apple. So innocent a face as I have rarely seen on any creature, and I have looked in face of many heifers. And as she took the apple from my hand, I caught the apple of her eye. She smelled as sweet as the clethra blossom. There was no sinister expression. And for horns, though she had them, they were so well disposed in the right place, bent neither up nor down, I do not now remember she had any. No horn was held toward me.

11, 67-68   1850

CATS, TAME AND WILD

Even the cat which lies on a rug all day commences to prowl about the fields at night, resumes her ancient forest habits. The most tenderly bred grimalkin steals forth at night,—watches some bird on its perch for an hour in the furrow, like a gun at rest. She catches no cold; it is her nature. Caressed by children and cherished with a saucer of milk. Even she can erect her back and expand her tail and spit at her enemies like the wild cat of the woods. Sweet Sylvia!

11, 184   30 Apr. 1851

MUSKRAT

I saw a muskrat come out of a hole in the ice. He is a man wilder than Ray or Melvin.* While I am looking at him, I am thinking what he is thinking of me. He is a different sort of a man, that is all. He would dive when I went nearer, then reappear again, and had kept open a place five or six feet square so that it had not frozen, by swimming about in it. Then he would sit on the edge of the ice and busy himself about something, I could not see whether it was a clam or not. What a cold-blooded fellow! thoughts at a low temperature, sitting perfectly still so long on ice covered with water, mumbling a cold, wet clam in its shell. What safe, low, moderate thoughts it must have! It does not get on to stilts. The generations of muskrats do not fail. They are not preserved by the legislature of Massachusetts.

II, III   25 Nov. 1850

WOOD FROGS

Southeast wind. Begins to sprinkle while I am sitting in Laurel Glen, listening to hear the earliest wood frogs croaking. I think they get under weigh a little earlier, *i. e.*, you will hear many of them sooner than you will hear many hylodes. Now, when the leaves get to be dry and rustle under your feet, dried by the March winds, the peculiar dry note, *wurrk wurrk wur-r-r-k wurk* of the wood frog is heard faintly by ears on the alert, borne up from some unseen pool in a woodland hollow which is open to the influences of the sun. It is a singular sound for awakening Nature to make, associated with the first warmer days, when you sit in some sheltered place in the woods amid the dried leaves. How moderate on her first awakening, how little demonstrative! You may sit half an hour before you will hear another. You doubt if the season will be long enough for such Oriental

* See "The Hunter," p. 46.

and luxurious slowness. But they get on, nevertheless, and by to-morrow, or in a day or two, they croak louder and more frequently. Can you ever be sure that you have heard the very first wood frog in the township croak? Ah! how weather-wise must he be! There is no guessing at the weather with him. He makes the weather in his degree; he encourages it to be mild. The weather, what is it but the tempera-ment of the earth? and he is wholly of the earth, sensitive as its skin in which he lives and of which he is a part. His life relaxes with the thawing ground. He pitches and tunes his voice to chord with the rustling leaves which the March wind has dried. Long before the frost is quite out, he feels the influence of the spring rains and the warmer days. His is the very voice of the weather. He rises and falls like quicksilver in the thermometer. You do not perceive the spring so surely in the actions of men, their lives are so artificial. They may make more fire or less in their parlors, and their feelings accordingly are not good thermometers. The frog far away in the wood, that burns no coal nor wood, perceives more surely the general and universal changes.

XII, 78-79   24 Mar. 1859

TOADS

My dream frog turns out to be a toad. I watched half a dozen a long time at 3.30 this afternoon in Hubbard's Pool, where they were frogging (?) lustily. They sat in the shade, either partly in the water, or on a stick; looked larger and narrower in proportion to their length than toads usually do, and moreover are aquatic. I see them jump into the ditches as I walk. After an interval of silence, one appeared to be gulping the wind into his belly, inflating himself so that he was con-siderably expanded; then he discharged it all into his throat while his body or belly collapsed suddenly, expanding his throat to a remarkable size. Was nearly a minute inflating itself; then swelled out its sac, which is rounded and reminded me of the bag to a work-table, hold-ing its head up the while. It is whitish specked (the bag) on a dull bluish or slate ground, much bigger than all the rest of the head, and nearly an inch in diameter. It was a ludicrous sight, with their so serious prominent eyes peering over it; and a deafening sound, when several were frogging at once, as I was leaning over them. The mouth [seemed] to be shut always, and perhaps the air was expelled through the nostrils. The strain appeared prolonged as long as the air lasted, and was sometimes quavered or made intermittent, apparently by clos-ing the orifice, whatever it was, or the blast. One, which I brought home, answers well enough to the description of the common toad (*Bufo Americanus*), though it is hardly so gray. Their piping (?) was evidently connected with their loves. Close by, it is an unmusical monotonous deafening sound, a steady blast,—not a peep nor a croak, but a *kind* of piping,—but, far away, it is a dreamy, lulling sound, and fills well the crevices of nature.

IV, 24·25   6 May 1852

TORTOISE LAYING EGGS

At 3 P.M., as I walked up the bank by the Hemlocks, I saw a painted tortoise just beginning its hole; then another a dozen rods from the river on the bare barren field near some pitch pines, where the earth was covered with cladonias, cinquefoil, sorrel, etc. Its hole was about two thirds done. I stooped down over it, and, to my surprise, after a slight pause it proceeded in its work, directly under and within eighteen inches of my face. I retained a constrained position for three quarters of an hour or more for fear of alarming it. It rested on its fore legs, the front part of its shell about one inch higher than the rear, and this position was not changed essentially to the last. The hole was oval, broadest behind, about one inch wide and one and three quarters long, and the dirt already removed was quite wet or moistened. It made the hole and removed the dirt with its hind legs only, not using its tail or shell, which last of course could not enter the hole, though there was some dirt on it. It first scratched two or three times with one hind foot; then took up a pinch of the loose sand and deposited it directly behind that leg, pushing it backward to its full length and then deliberately opening it and letting the dirt fall; then the same

with the other hind foot. This it did rapidly, using each leg alternately
with perfect regularity, standing on the other one the while, and thus
tilting up its shell each time, now to this side, then to that. There was
half a minute or a minute between each change. The hole was made
as deep as the feet could reach, about two inches. It was very neat
about its work, not scattering the dirt about any more than was necessary. The completing of the hole occupied perhaps five minutes.

It then without any pause drew its head completely into its shell,
raised the rear a little, and protruded and dropped a wet flesh-colored
egg into the hole, one end foremost, the red skin of its body being
considerably protruded with it. Then it put out its head again a little,
slowly, and placed the egg at one side with one hind foot. After a
delay of about two minutes it again drew in its head and dropped another, and so on to the fifth—drawing in its head each time, and pausing somewhat longer between the last. The eggs were placed in the
hole without any *particular* care,—only well down flat and [each] out
of the way of the next,—and I could plainly see them from above.

After these ten minutes or more, it without pause or turning began to scrape the moist earth into the hole with its hind legs, and,
when it had half filled it, it carefully pressed it down with the edges
of its hind feet, dancing on them alternately, for some time, as on its
knees, tilting from side to side, pressing by the whole weight of the
rear of its shell. When it had drawn in thus all the earth that had been
moistened, it stretched its hind legs further back and to each side, and
drew in the dry and lichen-clad crust, and then danced upon and
pressed that down, still not moving the rear of its shell more than one
inch to right or left all the while, or changing the position of the forward part at all. The thoroughness with which the covering was done
was remarkable. It persevered in drawing in and dancing on the dry
surface which had never been disturbed, long after you thought it had
done its duty, but it never moved its fore feet, nor once looked round,
nor saw the eggs it had laid. There were frequent pauses throughout
the whole, when it rested, or ran out its head and looked about cir-
cumspectly, at any noise or motion. These pauses were especially long
during the covering of its eggs, which occupied more than half an
hour. Perhaps it was hard work.

When it had done, it immediately started for the river at a pretty rapid rate (the suddenness with which it made these transitions was amusing), pausing from time to time, and I judged that it would reach it in fifteen minutes. It was not easy to detect that the ground had been disturbed there. An Indian could not have made his cache more skillfully. In a few minutes all traces of it would be lost to the eye.

VII, 425-427   18 June 1855

MOTHER TURTLE AND WORLD TURTLE

This morning I find a little hole, three quarters of an inch or an inch over, above my small tortoise eggs,* and find a young tortoise coming out (apparently in the rainy night) just beneath. It is the *Sternothœrus odoratus*—already has the strong scent—and now has drawn in its head and legs. I see no traces of the yolk, or what-not, attached. It may have been out of the egg some days. *Only one* as yet. I buried them in the garden June 15th.

I am affected by the thought that the earth nurses these eggs. They are planted in the earth, and the earth takes care of them; she is genial to them and does not kill them. It suggests a certain vitality and intelligence in the earth, which I had not realized. This mother is not merely inanimate and inorganic. Though the immediate mother turtle abandons her offspring, the earth and sun are kind to them. The old turtle on which the earth rests takes care of them while the other waddles off. Earth was not made poisonous and deadly to them. The earth has some virtue in it; when seeds are put into it, they germinate; when turtles' eggs, they hatch in due time. Though the mother turtle remained and brooded them, it would still nevertheless be the universal world turtle † which, through her, cared for them as now. Thus the earth is the mother of all creatures.

II, 28-29   9 Sept. 1850

* Not to be confused with the eggs of the painted tortoise described in the preceding miniature.

† In the Hindu myth of creation the world rests on the back of a giant turtle. Vishnu, the Creator, sometimes took the form of a turtle.

YOUNG TURTLE

Opened one of my snapping turtle's eggs.* The egg was not warm to the touch. The young is now larger and darker-colored, shell and all, more than a hemisphere, and the yolk which maintains it is much reduced. Its shell, very deep, hemispherical, fitting close to the shell of the egg, and, if you had not just opened the egg, you would say it could not contain so much. Its shell is considerably hardened, its feet and claws developed, and also its great head, though held in for want of room. Its eyes are open. It puts out its head, stretches forth its claws, and liberates its tail, though all were enveloped in a gelatinous fluid. With its great head it has already the ugliness of the fullgrown, and is already a hieroglyphic of snappishness. It may take a fortnight longer to hatch it.

How much lies quietly buried in the ground that we wot not of! We unconsciously step over the eggs of snapping turtles slowly hatching the summer through. Not only was the surface perfectly dry and trackless there, but blackberry vines had run over the spot where these eggs were buried and weeds had sprung up above. If Iliads are not composed in our day, snapping turtles are hatched and arrive at maturity. It already thrusts forth its tremendous head,—for the first time in this sphere,—and slowly moves from side to side,—opening its small glistening eyes for the first time to the light,—expressive of dull rage, as if it had endured the trials of this world for a century. When I behold this monster thus steadily advancing toward maturity, all nature abetting, I am convinced that there must be an irresistible necessity for mud turtles. With what tenacity Nature sticks to her idea! These eggs, not warm to the touch, buried in the ground, so slow to hatch, are like the seeds of vegetable life.

VI, 474-475   26 Aug. 1854

*   A third variety.

IANT TURTLE

As I was returning over the [flooded] meadow this side of the Island, I saw the snout of a mud turtle above the surface,—little more than an inch of the point,—and paddled toward it. Then, as he moved slowly on the surface, different parts of his shell and head just appearing looked just like the scalloped edges of some pads which had just reached the surface. I pushed up and found a large snapping turtle on the bottom. He appeared of a dirty brown there, very nearly the color of the bottom at present. With his great head, as big as an infant's, and his vigilant eyes as he paddled about on the bottom in his attempts to escape, he looked not merely repulsive, but to some extent terrible even as a crocodile. At length, after thrusting my arm in up to the shoulder two or three times, I succeeded in getting him into the boat, where I secured him with a lever under a seat. I could get him from the landing to the house only by turning him over and drawing him by the tail, the hard crests of which afforded a good hold; for he was so heavy that I could not hold him off so far as to prevent his snapping at my legs. He weighed thirty and a half pounds. . . . He had surprisingly stout hooked jaws, of a gray color or bluish-gray, the upper shutting over the under, a more or less sharp triangular beak corresponding to one below; and his flippers were armed with very stout claws 1¼ inches long. He had a very ugly and spiteful face (with a vigilant gray eye, which was never shut in any position of the head), surrounded by the thick and ample folds of the skin about his neck. His shell was comparatively smooth and free from moss,—a dirty black. He was a *dirty* or speckled white beneath. He made the most remarkable and awkward appearance when walking. The edge of his shell was lifted about eight inches from the ground, tilting now to this side, then to that, his great scaly legs or flippers hanging with flesh and loose skin,—slowly and gravely (?) hissing the while. His walking was perfectly elephantine. Thus he stalked along,—a low conical mountain,—dragging his tail, with his head turned upward with the ugliest and most venomous look, on his flippers, half leg half fin. But he did not proceed far before he sank down to rest. If he could support a world on his back when lying down, he certainly could not stand up under it. All said that he walked like an elephant. . . .

The turtle's snapping impressed me as something mechanical, like a spring, as if there were no volition about [it]. Its very suddenness seemed too great for a conscious movement. Perhaps in these cold-blooded and sluggish animals there is a near approach to the purely material and mechanical. Their very tenacity of life seems to be owing to their insensibility or small amount of life,—indeed, to be an irritation of the muscles. One man tells me of a turtle's head which, the day after it was cut off, snapped at a dog's tail and made him run off yelping, and I have witnessed something similar myself. I can think of nothing but a merely animated jaw, as it were a piece of mechanism. There is in this creature a tremendous development of the jaw, and, long after the head is cut off, this snaps vigorously when irritated, like a piece of mechanism. A naturalist tells me that he dissected one and laid its heart aside, and he found it beating or palpitating the next morning. They are sometimes baited with eels and caught with a hook. Apparently the best time to hunt them is in the morning when the water is smooth.

VI, 271-273, 276   17 May 1854

ATER ADDER

A man mowing in the Great Meadows killed a great water adder (?) the other day, said to be four feet long and as big as a man's wrist. It ran at him. They find them sometimes when they go to open their hay. I tried to see it this morning, but some boys had chopped it up and buried it. They said that they found a *great many* young ones in it. That probably accounts for its being so large round. . . . The mower on the river meadows, when [he] comes to open his hay these days, encounters some overgrown water adder full of young (?) and bold in defense of its progeny, and tells a tale when he comes home at night which causes a shudder to run through the village,—

how it came at him, and he ran, and it pursued and overtook him, and he transfixed it with a pitchfork and laid it on a cock of hay, but it revived and came at him again. This is the story he tells in the shops at evening. The big snake is a sort of fabulous animal. It is always as big as a man's arm and of indefinite length. Nobody knows exactly how deadly its bite, but nobody is known to have been bitten and recovered. Irishmen introduced into these meadows for the first time, on seeing a snake, a creature which they have seen only in pictures before, lay down their scythes and run as if it were the evil one himself, and cannot be induced to return to their work. They sigh for Ireland, where they say there is no venomous thing that can hurt you.

v, 354-355   7 Aug. 1853

CRICKETS

I fear that the character of my knowledge is from year to year becoming more distinct and scientific; that, in exchange for views as wide as heaven's cope, I am being narrowed down to the field of the microscope. I see details, not wholes nor the shadow of the whole. I count some parts, and say, "I know." The cricket's chirp now fills the air in dry fields near pine woods. . . .

I hear a cricket in the Depot Field, walk a rod or two, and find the note proceeds from near a rock. Partly under a rock, between it and the roots of the grass, he lies concealed,—for I pull away the withered grass with my hands,—uttering his night-like creak, with a vibratory motion of his wings, and flattering himself that it is night, because he has shut out the day. He was a black fellow nearly an inch long, with two long, slender feelers. They plainly avoid the light and hide their heads in the grass. At any rate they regard this as the evening of the year. They are remarkably secret and unobserved, considering how much noise they make. Every milkman has heard them all his life; it is the sound that fills his ears as he drives along. But what one has ever got off his cart to go in search of one? I see smaller ones moving stealthily about, whose note I do not know. Who ever distinguished their various notes, which fill the crevices in each other's song? It would be a curious ear, indeed, that distinguished the species of the crickets which it heard, and traced even the earth-song home, each part to its particular performer. I am afraid to be so knowing. They are shy as birds, these little bodies. Those nearest me continually cease their song as I walk, so that the singers are always a rod distant, and I cannot easily detect one. It is difficult, moreover, to judge correctly whence the sound proceeds. Perhaps this wariness is necessary to save them from insectivorous birds, which would otherwise speedily find out so loud a singer. They are somewhat protected by the universalness of the sound, each one's song being merged and lost in the general concert, as if it were the creaking of earth's axle. They are very numerous in oats and other grain, which conceals them and yet affords a clear passage. I never knew any drought or sickness so to prevail as to quench the song of the crickets; it fails not in its season, night or day.

II, 406-409   19-20 Aug. 1851

CRICKET AS SYMBOL

The first cricket's chirrup which I have chanced to hear now falls on my ear and makes me forget all else; all else is a thin and movable crust down to that depth where he resides eternally. He already foretells autumn. Deep under the dry border of some rock in this hillside he sits, and makes the finest singing of birds outward and insignificant, his own song is so much deeper and more significant. His voice has set me thinking, philosophizing, moralizing at once. It is not so wildly melodious, but it is wiser and more mature than that of the wood thrush. With this elixir I see clear through the summer now to autumn, and any summer work seems frivolous. I am disposed to ask this humblebee that hurries humming past so busily if he knows what he is about. At one leap I go from the just opened buttercup to the life-everlasting. This singer has antedated autumn. His strain is superior (inferior?)[1] to seasons. It annihilates time and space; the summer is for time-servers.

v, 158   15 May 1853

GULL AND SUCKER

Thinking of the value of the gull to the scenery of our river in the spring, when for a few weeks, they are seen circling about so deliberately and heavily yet gracefully, without apparent object, beating like a vessel in the air, Gilpin[*] says something to the purpose, that water-fowl "discover in their flight some determined aim. They eagerly coast the river, or return to the sea; bent on some purpose, of which they never lose sight. But the evolutions of the gull appear capricious, and undirected, both when she flies alone, and, as she often does, in large companies.—The more however her character suffers as a loiterer, the more it is raised in picturesque value, by her continuing longer before the eye; and displaying, in her elegant sweeps along the air, her sharp-pointed wings, and her bright silvery hue.—She is beautiful also, not only on the wing, but when she floats, in numerous assemblies on the water; or when she rests on the shore, dotting either one, or the other with white spots; which, minute as they are, are very picturesque: . . . giving life and spirit to a view."

He seems to be describing our very bird. I do not *remember* to have seen them over or in our river meadows when there was not ice there. They come annually a-fishing here like royal hunters, to remind us of the sea and that our town, after all, lies but further up a creek of the universal sea, above the head of the tide. So ready is a deluge to overwhelm our lands, as the gulls to circle hither in the spring freshets. To see a gull beating high over our meadowy flood in chill and windy March is akin to seeing a mackerel schooner on the coast. It is the nearest approach to sailing vessels in our scenery. I never saw one at Walden. Oh, how it salts our fresh, our sweet

---

[1]   Exaltedly inferior [Thoreau's note].

[*]   William Gilpin, eighteenth-century English writer on nature and art, best known for his essays on the picturesque.

watered Fair Haven all at once to see this sharp-beaked, greedy sea-
bird beating over it! For a while the water is brackish to my eyes. It
is merely some herring pond, and if I climb the eastern bank I expect
to see the Atlantic there covered with countless sails. We are so far
maritime, do not dwell beyond the range of the seagoing gull, the
littoral birds. Does not the gull come up after those suckers which I
see? He is never to me perfectly in harmony with the scenery, but,
like the high water, something unusual.

What a novel life, to be introduced to a dead sucker floating on
the water in the spring! Where was it spawned, pray? The sucker is
so recent, so unexpected, so unrememberable, so unanticipatable a
creation. While so many institutions are gone by the board, and we
are despairing of men and of ourselves, there seems to be life even in a
dead sucker, whose fellows at least are alive. The world never looks
more recent or promising—religion, philosophy, poetry—than when
viewed from this point. To see a sucker tossing on the spring flood,
its swelling, imbricated breast heaving up a bait to not-despairing
gulls! It is a strong and a strengthening sight. Is the world coming to
an end? Ask the chubs. As long as fishes spawn, glory and honor to
the cold-blooded who despair! As long as ideas are expressed, as long
as friction makes bright, as long as vibrating wires make music of
harps, we do not want redeemers. What a volume you might [write]
on the separate virtues of the various animals, the black duck and
the rest!

III, 416-417   15 Apr. 1852

SUCKER AS SYMBOL

The sight of the sucker floating on the meadow at this season
affects me singularly, as if it were a fabulous or mythological fish,
realizing my *idea* of a fish. It reminds me of pictures of dolphins or of
Proteus. I see it for what is is,—not an actual terrene fish, but the fair
symbol of a divine idea, the design of an artist. Its color and form, its
gills and fins and scales, are perfectly beautiful, because they completely express to my mind what they were intended to express. It is

as little fishy as a fossil fish. Such a form as is sculptured on ancient monuments and will be to the end of time; made to point a moral. I am serene and satisfied when the birds fly and the fishes swim as in fable, for the moral is not far off; when the migration of the goose is significant and has a moral to it; when the events of the day have a mythological character, and the most trivial is symbolical.

III, 437-438   18 Apr. 1852

YNX

George Melvin came to tell me this forenoon that a strange animal was killed on Sunday, the 9th, near the north end of the town, and it was not known certainly what it was. From his description I judged it to be a Canada lynx. In the afternoon I went to see it. It was killed on Sunday morning by John Quincy Adams, who lives in Carlisle about half a mile (or less) from the Concord line,* on the Carlisle road. . . .

Adams had lost some of his hens, and had referred it to a fox or the like. He being out, his son told me that on Sunday he went out with his gun to look after the depredator, and some forty or fifty rods from his house northwesterly (on Dr. Jones's lot, which I surveyed) in the woods, this animal suddenly dropped within two feet of him, so near that he could not fire. He had heard a loud hiss, but did not mind it. . . . He felt somewhat frightened. Struck him with the butt of his gun, but did not hurt him much, he was so quick. He jumped at once thirty feet, turned round, and faced him. He then fired, about thirty feet, at his eyes, and destroyed one,—perhaps put out the other, too. He then bounded out of sight. When he had loaded he found him crawling toward him on his belly as if to spring upon him; fired again, and thinks he mortally wounded him then. After loading, approached, and the lynx faced him, all alive. He then fired, and the lynx leapt up fifteen feet, fell, and died. Either at the second or last shot leapt within ten feet of him. He was much impressed by his eyes and the ruff standing out on the sides of his neck. . . .

* The boundary of the township, not the village.

[It was a female, weighing nineteen pounds, and measuring five feet in overall length and twenty inches in height; its fur brownish-gray with a dark-brown or black line down the back, its tail reddish and conspicuously black at the end.] . . .

It is remarkable how slow people are to believe that there are any wild animals in the neighborhood. . . . While the man that killed my lynx (and many others) thinks it came out of a menagerie, and the naturalists call it the Canada lynx, and at the White Mountains they call it the Siberian lynx,—in each case forgetting, or ignoring, that it belongs here—I call it the Concord lynx.

XIV, 78-79, 83-84, 87   11, 13 Sept. 1860

LYNX, P. S.

You would say that some men had been tempted to live in this world at all only by the offer of a bounty by the general government —a bounty on living—to any one who will consent to be *out* at this era of the world, the object of the governors being to create a nursery for their navy. I told such a man the other day that I had got a Canada lynx here in Concord, and his instant question was, "Have you got the reward for him?" What reward? Why, the ten dollars which the State offers. As long as I saw him he neither said nor thought anything about the lynx, but only about this reward. "Yes," said he, "this State offers ten dollars reward." You might have inferred that ten dollars was something rarer in his neighborhood than a lynx even, and he was anxious to see it on that account. I have thought that a lynx was a bright-eyed, four-legged, furry beast of the cat kind, very *current*, indeed, though its natural gait is by leaps. But he knew it to be a draught drawn by the cashier of the wildcat bank on the State treasury, payable at sight. Then I reflected that the first money was of leather, or a whole creature (whence *pecunia*, from *pecus*, a herd), and, since leather was at first furry, I easily understood the connection between a lynx and ten dollars, and found that all money was traceable right back to the original wildcat bank. But the fact was that, instead of receiving ten dollars for the lynx which I had got, I had paid away some dollars in order to get him. So, you see, I was away back in a gray antiquity behind the institution of money,—further than history goes.

This reminded me that I once saw a cougar recently killed at the Adirondacks which had had its ears clipped. This was a ten-dollar cougar.

   xiv, 282-283   29 Nov. 1860

Events

SQUIRREL STRIPPING A PINE CONE

This plucking and stripping a pine cone is a business which he and his family understand perfectly. That is their *forte*. I doubt if you could suggest any improvement. After ages of experiment their instinct has settled on the same method that our reason would finally, if we had to open a pine cone with our teeth; and they were thus accomplished before our race knew that a pine cone contained any seed.

He does not prick his fingers, nor pitch his whiskers, nor gnaw the solid core any more than is necessary. Having sheared off the twigs and needles that may be in his way,—for like a skillful wood-chopper he first secures room and verge enough,—he neatly cuts off the stout stem of the cone with a few strokes of his chisels, and it is his. To be sure, he may let it fall to the ground and look down at it for a moment curiously, as if it were not his; but he is taking note where it lies and adding it to a heap of a hundred more like it in his mind, and it now is only so much the more his for his seeming carelessness. And, when the hour comes to open it, observe how he proceeds. He holds it in his hands,—a solid embossed cone, so hard it almost rings at the touch of his teeth. He pauses for a moment perhaps,—but not because he does not know how to begin,—he only listens to hear what is in the wind, not being in a hurry. He knows better than try to cut off the tip and work his way downward against a *chevaux-de-frise* of advanced scales and prickles, or to gnaw into the side for three quarters of an inch in the face of many armed shields. But he does not have to think of what he knows, having heard the latest æolian rumor. If there ever was an age of the world when the squirrels opened their cones wrong end foremost, it was not the golden age at any rate. He whirls the cone bottom upward in a twinkling, where the scales are smallest and the prickles slight or none and the short stem is cut so close as not to be in his way, and then he proceeds to cut through the thin and tender bases of the scales, and each stroke tells, laying bare at once a couple of seeds. And then he strips it as easily as if its scales were chaff, and so rapidly, twirling it as he advances, that you cannot tell how he does it till you drive him off and inspect his unfinished work.

SNAKE CLIMBING A TREE

Sat down in the sun in the path through Wright's wood-lot above Goose Pond, but soon, hearing a slight rustling, I looked round and saw a very large black snake about five feet long on the dry leaves, about a rod off. When I moved, it vibrated its tail very rapidly and smartly, which made quite a loud rustling or rattling sound, reminding me of the rattlesnake, as if many snakes obeyed the same instinct as the rattlesnake when they vibrate their tails. Once I thought I heard a low hiss. It was on the edge of a young wood of oaks and a few white pines from ten to eighteen feet high, the oaks as yet bare of leaves. As I moved toward the snake, I thought it would take refuge in some hole, but it appeared that it was out on a scout and did not know of any place of refuge near. Suddenly, as it moved along, it erected itself half its length, and when I thought it was preparing to strike at me, to my surprise it glided up a slender oak sapling about an inch in diameter at the ground and ten feet high. It ascended this easily and quickly, at first, I think, slanting its body over the lowest twig of the next tree. There were seven little branches for nine feet, averaging about the size of a pipe-stem. It moved up in a somewhat zigzag manner, availing itself of the branches, yet also in part spirally about the main stem. It finds a rest (or hold if necessary) for its neck or forward part of its body, moving crosswise the small twigs, then draws up the rest of its body. From the top of this little oak it passed into the top of a white pine of the same height an inch and a half in diameter at the ground and two feet off; from this into another oak, fifteen feet high and three feet from the pine; from this to another oak, three feet from the last and about the same height; from this to a large oak about four feet off and three or four inches in diameter, in which it was about fourteen feet from the ground; thence through two more oaks, a little lower, at intervals of four feet, and so into a white pine; and at last into a small white pine and thence to the ground. The distance in a straight line from where it left the ground to where it descended was about twenty-five feet, and the greatest height it reached, about fourteen feet. It moved quite deliberately for the most part, choosing its

course from tree to tree with great skill, and resting from time to time
while it watched me, only my approach compelling it to move again.
It surprised me very much to see it cross from tree to tree exactly like a
squirrel, where there appeared little or no support for such a body. It
would glide down the proper twig, its body resting at intervals of a
foot or two, on the smaller side twigs, perchance, and then would easily cross an interval of two feet, sometimes in an ascending, sometimes
a descending, direction. If the latter, its weight at last bent the first twig
down nearer to the opposite one. It would extend its neck very much,
as I could see by the increased width of the scales exposed, till its neck
rested across the opposite twig, hold on all the while tightly to some
part of the last twig by the very tip of its tail, which was curled round
it just like a monkey's. I have hardly seen a squirrel *rest* on such slight
twigs as it would rest on in mid-air, only two or three not bigger than
a pipe-stem, while its body stretched *clear* a foot at least between two
trees. It was not at all like creeping over a coarse basketwork, but suggested long practice and skill, like the rope-dancer's. There were no
limbs for it to use comparable for size with its own body, and you
hardly noticed the few slight twigs it rested on, as it glided through the
air. When its neck rested on the opposite twig, it was, as it were, glued
to it. It helped itself over or up them as surely as if it grasped with a
hand. There were, no doubt, rigid kinks in its body when they were
needed for support. It is a sort of endless hook, and, by its ability to
bend its body in every direction, it finds some support on every side.
Perhaps the edges of its scales give it a hold also. It is evident that it
can take the young birds out of a sapling of any height, and no twigs
are so small and pliant as to prevent it. Pendulous sprays would be the
most difficult for it, where the twigs are more nearly parallel with the
main one, as well as nearly vertical, but even then it might hold on by
its tail while its head hung below. I have no doubt that this snake could
have reached many of the oriole-nests which I have seen. I noticed that
in its anger its rigid neck was very much flattened or compressed ver-
tically. At length it coiled itself upon itself as if to strike, and, I pre-
senting a stick, it struck it smartly and then darted away, running
swiftly down the hill toward the pond.

     x, 423-426   16 May 1858

HEARING A WILD GOOSE

Minott * has a sharp ear for the note of any migrating bird. Though confined to his dooryard by the rheumatism, he commonly hears them sooner than the widest rambler. Maybe he listens all day for them, or they come and sing over his house,—report themselves to him and receive their season ticket. He is never at fault. If he says he heard such a bird, though sitting by his chimney-side, you may depend on it. He can swear through glass. He has not spoiled his ears by attending lectures and caucuses, etc. The other day the rumor went that a flock of geese had been seen flying north over Concord, mid-winter as it was, by the almanac. I traced it to Minott, and yet I was compelled to doubt. I had it directly that he had heard them within a week. I saw him,—I made haste to him. His reputation was at stake. He said that he stood in his shed,—it was one of the late warm, muggy, April-like mornings,—when he heard one short but distinct *honk* of a goose. He went into the house, he took his cane, he exerted himself, or that sound imparted strength to him. Lame as he was, he went up on to the hill,—he had not done it for a year,—that he might hear all around. He saw nothing, but he heard the note again. It came from over the brook. It was a wild goose, he was sure of it. And hence the rumor spread and grew. He thought that the back of the winter was broken,—if it had any this year,—but he feared such a winter would kill him too.

I was silent; I reflected; I drew into my mind all its members, like the tortoise; I abandoned myself to unseen guides. Suddenly the truth flashed on me, and I remembered that within a week I had heard of a box at the tavern, which had come by railroad express, containing three wild geese and directed to his neighbor over the brook. The April-like morning had excited one so that he honked; and Minott's reputation acquired new lustre.

x, 264-266   28 Jan. 1858

* George Minott (see "Minott, the Poetical Farmer," p. 31).

CAPTURING AN OWL

As I paddle under the Hemlock bank this cloudy afternoon, about 3 o'clock, I see a screech owl sitting on the edge of a hollow hemlock stump about three feet high, at the base of a large hemlock. It sits with its head drawn in, eying me, with its eyes partly open, about twenty feet off. When it hears me move, it turns its head toward me, perhaps one eye only open, with its great glaring golden iris. You see two whitish triangular lines above the eyes meeting at the bill, with a sharp reddish-brown triangle between and a narrow curved line of black under each eye. At this distance and in this light, you see only a black spot where the eye is, and the question is whether the eyes are open or not. It sits on the lee side of the tree this raw and windy day. You would say that this was a bird without a neck. Its short bill, which rests upon its breast, scarcely projects at all, but in a state of rest the whole upper part of the bird from the wings is rounded off smoothly, excepting the horns, which stand up conspicuously or are slanted back. After watching it ten minutes from the boat, I landed two rods above, and, stealing quietly up behind the hemlock, though from the windward, I looked carefully around it, and, to my surprise, saw the owl still sitting there. So I sprang round quickly, with my arm outstretched, and caught it in my hand. It was so surprised that it offered no resistance at first, only glared at me in mute astonishment with eyes as big as saucers. But ere long it began to snap its bill, making quite a noise, and, as I rolled it up in my handkerchief and put it in my pocket, it bit my finger slightly. I soon took it out of my pocket and, tying the handkerchief, left it on the bottom of the boat. So I carried it home and made a small cage in which to keep it, for a night. When I took it up, it clung so tightly to my hand as to sink its claws into my fingers and bring blood.

When alarmed or provoked most, it snaps its bill and hisses. It puffs up its feathers to nearly twice its usual size, stretches out its neck, and, with wide-open eyes, stares this way and that, moving its head slowly and undulatingly from side to side with a curious motion. While I write this evening, I see that there is ground for much superstition in it. It looks out on me from a dusky corner of its box with its great solemn eyes, so perfectly still itself. I was surprised to find that I could imitate its note as I remember it, by a *guttural* whinner, ing. . . .

Carried my owl to the hill again. Had to shake him out of the box, for he did not go of his own accord. (He had learned to alight on his perch, and it was surprising how lightly and noiselessly he would hop upon it.) There he stood on the grass, at first bewildered, with his horns pricked up and looking toward me. In this strong light the pupils of his eyes suddenly contracted and the iris expanded till they were two great brazen orbs with a centre spot merely. His attitude expressed astonishment more than anything. I was obliged to toss him up a little that he might feel his wings, and then he flapped away low and heavily to a hickory on the hillside twenty rods off. (I had let him out in the plain just east of the hill.) Thither I followed and tried to start him again. He was now on the *qui vive*, yet would not start. He erected his head, showing some neck, narrower than the round head above. His eyes were broad brazen rings around bullets of black. His horns stood quite an inch high, as not before. As I moved around him, he turned his head always toward me, till he looked *directly* behind himself as he sat crosswise on a bough. He behaved as if bewildered and dazzled, gathering all the light he could and ever straining his great eyes toward [you] to make out who you are, but not inclining to fly. I had to lift him again with a stick to make him fly, and then he only rose to a higher perch, where at last he seemed to seek the shelter of a thicker cluster of the sere leaves, partly crouching there. He never appeared so much alarmed as surprised and astonished.

VII, 522-525   28-29 Oct. 1855

TAMING A WOODCHUCK

As I turned round the corner of Hubbard's Grove, saw a woodchuck, the first of the season, in the middle of the field, six or seven rods from the fence which bounds the wood, and twenty rods distant. I ran along the fence and cut him off, or rather overtook him, though he started at the same time. When I was only a rod and a half off, he stopped, and I did the same; then he ran again, and I ran up within three feet of him, when he stopped again, the fence being between us. I squatted down and surveyed him at my leisure. His eyes were dull black and rather inobvious, with a faint chestnut (?) iris, with but little expression and that more of resignation than of anger. The general aspect was a coarse grayish brown, a sort of grisel (?). A lighter brown next the skin, then black or very dark brown and tipped with whitish rather loosely. The head between a squirrel and a bear, flat on the top and dark brown, and darker still or black on the tip of the nose. The whiskers black, two inches long. The ears very small and roundish, set far back and nearly buried in the fur. Black feet, with long and slender claws for digging. It appeared to tremble, or perchance shivered with cold. When I moved, it gritted its teeth quite loud, sometimes striking the under jaw against the other chatteringly, sometimes grinding one jaw on the other, yet as if more from instinct than anger. Whichever way I turned, that way it headed. I took a twig a foot long and touched its snout, at which it started forward and bit the stick, lessening the distance between us to two feet, and still it held all the ground it gained. I played with it tenderly awhile with the stick, trying to open its gritting jaws. Ever its long incisors, two above and two below, were presented. But I thought it would go to sleep if I stayed long enough. It did not sit up-right as sometimes, but *standing* on its fore feet with its head down, *i. e.* half sitting, half standing. We sat looking at one another about half an hour, till we began to feel mesmeric influences. When I was tired, I moved away, wishing to see him run, but I could not start him. He would not stir as long as I was looking at him or could see him. I walked round him; he turned as fast and fronted me still. I sat down by his side within a foot. I talked to him *quasi* forest lingo, baby-talk, at any rate in a conciliatory tone, and thought that I had some influ-ence on him. He gritted his teeth less. I chewed checkerberry leaves and presented them to his nose at last without a grit; though I saw that by so much gritting of the teeth he had worn them rapidly and they were covered with a fine white powder, which, if you measured it thus, would have made his anger terrible. He did not mind any

noise I might make. With a little stick I lifted one of his paws to examine it, and held it up at pleasure. I turned him over to see what
color he was beneath (darker or more purely brown), though he
turned himself back again sooner than I could have wished. His tail
was also all brown, though not very dark, rat-tail like, with loose hairs
standing out on all sides like a caterpillar brush. He had a rather mild
look. I spoke kindly to him. I reached checkerberry leaves to his
mouth. I stretched my hands over him, though he turned up his head
and still gritted a little. I laid my hand on him, but immediately took
it off again, instinct not being wholly overcome. If I had had a few
fresh bean leaves, thus in advance of the season, I am sure I should
have tamed him completely. It was a frizzly tail. His is a humble, terrestrial color like the partridge's, well concealed where dead wiry grass
rises above darker brown or chestnut dead leaves,—a modest color. If
I had had some food, I should have ended with stroking him at my
leisure. Could easily have wrapped him in my handkerchief. He was
not fat nor particularly lean. I finally had to leave him without seeing
him move from the place. A large, clumsy, burrowing squirrel. *Arc-
tomys*, bear-mouse. I respect him as one of the natives. He lies there,
by his color and habits so naturalized amid the dry leaves, the withered
grass, and the bushes. A sound nap, too, he has enjoyed in his native
fields, the past winter. I think I might learn some wisdom of him. His
ancestors have lived here longer than mine. He is more thoroughly
acclimated and naturalized than I. Bean leaves the red man raised for
him, but he can do without them.

III, 420-423   15-16 Apr. 1852

FOX CHASE

Suddenly, looking down the river, I saw a fox some sixty rods
off, making across to the hills on my left. As the snow lay five inches
deep, he made but slow progress, but it was no impediment to me. So,
yielding to the instinct of the chase, I tossed my head aloft and
bounded away, snuffing the air like a fox-hound, and spurning the
world and the Humane Society at each bound. It seemed the woods

rang with the hunter's horn, and Diana and all the satyrs joined in the chase and cheered me on. Olympian and Elean * youths were waving palms on the hills. In the meanwhile I gained rapidly on the fox; but he showed a remarkable presence of mind, for, instead of keeping up the face of the hill, which was steep and unwooded in that part, he kept along the slope in the direction of the forest, though he lost ground by it. Notwithstanding his fright, he took no step which was not beautiful. The course on his part was a series of most graceful curves. It was a sort of leopard canter, I should say, as if he were no-wise impeded by the snow, but were husbanding his strength all the while. When he doubled I wheeled and cut him off, bounding with fresh vigor, and Antæus-like, recovering my strength each time I touched the snow. Having got near enough for a fair view, just as he was slipping into the wood, I gracefully yielded him the palm. He ran as though there were not a bone in his back, occasionally dropping his muzzle to the snow for a rod or two, and then tossing his head aloft when satisfied of his course. When he came to a declivity he put his fore feet together and slid down it like a cat. He trod so softly that you could not have heard it from any nearness, and yet with such expression that it would not have been quite inaudible at any distance. So, hoping this experience would prove a useful lesson to him, I returned to the village by the highway of the river.

    1, 186-187   30 Jan. 1841

ORIGIN OF AESOP

Yesterday I skated after a fox over the ice. Occasionally he sat on his haunches and barked at me like a young wolf. It made me think of the bear and her cubs mentioned by Captain Parry, † I think.

---

*   Elea was the seat of a Greek school of philosophy teaching the universal unity of being: that the All is One.

†   Sir William Edward Parry (1790–1855); his *Narrative of an Attempt to Reach the North Pole* was published in 1827.

    Pilpay, mentioned in the next sentence, was a popular name for the famous Hindu volume of animal fables, the *Heetopadees of Veeshnoo-Sarma*.

All brutes seem to have a genius for mystery, an Oriental aptitude for symbols and the language of signs; and this is the origin of Pilpay and Æsop. The fox manifested an almost human suspicion of mystery in my actions. While I skated directly after him, he cantered at the top of his speed; but when I stood still, though his fear was not abated, some strange but inflexible law of his nature caused him to stop also, and sit again on his haunches. While I still stood motionless, he would go slowly a rod to one side, then sit and bark, then a rod to the other side, and sit and bark again, but did not retreat, as if spell-bound. When, however, I commenced the pursuit again, he found himself released from his durance.

Plainly the fox belongs to a different order of things from that which reigns in the village. Our courts, though they offer a bounty for his hide, and our pulpits, though they draw many a moral from his cunning, are in few senses contemporary with his free forest life.

I, 470   1837-1847

WEASEL AND HAWK

Farmer * says that he remembers his father's saying that as he stood in a field once, he saw a hawk soaring above and eying something on the ground. Looking round, he saw a weasel there eying the hawk. Just then the hawk swooped, and the weasel at the same instant sprang upon him, and up went the hawk with the weasel; but by and by the hawk began to come down as fast as he went up, rolling over and over, till he struck the ground. His father, going up, raised him up, when out hopped the weasel from under his wing and ran off none the worse for his fall.

XIII, 88   13 Jan. 1860

* Jacob Farmer, who shared Thoreau's interests as an amateur naturalist.

SNAKE AND TOAD

I saw a snake by the roadside and touched him with my foot to see if he were alive. He had a toad in his jaws, which he was preparing to swallow with his jaws distended to three times his width, but he relinquished his prey in haste and fled; and I thought, as the toad jumped leisurely away with his slime-covered hind-quarters glistening in the sun, as if I, his deliverer, wished to interrupt his meditations,—without a shriek or fainting,—I thought what a healthy indifference he manifested. Is not this the broad earth still? he said.

II, 423   23 Aug. 1851

MUSKRAT AND CLAM

Some of the clamshells, freshly opened by the muskrats and left lying on their half-sunken cabins, where they are kept wet by the waves, show very handsome rainbow tints. I examined one such this afternoon. The hinge of the shell was not broken, and I could discover no injury to the shell, except a little broken off the edges at the broadest end, as if by the teeth of the rat in order to get hold, insert its incisors. The fish is confined to the shell by strong muscles at each end of each valve, and the rat must dissolve the union between both of these and one side of the shell before he can get it open, unless the fish itself opens it, which perhaps it cannot wide enough. I could not open one just dead without separating the muscle from the shell. The growth of the mussel's shell appears to be in concentric layers or additions to a small shell or eye. . . .

It is a somewhat saddening reflection that the beautiful colors of this shell for want of light cannot be said to exist, until its inhabitant has fallen a prey to the spoiler, and it is thus left a wreck upon the strand. Its beauty then beams forth, and it remains a splendid cenotaph to its departed tenant, symbolical of those radiant realms of light to which the latter has risen,—what glory he has gone to. . . .

It is as if the occupant had not begun to live until the light, with whatever violence, is let into its shell with these magical results. It is rather a resurrection than a death. These beaming shells, with the tints of the sky and the rainbow commingled, suggest what pure serenity has occupied it.

VI, 7-8   3 Dec. 1853

THE "MINISTER"* SQUEAKED HIS LAST

I have been surprised to discover the amount and the various kinds of life which a single shallow swamp will sustain. On the south side of the pond, not more than a quarter of a mile from it, is a small [flooded] meadow of ten or a dozen acres in the woods, considerably lower than Walden, and which by some is thought to be fed by the former by a subterranean outlet,—which is very likely, for its shores are quite springy and its supply of water is abundant and unfailing. . . . I heard a splashing in the shallow and muddy water and stood awhile to observe the cause of it. Again and again I heard and saw the commotion, but could not guess the cause of it,—what kind of life had its residence in that insignificant pool. [I] sat down on the hillside. Ere long a muskrat came swimming by as if attracted by the same disturbance, and then another and another, till three had passed, and I began to suspect that they were at the bottom of it. Still ever and anon I observed the same commotion in the waters over the same spot, and at length I observed the snout of some creature slyly raised above the surface after each commotion, as if to see if it were observed by foes, and then but a few rods distant I saw another snout above the water and began to divine the cause of the disturbance. Putting off my shoes and stockings, I crept stealthily down the hill and waded out slowly and noiselessly about a rod from the firm land, keeping behind the tussocks, till I stood behind the tussock near which I had observed the splashing. Then, suddenly stooping over it, I saw through the

---

*   Another name for the horned pout, or common catfish (M. M. Mathews, *Dictionary of Americanisms*).

shallow but muddy water that there was a mud turtle there, and thrust-ing in my hand at once caught him by the claw, and, quicker than I can tell it, heaved him high and dry ashore; and there came out with him a large pout just dead and partly devoured, which he held in his jaws. It was the pout in his flurry and the turtle in his struggles to hold him fast which had created the commotion. There he had lain, prob-ably buried in the mud at the bottom up to his eyes, till the pout came sailing over, and then this musky lagune had put forth in the direction of his ventral fins, expanding suddenly under the influence of a more than vernal heat,—there are sermons in stones,* aye and mud turtles at the bottoms of the pools,—in the direction of his ventral fins, his tender white belly, where he kept no eye; and the minister squeaked his last. Oh, what an eye was there, my countrymen! buried in mud up to the lids, meditating on what? sleepless at the bottom of the pool, at the top of the bottom, directed heavenward, in no danger from motes. Pouts expect their foes not from below. Suddenly a mud vol-cano swallowed him up, seized his midriff; he fell into those relentless jaws from which there is no escape, which relax not their hold even in death. There the pout might calculate on remaining until nine days after the head was cut off. Sculled through Heywood's shallow meadow, not thinking of foes, looking through the water up into the sky. I saw his [the turtle's] brother sunning and airing his broad back like a ship bottom up which had been scuttled,—foundered at sea. I had no idea that there was so much going on in Heywood's meadow.

II, 13·15   1850

TURTLE KILLED BY A HERON

Landing on Tall's Island, I perceive a sour scent from the wilted leaves and scraps of leaves which were blown off yesterday and strew the ground in all woods.

Just within the edge of the wood there, I see a small painted turtle on its back, with it head stretched out as if to turn over. Sur-prised by the sight, I stooped to investigate the cause. It drew in its

* *As You Like It,* II.1.7.

head at once, but I noticed that its shell was partially empty. I could see through it from side to side as it lay, its entrails having been extracted through large openings just before the hind legs. The dead leaves were flattened for a foot over, where it had been operated on, and were a little bloody. Its paunch lay on the leaves, and contained much vegetable matter,—old cranberry leaves, etc. Judging by the striæ, it was not more than five or six years old,—or four or five. Its fore parts were quite alive, its hind legs apparently dead, its inwards gone; apparently its spine perfect. The flies had entered it in numbers. What creature could have done this which it would be difficult for a man to do? I thought of a skunk, weazel, mink, but I do not believe that they could have got their snouts into so small a space as that in front of the hind legs between the shells. The hind legs themselves had not been injured nor the shell scratched. I thought it most likely that it was done by some bird of the heron kind which has a long and powerful bill. And probably this accounts for the many dead turtles which I have found and thought died from disease. Such is Nature, who gave one creature a taste or yearning for another's entrails as its favorite tidbit!! I thought the more of a bird, for, just as we were shoving away from this isle, I heard a sound just like a small dog barking hoarsely, and, looking up, saw it was made by a bittern (*Ardea minor*), a pair of which were flapping over the meadows and probably had a nest in some tussock thereabouts. No wonder the turtle is wary, for, notwithstanding its horny shell, when it comes forth to lay its eggs it runs the risk of having its entrails plucked out. That is the reason that the box turtle, which lives on the land, is made to shut itself up entirely within the shell, and I suspect that the mud tortoise only comes forth by night. What need the turtle has of some horny shield over those tender parts and avenues to its entrails! I saw several of these painted turtles dead on the bottom.

XIII, 345·347   11 June 1860

MURDER MYSTERY: RABBIT, FOX, OWL

In Hosmer's pitch pine wood just north of the bridge, I find myself on the track of a fox—as I take it—that has run about a great deal. Next I come to the tracks of rabbits, see where they have travelled back and forth, making a well-trodden path in the snow; and soon after I see where one has been killed and apparently devoured. There are to be seen only the tracks of what I take to be the fox. The snow is much trampled, or rather flattened by the body of the rabbit. It is somewhat bloody and is covered with flocks of slate-colored and brown fur, but only the rabbit's tail, a little ball of fur, an inch and a half long and about as wide, white beneath, and the contents of its paunch or of its entrails are left,—nothing more. Half a dozen rods further, I see where the rabbit has been dropped on the snow again, and some fur is left, and there are the tracks of the fox to the spot and about it. There, or within a rod or two, I notice a considerable furrow in the snow, three or four inches wide and some two rods long, as if one had drawn a stick along, but there is no other mark or track whatever; so I conclude that a partridge, perhaps scared by the fox, had dashed swiftly along so low as to plow the snow. But two or three rods further on one side I see more sign[s], and lo! there is the remainder of the rabbit,—the whole, indeed, but the tail and the inward or soft parts,—all frozen stiff; but here there is no distinct track of any creature, only a few scratches and marks where some great bird of prey—a hawk or owl—has struck the snow with its primaries on each side, and one or two holes where it has stood. Now I understand how that long furrow was made, the bird with the rabbit in its talons flying low there, and now I remember that at the first bloody spot I saw some of these quill-marks; and therefore it is certain that the bird had it there, and probably he killed it, and he, perhaps disturbed by the fox, carried it to the second place, and it is certain that he (probably disturbed by the fox again) carried it to the last place, making a furrow on the way.

If it had not been for the snow on the ground I probably should not have noticed any signs that a rabbit had been killed. Or, if I had chanced to see the scattered fur, I should not have known what crea-ture did it, or how recently. . . . There were many tracks of the fox about that place, and I had no doubt then that he had killed that rab-bit, and I supposed that some scratches which I saw might have been made by his frisking some part of the rabbit back and forth, shaking it in his mouth. I thought, Perhaps he has carried off to his young, or buried, the rest. But as it turned out, though the circumstantial evi-dence against the fox was very strong, I was mistaken. I had made him kill the rabbit, and shake and tear the carcass, and eat it all up but the tail (almost); but it seems that he didn't do it at [all], and apparently never got a mouthful of the rabbit. . . .

The circumstantial evidence against that fox was very strong, for the deed was done since the snow fell and I saw no other tracks but his at the first places. Any jury would have convicted him, and he would have been hung, if he could have been caught.

XIII, 73·76   4 Jan. 1860

PERAMBULATING THE BOUNDS OF CONCORD

On Monday, the 15th instant, I am going to perambulate the bounds of the town. As I am partial to across-lot routes, this appears to be a very proper duty for me to perform,* for certainly no route can well be chosen which shall be more across-lot, since the roads in no case run round the town but ray out from its centre, and my

* Thoreau sometimes made a living by surveying. A "town" in New England is similar to a township or small county in other states. The "town" of Concord here referred to comprised an area about five by eight miles, including not only the village of Concord but several ham-lets, Walden Pond and a half-dozen others.

The reference in the next paragraph is presumably to *A Critical Pronouncing Dictionary of the English Language* (1791) by John Walker, a lexicographer who enjoyed the patronage of Dr. Samuel Johnson; their dictionaries remained standard works until well into the nineteenth century.

course will lie across each one. It is almost as if I had undertaken to walk round the town at the greatest distance from its centre and at the same time from the surrounding villages. There is no public house near the line. It is a sort of reconnoissance of its frontiers authorized by the central government of the town, which will bring the surveyor in contact with whatever wild inhabitant or wilderness its territory embraces.

This appears to be a very ancient custom, and I find that this word "perambulation" has exactly the same meaning that it has at present in Johnson and Walker's dictionary. A hundred years ago they went round the towns of this State every three years. And the old selectmen tell me that, before the present split stones were set up in 1829, the bounds were marked by a heap of stones, and it was customary for each selectman to add a stone to the heap. . . .

Sept. 26. Since I perambulated the bounds of the town, I find that I have in some degree confined myself,—my vision and my walks. On whatever side I look off I am reminded of the mean and narrow-minded men whom I have lately met there. What can be uglier than a country occupied by grovelling, coarse, and low-lived men? No scenery will redeem it. What can be more beautiful than any scenery inhabited by heroes? Any landscape would be glorious to me, if I were assured that its sky was arched over a single hero. Hornets, hyenas, and baboons are not so great a curse to a country as men of a similar character. It is a charmed circle which I have drawn around my abode, having walked not with God but with the devil. I am too well aware when I have crossed this line.

    II, 498-499; III, 23-24   12, 26 Sept. 1857

PERAMBULATING THE BOUNDS OF IMAGINATION

As I go through the fields, endeavoring to recover my tone and sanity and to perceive things truly and simply again, after having been perambulating the bounds of the town all the week, and dealing with the most commonplace and worldly-minded men, and emphatically *trivial* things, I feel as if I had committed suicide in a sense. I am again forcibly struck with the truth of the fable of Apollo serving King Admetus,* its universal applicability. A fatal coarseness is the result of mixing in the trivial affairs of men. Though I have been associating even with the *select* men of this and the surrounding towns, I feel inexpressibly begrimed. My Pegasus has lost his wings; he has turned a reptile and gone on his belly. Such things are compatible only with a cheap and superficial life.

The poet must keep himself unstained and aloof. Let him perambulate the bounds of Imagination's provinces, the realms of faery, and not the insignificant boundaries of towns. The excursions of the imagination are so boundless, the limits of towns are so petty.

III, 5   20 Sept. 1851

THE DIVINE FLUTE-PLAYER

I hear now from Bear Garden Hill—I rarely walk by moonlight without hearing—the sound of a flute, or a horn, or a human voice. It is a performer I never see by day; should not recognize him if pointed out; but you may hear his performance in every horizon. He plays but one strain and goes to bed early, but I know by the character of that single strain that he is deeply dissatisfied with the manner in which he spends his day. He is a slave who is purchasing his freedom. He is Apollo watching the flocks of Admetus * on every hill, and this strain he plays every evening to remind him of his heavenly descent. It is all that saves him,—his one redeeming trait. It is a reminiscence; he loves to remember his youth. He is sprung of a noble family. He is highly related, I have no doubt; was tenderly nurtured in his infancy, poor hind as he is. That noble strain he utters, instead of any jewel on his finger, or precious locket fastened to his breast, or purple garments that came with him. The elements recognize him, and echo his strain. All the dogs know him their master, though lords and ladies, rich men and learned, know him not. He is

* Thoreau frequently used this fable to symbolize the poet's servitude in having to earn a living, and so compared himself to Apollo.

the son of a rich man, of a famous man who served his country well. He has heard his sire's stories. I thought of the time when he would discover his parentage, obtain his inheritance and sing a strain suited to the morning hour. He cherishes hopes. I never see the man by day who plays that clarionet.

II, 373-374   5 Aug. 1851

EXCHANGING STARES

As I approached the pond, I saw a hind in a potato-field (digging potatoes), who stood stock-still for ten minutes to gaze at me in mute astonishment, till I had sunk into the woods amid the hills about the pond, and when I emerged again, there he was motionless still, on the same spot, with his eye on me, resting on his idle hoe, as one might watch at the mouth of a fox's hole to see him come out. Perchance he may have thought *nihil humanum*,* etc., or else he was transfixed with thought,—which is worth a bushel or two of potatoes, whatever his employer may say,—contrasting his condition with my own, and though he stood so still, civilization made some progress. But I must hasten away or he'll lose his day. I was as indifferent to his eyeshot as a tree walking, for I am used to such things. Perchance he will relate his adventure when he gets home at night, and what he has seen, though he did not have to light a candle this time. I am in a fair way to become a valuable citizen to him, as he is to me. He raises potatoes in the field for me; I raise curiosity in him. He stirs the earth; I stir him. What a power am I! I cause the potatoes to rot in the ground. I affect distant markets surely. But he shall not spoil my day; I will get in my harvest nevertheless. This will be nuts to him when the winter evenings come; he will tell his dream then. Talk of reaping-machines! I did not go into that field at all. I did not meddle with the

* Terence's line (*Heauton Timorumenos*, 77)—"Homo sum: humani nil a me alienum puto" (I am a man: nothing human can be alien to me)—is subverted here and put in the mouth of the rustic (hind) who is the butt of this little satire.

potatoes. He was the only crop I gathered at a glance. Perchance he thought, "I harvest potatoes; he harvests me!"

 XI, 230-231   20 Oct. 1858

WALKING AND TALKING

I know of but one or two persons with whom I can afford to walk. With most the walk degenerates into a mere vigorous use of your legs, ludicrously purposeless, while you are discussing some mighty argument, each one having his say, spoiling each other's day, worrying one another with conversation, hustling one another with our conversation. I know of no use in the walking part in this case, except that we may seem to be getting on together toward some goal; but of course we keep our original distance all the way. Jumping every wall and ditch with vigor in the vain hope of shaking your companion off. Trying to kill two birds with one stone, though they sit at opposite points of [the] compass, to see nature and do the honors to one who does not.

 XI, 296-297   8 Nov. 1858

WALKING IN SOLITUDE

It is surprising how much room there is in nature,—if a man will follow his proper path. In these broad fields, in these extensive woods, on this stretching river, I never meet a walker. Passing behind the farmhouses, I see no man out. Perhaps I do not meet so many men as I should have met three centuries ago, when the Indian hunter roamed these woods. I enjoy the retirement and solitude of an early settler. Men have cleared some of the earth, which no doubt is an advantage to the walker. I see a man sometimes chopping in the woods, or planting or hoeing in a field, at a distance; and yet there may be a lyceum* in the evening, and there is a book-shop and library in the village, and five times a day I can be whirled to Boston within an hour.

IV, 478-479   26 Jan. 1853

WALKING IN THE MIST

I find it good to be out this still, dark, mizzling afternoon; my walk or voyage is more suggestive and profitable than in bright weather. The view is contracted by the misty rain, the water is perfectly smooth, and the stillness is favorable to reflection. I am more open to impressions, more sensitive (not calloused or indurated by sun and wind), as if in a chamber still. My thoughts are concentrated; I am all compact. The solitude is real, too, for the weather keeps other men at home. This mist is like a roof and walls over and around, and I walk with a domestic feeling. The sound of a wagon going over an unseen bridge is louder than ever, and so of other sounds. I am *compelled* to look at near objects. All things have a soothing effect; the very clouds and mists brood over me. My power of observation and contemplation is much increased. My attention does not wander. The world and my life are simplified. What now of Europe and Asia?

VIII, 14   7 Nov. 1855

FLUVIAL WALKING

Now for another fluvial walk. There is always a current of air above the water, blowing up or down the course of the river, so that this is the coolest highway. Divesting yourself of all clothing but your shirt and hat, which are to protect your exposed parts from the sun, you are prepared for the fluvial excursion. You choose what depths

* The Concord Lyceum was a famous one in the period from 1840 to 1860, with many Transcendentalist lecturers, including Thoreau as well as Emerson, Alcott, Channing, Theodore Parker, and others.

you like, tucking your toga higher or lower, as you take the deep middle of the road or the shallow sidewalks. Here is a road where no dust was ever known, no intolerable drouth. Now your feet expand on a smooth sandy bottom, now contract timidly on pebbles, now slump in genial fatty mud—greasy, saponaceous—amid the pads. You scare out whole schools of small breams and perch, and some-times a pickerel, which have taken shelter from the sun under the pads. This river is so clear compared with the South Branch, or main stream, that all their secrets are betrayed to you. Or you meet with and interrupt a turtle taking a more leisurely walk up the stream. Ever and anon you cross some furrow in the sand, made by a muskrat, leading off to right or left to their galleries in the bank, and you thrust your foot into the entrance, which is just below the surface of the water and is strewn with grass and rushes, of which they make their nests. In shallow water near the shore, your feet at once detect the presence of springs in the bank emptying in, by the sudden coldness of the water, and there, if you are thirsty, you dig a little well in the sand with your hands, and when you return, after it has settled and clarified itself, get a draught of pure cold water there. The fishes are very forward to find out such places, and I have observed that a frog will occupy a cool spring, however small.

IV, 220-221   12 July 1852

WALKING ON THE SKY

I walk over a smooth green sea, or *aequor*, the sun just disap-pearing in the cloudless horizon, amid thousands of these flat isles as purple as the petals of a flower. It would not be more enchanting to walk amid the purple clouds of the sunset sky. And, by the way, this is but a sunset sky under our feet, produced by the same law, the same slanting rays and twilight. Here the clouds are these patches of snow or frozen vapor, and the ice is the greenish sky between them. Thus all of heaven is realized on earth. You have seen those purple fortunate isles in the sunset heavens, and that green and amber sky between them. Would you believe that you could ever walk amid those isles? You can on many a winter evening. I have done so a hundred times. The ice is a solid crystalline sky under our feet. . . .

Thus the sky and the earth sympathize, and are subject to the same laws, and in the horizon they, as it were, meet and are seen to be one.

I have walked in such a place and found it hard as marble.

Not only the earth but the heavens are made our footstool. That is what the phenomenon of ice means. The earth is annually inverted and we walk upon the sky. The ice reflects the blue of the sky. The waters become solid and made a sky below. The clouds grow heavy and fall to earth, and we walk on them. We live and walk on solidified fluids.

We have such a habit of looking away that we see not what is around us. How few are aware that in winter, when the earth is covered with snow and ice, the phenomenon of the sunset sky is double! The one is on the earth around us, the other in the horizon. These snow-clad hills answer to the rosy isles in the west. The winter is coming when I shall walk the sky. The ice is a solid sky on which we walk. It is the inverted year. There is an annual light in the darkness of the winter night. The shadows are blue, as the sky is forever blue. In winter we are purified and translated. The earth does not absorb our thoughts. It becomes a Valhalla.

XIII, 140-142   12 Feb. 1860

BOATING

It is pleasant to embark on a voyage, if only for a short river excursion, the boat to be your home for the day, especially if it is neat and dry. A sort of moving studio it becomes, you can carry so many things with you. It is almost as if you put oars out at your windows and moved your house along. A sailor, I see, easily becomes attached to his vessel. How continually we [are] thankful to the boat if it does not leak! We move now with a certain pomp and circumstance, with planetary dignity. The pleasure of sailing is akin to that which a planet feels. It seems a more complete adventure than a walk. We make believe embark our all,—our house and furniture. We are further from the earth than the rider; we receive no jar from it. We can carry many things with us. . . .

How much he knows of the wind, its strength and direction, whose steed it is,—the sailor. With a good gale he advances rapidly; when it dies away he is at a standstill. The very sounds made by moving the furniture of my boat are agreeable, echoing so distinctly and sweetly over the water; they give the sense of being abroad. I find myself *at home* in new scenery. I carry more of myself with me; I am more entirely abroad, as when a man takes his children into the fields with him. I carry so many me's with [me]. This large basket of melons, umbrella, flowers, hammer, etc., etc., all go with me to the end of the voyage without being the least incumbrance, and preserve their relative distances. Our capacity to carry our furniture with us is so much increased. There is little danger of overloading the steed. We can go completely equipped to fields a dozen miles off. The tent and the chest can be taken as easily as not. We embark; we go aboard a boat; we sit or we stand. If we sail, there is no exertion necessary. If we move in the opposite direction, we nevertheless progress. And if we row, we sit to an agreeable exercise, akin to flying. A student, of course, if it were perfectly convenient, would always move with his escritoire and his library about him. If you have a cabin and can descend into that, the charm is double. . . .

All the fields and meadows are shorn. I would like to go into perfectly new and wild country where the meadows are rich in decaying and rustling vegetation, present a wilder luxuriance. I wish to lose myself amid reeds and sedges and wild grasses that have not been touched. If haying were omitted for a season or two, a voyage up this river in the fall, methinks, would make a much wilder impression. I sail and paddle to find a place where the bank has a more neglected look. I wish to bury myself amid reeds. I pine for the luxuriant vegetation of the river-banks.

IV, 325-329   31 Aug. 1852

KATING

I think more of skates than of the horse or locomotive as anni-hilators of distance, for while I am getting along with the speed of the horse, I have at the same times the satisfaction of the horse and his rider, and far more adventure and variety than if I were riding. We never cease to be surprised when we observe how swiftly the skater glides along. Just compare him with one walking or running. The walker is but a snail in comparison, and the runner gives up the con-test after a few rods. The skater can afford to follow all the windings of a stream, and yet soon leaves far behind and out of sight the walker who cuts across. Distance is hardly an obstacle to him. . . . The briskest walkers appear to be stationary to the skater. The skater has wings, *talaria,* to his feet. Moreover, you have such perfect control of your feet that you can take advantage of the narrowest and most winding and sloping bridge of ice in order to pass between the button-bushes and the open stream or under a bridge on a narrow shelf, where the walker cannot go at all. You can glide securely within an inch of destruction on this the most slippery of surfaces, more securely than you could walk there, perhaps, on any other material. You can pursue swiftly the most intricate and winding path, even leaping obstacles which suddenly present themselves.

XI, 381-382   29 Dec. 1858

ARVESTING THE MEADOWS

The farmers are just finishing their meadow-haying. (To-day is Sunday.) Those who have early potatoes may be digging them, or doing any other job which the haying has obliged them to postpone. For six weeks or more this has been the farmer's work, to shave the surface of the fields and meadows clean. This is done all over the country. The razor is passed over these parts of nature's face the country over. A thirteenth labor which methinks would have broken the back of Hercules, would have given him a memorable sweat, ac-complished with what sweating of scythes and early and late! I chance [to] know one young man who has lost his life in this season's cam-paign, by overdoing. In haying time some men take double wages, and they are engaged long before in the spring. To shave all the fields and meadows of New England clean! If men did this but once, and not every year, we should never hear the last of that labor; it would be more famous in each farmer's case than Buonaparte's road over the Simplon. It has no other bulletin but the truthful "Farmer's Al-manac." Ask them where scythe-snaths are made and sold, and rifles too, if it is not a real labor. In its very weapons and its passes it has the semblance of war. Mexico was won with less exertion and less true valor than are required to do one season's haying in New Eng-land. The former work was done by those who played truant and ran away from the latter. Those Mexicans were mown down more easily than the summer's crop of grass in many a farmer's fields. Is there not some work in New England men? This haying is no work for marines, nor for deserters; nor for United States troops, so called, nor for West Point cadets. It would wilt them, and they would desert. Have they not deserted? and run off to West Point? Every field is a battle-field to the mower,—a pitched battle too,—and whole win-rows of dead have covered it in the course of the season. Early and late the farmer has gone forth with his formidable scythe, weapon of time, Time's weapon, and fought the ground inch by inch. It is the summer's enterprise. And if we were a more poetic people, horns would be blown to celebrate its completion. There might be a Hay-makers' Day. New England's peaceful battles. At Bunker Hill* there were some who stood at the rail-fence and behind the winrows of new-mown hay. They have not yet quitted the field. They stand there still; they alone have not retreated.

11, 393-395   17 Aug. 1851

*   In this famous Revolutionary War battle Stark and his companions met the enemy in a hay-field. The Mexican War (1845–1847), re-ferred to above, gave Thoreau an opportunity for satirical contrast; it was fought for the extension of slavery, in his opinion, instead of for in-dependence and freedom from tyranny.

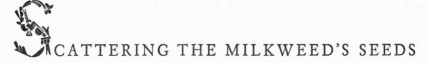

SCATTERING THE MILKWEED'S SEEDS

At Clematis Brook I perceive that the pods or follicles of the *Asclepias Syriaca* now point upward. Did they before all point down? Have they turned up? They are already bursting. I release some seeds with the long, fine silk attached. The fine threads fly apart at once, open with a spring, and then ray themselves out into a hemispherical form, each thread freeing itself from its neighbor and all reflecting prismatic or rainbow tints. The seeds, besides, are furnished with wings, which plainly keep them steady and prevent their whirling round. I let one go, and it rises slowly and uncertainly at first, now driven this way, then that, by currents which I cannot perceive, and I fear it will make shipwreck against the neighboring wood; but no, as it approaches it, it surely rises above it, and then, feeling the strong north wind, it is borne off rapidly in the opposite direction, ever rising higher and higher and tossing and heaved about with every fluctuation of the air, till, at a hundred feet above the earth and fifty rods off, steering south, I lose sight of it. How many myriads go sailing away at this season, high over hill and meadow and river, on various tacks until the wind lulls, to plant their race in new localities, who can tell how many miles distant! And for this end these silken streamers have been perfecting all summer, snugly packed in this light chest,—a perfect adaptation to this end, a prophecy not only of the fall but of future springs. Who could believe in prophecies of Daniel or of Miller* that the world would end this summer, while one milkweed with faith matured its seeds?

I did not see but the seeds of the milkweed would be borne many hundred miles, and those which were ripened in New England might plant themselves in Pennsylvania. Densely packed in a little oblong chest armed with soft downy prickles and lined with a smooth silky lining, lie some one or two hundreds such pear-shaped seeds (or

---

* William Miller, an American preacher with many followers during the 1840's, prophesied that the end of the world and the second coming of Christ were at hand. (Daniel presumably refers to The Old Testament prophet.)

like a steelyards poise), which have derived their nutriment through a band of extremely fine silken threads attached by their extremities to the core. At length, when the seeds are matured and cease to require nourishment from the parent plant, being weaned, and the pod with dryness and frost bursts, the extremities of the silken threads detach themselves from the core, and from being the conduits of nutriment to the seed become the buoyant balloon which, like some spiders' webs, bear the seeds to new and distant fields. They merely serve to buoy up the full-fed seed. Far finer than the finest thread. Think of the great variety of balloons which at this season are buoyed up by similar means! I am interested in the fate or success of every such venture which the autumn sends forth.

III, 17-20   24-25 Sept. 1851

DEATH OF A PINE

This afternoon, being on Fair Haven Hill, I heard the sound of a saw, and soon after from the Cliff saw two men sawing down a noble pine beneath, about forty rods off. I resolved to watch it till it fell, the last of a dozen or more which were left when the forest was cut and for fifteen years have waved in solitary majesty over the sprout-land. I saw them like beavers or insects gnawing at the trunk of this noble tree, the diminutive manikins with their cross-cut saw which could scarcely span it. It towered up a hundred feet as I afterward found by measurement, one of the tallest probably in the township and straight as an arrow, but slanting a little toward the hillside, its top seen against the frozen river and the hills of Conantum. I watch closely to see when it begins to move. Now the sawers stop, and with an axe open it a little on the side toward which it leans, that it may break the faster. And now their saw goes again. Now surely it is going; it is inclined one quarter of the quadrant, and, breathless, I expect its crashing fall. But no, I was mistaken; it has not moved an inch; it stands at the same angle as at first. It is fifteen minutes yet to its fall. Still its branches wave in the wind, as if it were destined to stand for a century, and the wind soughs through its needles as of yore; it is still a forest tree, the most majestic tree that waves over Musketaquid. The silvery sheen of the sunlight is reflected from its needles; it still affords an inaccessible crotch for the squirrel's nest; not a lichen has forsaken its mast-like stem, its raking mast,—the hill is the hulk. Now, now's the moment! The manikins at its base are fleeing from their crime. They have dropped the guilty saw and axe. How slowly and majestically it starts! as if it were only swayed by a summer breeze, and would return without a sigh to its location in the air. And now it fans the hillside with its fall, and it lies down to its bed in the valley, from which it is never to rise, as softly as a feather, folding its green mantle about it like a warrior, as if, tired of standing, it embraced the earth with silent joy, returning its elements to the dust again. But hark! there you only saw, but did not hear. There now comes up a deafening crash to these rocks, advertising you that even trees do not die without a groan. It rushes to embrace the earth, and mingle its elements with the dust. And now all is still once more and forever, both to eye and ear.

I went down and measured it. It was about four feet in diameter where it was sawed, about one hundred feet long. Before I had reached it the axemen had already half divested it of its branches. Its gracefully spreading top was a perfect wreck on the hillside as if it had been made of glass, and the tender cones of one year's growth upon its summit appealed in vain and too late to the mercy of the chopper. Already he has measured it with his axe, and marked off the mill-logs it will make. And the space it occupied in upper air is vacant for the next two centuries. It is lumber. He has laid waste the air. When the fish hawk in the spring revisits the banks of the Musketaquid, he will circle in vain to find his accustomed perch, and the hen-hawk will mourn for the pines lofty enough to protect her brood. A plant which it has taken two centuries to perfect, rising by slow stages into the heavens, has this afternoon ceased to exist. Its sapling top had expanded to this January thaw as the forerunner of summers to come. Why does not the village bell sound a knell? I hear no knell tolled. I see no procession of mourners in the streets, or the woodland aisles. The squirrel has leaped to another tree; the hawk has cricled further off, and has now settled upon a new eyrie, but the woodman is preparing [to] lay his axe at the root of that also.

III, 162-164   30 Dec. 1851

STUMPS BURNING

As I went up the Groton road, I saw a dim light at a distance, where no house was, which appeared to come from the earth. Could it be a traveller with a lanthorn? Could it be a will-o'-the-wisp? (Who ever saw one? Are not they a piece of modern mythology?) You wonder if you will ever reach it; already it seems to recede. Is it the reflection of the evening star in water? or what kind of phosphorescence? But now I smell the burning. I see the sparks go up in the dark.— It is a heap of stumps half covered with earth, left to smoulder and consume in the newly plowed meadow, now burst forth into dull internal flames. Looks like a gipsy encampment. I sit on the untouched end of a stump, and warm me by it, and write by the light, the moon not having risen. What a strange, Titanic thing this Fire, this Vulcan, here at work in the night in this bog, far from men, dangerous to them, consuming earth, gnawing at its vitals! The heap glows within. Here sits hungry Fire with the forest in his mouth. On the one side is the solid wood; on the other, smoke and sparks. Thus he works. The farmer designs to consume, to destroy, this wood, remains of trees. He gives them to his dog or vulture Fire. They burn like spunk, and I love the smell of the smoke. The frogs peep and dream around. Within are fiery caverns, incrusted with fire as a cave with saltpetre. No wonder at salamanders. It suggests a creature that lives in it, generated by it.

IV, 22-23   5 May 1852

LIGHTNING

Saw a very large white ash tree, three and a half feet in diameter, in front of the house which White formerly owned, under this hill, which was struck by lightning the 22d, about 4 P.M. The lightning apparently struck the top of the tree and scorched the bark and leaves for ten or fifteen feet downward, then began to strip off the bark and

enter the wood, making a ragged narrow furrow or crack, till, reaching one of the upper limbs, it apparently divided, descending on both
sides and entering deeper and deeper into the wood. At the first general branching, it had got full possession of the tree in its centre and
tossed off the main limbs butt foremost, making holes in the ground
where they struck; and so it went down in the midst of the trunk to
the earth, where it apparently exploded, rending the trunk into six
segments, whose tops, ten or twenty feet long, were rayed out on
every side at an angle of about 30° from a perpendicular, leaving the
ground bare directly under where the tree had stood, though they
were still fastened to the earth by their roots. The lightning appeared
to have gone off through the roots, furrowing them as the branches,
and through the earth, making a furrow like a plow, four or five rods
in one direction, and in another passing through the cellar of the
neighboring house, about thirty feet distant, scorching the tin milk-
pans and throwing dirt into the milk, and coming out the back side of
the house in a furrow, splitting some planks there. The main body
of the tree was completely stripped of bark, which was cast in every
direction two hundred feet; and large pieces of the inside of the tree,
fifteen feet long, were hurled with tremendous force in various directions, one into the side of [a] shed, smashing it, another burying itself
in a wood-pile. The heart of the tree lay by itself. Probably a piece as
large as [a] man's leg could not have been sawn out of the trunk which
would not have had a crack in it, and much of it was very finely splin-
tered. The windows in the house were broken and the inhabitants
knocked down by the concussion. All this was accomplished in an instant by a kind of fire out of the heavens called lightning, or a thunderbolt, accompanied by a crashing sound. For what purpose? The ancients called it Jove's bolt, with which he punished the guilty, and we
moderns understand it no better. There was displayed a Titanic force,
some of that force which made and can unmake the world. The
brute forces are not yet wholly tamed. Is this of the character of a
wild beast, or is it guided by intelligence and mercy? If we trust our
natural impressions, it is a manifestation of brutish force or vengeance,
more or less tempered with justice. Yet it is our own consciousness of
sin, probably, which suggests the idea of vengeance, and to a righteous
man it would be merely sublime without being awful.

This is one of those instances in which a man hesitates to refer his safety to his prudence, as the putting up of a lightning-rod. There is no lightning-rod by which the sinner can finally avert the avenging Nemesis. Though I should put up a rod if its utility were satisfactorily demonstrated to me, yet, so mixed are we, I should feel myself safe or in danger quite independently of the senseless rod. Yet there is a degree of faith and righteousness in putting up a rod, as well as trust-ing without one, though the latter, which is the rarest, I feel to be [the] most effectual rod of the two. It only suggests that impunity in respect to all forms of death or disease, whether sickness or casualty, is only to be attained by moral integrity. It is the faith with which we take medicine that cures us. Otherwise we may be cured into greater disease. In a violent tempest, we both fear and trust. We are ashamed of our fear, for we know that a righteous man would not suspect dan-ger, nor incur any. Wherever a man feels fear, there is an avenger. The savage's and the civilized man's instincts are right. Science af-firms too much. Science assumes to show *why* the lightning strikes a tree, but it does not show us the moral *why* any better than our instincts did. It is full of presumption. Why should trees be struck? It is not enough to say because they are in the way. Science answers, *Non scio*, I am ignorant. All the phenomena of nature need [to] be seen from the point of view of wonder and awe, like lightning; and, on the other hand, the lightning itself needs to [be] re-garded with serenity, as the most familiar and innocent phenomena are. There runs through the righteous man's moral spinal column a rod with burnished points to heaven, which conducts safely away into the earth the flashing wrath of Nemesis, so that it merely clarifies the air. This moment the confidence of the righteous man erects a sure conductor within him; the next, perchance, a timid staple diverts the fluid to his vitals. If a mortal be struck with a thunderbolt *coelo sereno*, it is naturally felt to be more awful and vengeful. Men are probably nearer to the essential truth in their superstitions than in their science. Some places are thought to be particularly exposed to lightning, some oaks on hilltops, for instance.

IV, 155-158   27 June 1852

THUNDER

I hear it in mid-afternoon, muttering, crashing in the muggy air in mid-heaven, a little south of the village as I go through it, like the tumbling down of piles of boards, and get a few sprinkles in the sun. Nature has found her hoarse summer voice again, like the lowing of a cow let out to pasture. It is Nature's rutting season. Even as the birds sing tumultuously and glance by with fresh and brilliant plumage, so now is Nature's grandest voice heard, and her sharpest flashes seen. The air has resumed its voice, and the lightning, like a yellow spring flower, illumines the dark banks of the clouds. All the pregnant earth is bursting into life like a mildew, accompanied with noise and fire and tumult. Some œstrus stings her that she dashes headlong against the steeples and bellows hollowly, making the earth tremble. She comes dropping rain like a cow with overflowing udder. The winds drive her; the dry fields milk her. It is the familiar note of another warbler, just arrived, echoing amid the roofs.

VIII, 349   20 May 1856

WIND

Going up the hill through Stow's young oak woodland, I listen to the sharp, dry rustle of the withered oak leaves. This is the voice of the wood now. It would be comparatively still and more dreary here in other respects, if it were not for these leaves that hold on. It sounds like the roar of the sea, and is enlivening and inspiriting like that, suggesting how all the land is seacoast to the aerial ocean. It is the sound of the surf, the rut of an unseen ocean, billows of air break-ing on the forest like water on itself or on sand and rocks. It rises and falls, wells and dies away, with agreeable alternation as the sea surf does. Perhaps the landsman can foretell a storm by it. It is remarkable how universal these grand murmurs are, these backgrounds of sound, —the surf, the wind in the forest, waterfalls, etc.,—which yet to the

ear and in their origin are essentially one voice, the earth-voice, the
breathing or snoring of the creature. The earth is our ship, and this is
the sound of the wind in her rigging as we sail. Just as the inhabitant
of Cape Cod hears the surf ever breaking on its shores, so we countrymen hear this kindred surf on the leaves of the forest. Regarded as a
voice,—though it is not articulate,—as our articulate sounds are
divided into vowels (but this is nearer a consonant sound), labials,
dentals, palatals, sibilants, mutes, aspirate, etc., so this may be called
folial or *frondal*, produced by air driven against the leaves, and comes
nearest to our sibilants or aspirate.

xi, 384-385   2 Jan. 1859

ECHOES

There is a good echo from that wood to one standing on the
side of Fair Haven. It was particularly good to-day. The woodland
lungs seemed particularly sound to-day; they echoed your shout with
a fuller and rounder voice than it was given in, seeming to *mouth* it.
It was uttered with a sort of sweeping intonation half round a vast
circle, *ore rotundo*, by a broad dell among the tree-tops passing it
round to the entrance of all the aisles of the wood. You had to choose
the right key or pitch, else the woods would not echo it with any spirit,
and so with eloquence. Of what significance is any sound if Nature
does not echo it? It does not prevail. It dies away as soon as uttered.
I wonder that wild men have not made more of echoes, or that we do
not hear that they have made more. It would be a pleasant, a soothing
and cheerful mission to go about the country in search of them,—
articulating, speaking, vocal, oracular, resounding, sonorous, hollow,
prophetic places; places wherein to found an oracle, sites for oracles,
sacred ears of Nature.

I used to strike with a paddle on the side of my boat on Walden
Pond, filling the surrounding woods with circling and dilating sound,
awaking the woods, "stirring them up," as a keeper of a menagerie
his lions and tigers, a growl from all.* All melody is a sweet echo, as

* This sentence was used in *Walden*, p. 193.

it were coincident with [the] movement of our organs. We wake the echo of the place we are in, its slumbering music.

I should think that savages would have made a god of echo.

I will call that Echo Wood.

11, 81-82   1850

STANDING IN A RAINBOW

As I am going to the pond to bathe, I see a black cloud in the northern horizon and hear the muttering of thunder, and make haste. Before I have bathed and dressed, the gusts which precede the tempest are heard roaring in the woods, and the first black, gusty clouds have reached my zenith. Hastening toward town, I meet the rain at the edge of the wood, and take refuge under the thickest leaves, where not a drop reaches me, and, at the end of half an hour, the renewed singing of the birds alone advertises me that the rain has ceased, and it is only the dripping from the leaves which I hear in the woods. It was a splendid sunset that day, a celestial light on all the land, so that all people went to their doors and windows to look on the grass and leaves and buildings and the sky, and it was equally glorious in whatever quarter you looked; a sort of fulgor as of stereotyped lightning filled the air. Of which this is my solution. We were in the westernmost edge of the shower at the moment the sun was setting, and its rays shone through the cloud and the falling rain. We were, in fact, in a rainbow and it was here its arch rested on the earth. At a little distance we should have seen all the colors.

11, 382-383   7 Aug. 1851

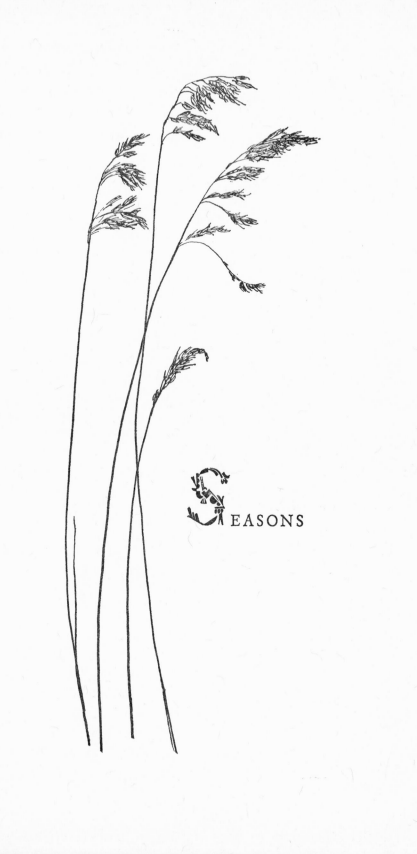

SEASONS

EACH SEASON AN INFINI-TESIMAL POINT

This is June, the month of grass and leaves. The deciduous trees are investing the evergreens and revealing how dark they are. Already the aspens are trembling again, and a new summer is offered me. I feel a little fluttered in my thoughts, as if I might be too late. Each season is but an infinitesimal point. It no sooner comes than it is gone. It has no duration. It simply gives a tone and hue to my thought. Each annual phenomenon is a reminiscence and prompting. Our thoughts and sentiments answer to the revolutions of the seasons, as two cog-wheels fit into each other. We are conversant with only one point of contact at a time, from which we receive a prompting and impulse and instantly pass to a new season or point of contact. A year is made up of a certain series and number of sensations and thoughts which have their language in nature. Now I am ice, now I am sorrel. Each experience reduces itself to a mood of the mind. I see a man grafting, for instance. What this imports chiefly is not apples to the owner or bread to the grafter, but a certain mood or train of thought to my mind. That is what this grafting is to me. Whether it is anything at all, even apples or bread, to anybody else, I cannot swear, for it would be worse than swearing *through glass*. For I only see those other facts as through a glass darkly.

IX, 406-407   6 June 1857

THE SEASONS ARE IN ME

These regular phenomena of the seasons get at last to be—they were *at first*, of course—simply and plainly phenomena or phases of my life. The seasons and all their changes are in me. I see not a dead eel or floating snake, or a gull, but it rounds my life and is like a line or accent in its poem. Almost I believe the Concord would not rise and overflow its banks again, were I not here. After a while I learn what my moods and seasons are. I would have nothing subtracted. I can imagine nothing added. My moods are thus periodical, not two days in my year alike. The perfect correspondence of Nature to man, so that he is at home in her!

X, 127   26 Oct. 1857

LIVE IN EACH SEASON

Live in each season as it passes; breathe the air, drink the drink, taste the fruit, and resign yourself to the influences of each. Let them be your only diet drink and botanical medicines. In August live on berries, not dried meats and pemmican, as if you were on shipboard making your way through a waste ocean, or in a northern desert. Be blown on by all the winds. Open all your pores and bathe in all the tides of Nature, in all her streams and oceans, at all seasons. Miasma and infection are from within, not without. The invalid, brought to the brink of the grave by an unnatural life, instead of imbibing only the great influence that Nature is, drinks only the tea made of a particular herb, while he still continues his unnatural life,—saves at the spile and wastes at the bung. He does not love Nature or his life, and so sickens and dies, and no doctor can cure him. Grow green with spring, yellow and ripe with autumn. Drink of each season's influence as a vial, a true panacea of all remedies mixed for your especial use. The vials of summer never made a man sick, but those which he stored in his cellar. Drink the wines, not of your bottling, but Nature's bottling; not kept in goat-skins or pig-skins, but the skins of a myriad fair berries. Let Nature do your bottling and your pickling and preserving. For all Nature is doing her best each moment to make us well. She exists for no other end. Do not resist her. With the least inclination to be well, we should not be sick. Men have discovered—or think they have discovered—the salutariness of a few wild things only, and not of all nature. Why, "nature" is but another name for health, and the seasons are but different states of health. Some men think that they are not well in spring, or summer, or autumn, or winter; it is only because they are not *well in* them.

v, 394·395   23 Aug. 1853

EASON OF RAIN

It is so mild and moist as I saunter along by the wall east of the Hill that I remember, or anticipate, one of those warm rain-storms in the spring, when the earth is just laid bare, the wind is south, and the cladonia lichens are swollen and lusty with moisture, your foot sinking into them and pressing the water out as from a sponge, and the sandy places also are drinking it in. You wander indefinitely in a beaded coat, wet to the skin of your legs, sit on moss-clad rocks and stumps, and hear the lisping of migrating sparrows flitting amid the shrub oaks, sit long at a time, still, and have your thoughts. A rain which is as serene as fair weather, suggesting fairer weather than was ever seen. You could hug the clods that defile you. You feel the fertilizing influence of the rain in your mind. The part of you that is wettest is fullest of life, like the lichens. You discover evidences of immortality not known to divines. You cease to die. You detect some buds and sprouts of life. Every step in the old rye-field is on virgin soil.

And then the rain comes thicker and faster than before, thawing the remaining frost in the ground, detaining the migrating bird; and you turn your back to it, full of serene, contented thought, soothed by the steady dropping on the withered leaves, more at home for being abroad, more comfortable for being wet, sinking at each step deep into the thawing earth, gladly breaking through the gray rotting ice. The dullest sounds seem sweetly modulated by the air. You leave your tracks in fields of spring rye, scaring the fox-colored sparrows along the wood-sides. You cannot go home yet; you stay and sit in the rain. You glide along the distant wood-side, full of joy and expectation, seeing nothing but beauty, hearing nothing but music, as free as the fox-colored sparrow, seeing far ahead, a courageous knight, a great philosopher, not indebted to any academy or college for this expansion, but chiefly to the April rain, which descendeth on all alike.*

x, 262-263   27 Jan. 1858

EASON OF DROUGHT AND HEAT

How far behind the spring seems now,—farther off, perhaps, than ever, for this heat and dryness is most opposed to spring. Where most I sought for flowers in April and May I do not think to go now; it is either drought and barrenness or fall there now. The reign of moisture is long since over. For a long time the year feels the influence of the snows of winter and the long rains of spring, but now how changed! It is like another and a fabulous age to look back on, when earth's veins were full of moisture, and violets burst out on every hillside. Spring is the reign of water; summer, of heat and dryness; winter, of cold. Whole families of plants that lately flourished have disappeared. Now the phenomena are tropical. Let our summer last long enough, and our land would wear the aspect of the tropics. The luxuriant foliage and growth of all kinds shades the earth and is converting every copse into a jungle. Vegetation is rampant. There is not such rapid growth, it is true, but it slumbers like a serpent that has swallowed its prey. Summer is one long drought. Rain is the exception. All the signs of it fail, for it is dry weather. Though it may seem so, the current year is not peculiar in this respect. It is a slight labor to keep count of all the showers, the rainy days, of a summer. You may keep it on your thumb nail.

v, 328-329   24 July 1853

* Possibly an allusion to Matthew 6.45: "[God] sendeth rain on the just and the unjust." It could also be an allusion (more suitable to the whole concept of this miniature) to the traditional medieval symbol of Christ as the gentle rain, falling on the earth in spring to make it green and fertile again, as in the anonymous fifteenth-century lyric: "He came . . . / As dew in April that falleth on the grass."

EASON OF GRASS

Do not the song of birds and the fireflies go with the grass? While the grass is fresh, the earth is in its vigor. The greenness of the grass is the best symptom or evidence of the earth's youth or health. Perhaps it will be found that when the grass ceases to be fresh and green, or after June, the birds have ceased to sing, and that the fireflies, too, no longer in *myriads* sparkle in the meadows. Perhaps a history of the year would be a history of the grass, or of a leaf, regarding the grass-blades as leaves, for it is equally true that the leaves soon lose their freshness and soundness, and become the prey of insects and of drought. Plants commonly soon cease to grow for the year, unless they may have a fall growth, which is a kind of second spring. In the feelings of the man, too, the year is already past, and he looks forward to the coming winter. His occasional rejuvenescence and faith in the current time is like the aftermath, a scanty crop. The enterprise which he has not already undertaken cannot be undertaken this year. The period of youth is past. The year may be in its summer, in its manhood, but it is no longer in the flower of its age. It is a season of withering, of dust and heat, a season of small fruits and trivial experiences. Summer thus answers to manhood. But there is an aftermath in early autumn, and some spring flowers bloom again, followed by an Indian summer of finer atmosphere and of a pensive beauty. May my life be not destitute of its Indian summer, a season of fine and clear, mild weather in which I may prolong my hunting before the winter comes, when I may once more lie on the ground with faith, as in spring, and even with more serene confidence. And then I will [wrap the] drapery of summer about me and lie down to pleasant dreams.* As one year passes into another through the medium of winter, so does this our life pass into another through the medium of death.

II, 481-482   8 Sept. 1857

* Bryant's "Thanatopsis" concludes with these lines:
    "Like one who wraps the drapery of his couch
    About him, and lies down to pleasant dreams."

SEASON OF FRUITS

What means this sense of lateness that so comes over one now,—
as if the rest of the year were down-hill, and if we had not performed
anything before, we should not now? The season of flowers or of
promise may be said to be over, and now is the season of fruits; but
where is our fruit? The night of the year is approaching. What have
we done with our talent?* All nature prompts and reproves us. How
early in the year it begins to be late! The sound of the crickets, even
in the spring, makes our hearts beat with its awful reproof, while it
encourages with its seasonable warning. It matters not by how little
we have fallen behind; it seems irretrievably late. The year is full of
warnings of its shortness, as is life. The sound of so many insects and
the sight of so many flowers affect us so,—the creak of the cricket
and the sight of the prunella and autumnal dandelion. They say,
"For the night cometh in which no man may work."

v, 378-379   18 Aug. 1853

FORETASTE OF AUTUMN

Cooler weather. Last Sunday we were sweltering here and one
hundred died of the heat in New York; to-day they have fires in this
village. After more rain, with wind in the night, it is now clearing up
cool. There is a broad, clear crescent of blue in the west, slowly increasing, and an agreeable autumnal coolness, both under the high,
withdrawn clouds and the edges of the woods, and a considerable
wind wafts us along with our one sail and two umbrellas, sitting in
thick coats. I was going to sit and write or mope all day in the house,
but it seems wise to cultivate animal spirits, to embark in enterprises
which employ and recreate the whole body. Let the divine spirits like
the huntsman with his bugle accompany the animal spirit that would

---

* An allusion to the well-known parable of the talents (Matthew
25.14–30). The quotation at the end of the paragraph is from John
9.4.

fain range the forest and meadow. Even the gods and goddesses, Apollo and Diana, are found in the field, though they are superior to the dog and the deer.

v, 378-379   19 Aug. 1853

THE PLUMES OF DEPARTING SUMMER

In the Lee farm swamp, by the old Sam Barrett mill site, I see two kinds of ferns still green and much in fruit. . . . In the summer you might not have noticed them. Now they are conspicuous amid the withered leaves. You are inclined to approach and raise each frond in succession, moist, trembling, fragile greenness. They linger thus in all moist clammy swamps under the bare maples and grape-vines and witch-hazels, and about each trickling spring which is half choked with fallen leaves. What means this persistent vitality, invul-nerable to frost and wet? Why were these spared when the brakes and osmundas were stricken down? They stay as if to keep up the spirits of the cold-blooded frogs which have not yet gone into the mud; that the summer may die with decent and graceful moderation, gradually. Is not the water of the spring improved by their presence? They fall back and droop here and there, like the plumes of depart-ing summer,—of the departing year. Even in them I feel an argument for immortality. Death is so far from being universal. The same de-stroyer does not destroy all. How valuable they are . . . for cheer-fulness. Greenness at the end of the year, after the fall of the leaf, as in a hale old age. To my eyes they are tall and noble as palm groves, and always some forest nobleness seems to have its haunt under their umbrage. Each such green tuft of ferns is a grove where some nobility dwells and walks. All that was immortal in the swamp's herbage seems here crowded into smaller compass,—the concentrated greenness of the swamp. How dear they must be to the chickadee and the rabbit! The cool, slowly retreating rear-guard of the swamp army. What virtue is theirs that enables them to resist the frost?

If you are afflicted with melancholy at this season, go to the swamp and see the brave spears of skunk-cabbage buds already advanced toward a new year. Their gravestones are not bespoken yet. Who shall be sexton to them? Is it the winter of their discontent?* Do they seem to have lain down to die, despairing of skunk-cabbage-dom? "Up and at 'em," "Give it to 'em," "Excelsior," "Put it through,"—these are their mottoes. Mortal human creatures must take a little respite in this fall of the year; their spirits do flag a little. There is a little questioning of destiny, and thinking to go like cowards to where the "weary shall be at rest." But not so with the skunk-cabbage. Its withered leaves fall and are transfixed by a rising bud. Winter and death are ignored; the circle of life is complete. Are these false prophets? Is it a lie or a vain boast underneath the skunk-cabbage bud, pushing it upward and lifting the dead leaves with it? They rest with spears advanced; they rest to shoot!

I say it is good for me to be here, slumping in the mud, a trap covered with withered leaves. See those green cabbage buds lifting the dry leaves in that watery and muddy place. There is no can't nor cant to them. They see over the brow of winter's hill. They see another summer ahead.

X, 149-151   31 Oct. 1857

SIGNS OF SPRING IN AUTUMN

. . . Each season is . . . drawn out and lingers in certain localities, as the birds and insects know very well. If you penetrate to some warm recess under a cliff in the woods, you will be astonished at the amount of summer life that still flourishes there. No doubt more of the summer's life than we are aware thus slips by and outmanœvres the winter, gliding from fence to fence. I have no doubt that a diligent search in proper places would discover many more of our summer flowers thus lingering till the snow came, than we suspect. It is as if the plant made no preparation for winter.

II, 104   19 Nov. 1850

* *Henry VI, Part Three*, V.5.81. The reference four sentences below is to Job 3.17.

PANORAMA" OF THE SEASONS

As the afternoons grow shorter, and the early evening drives us home to complete our chores, we are reminded of the shortness of life, and become more pensive, at least in this twilight of the year. We are prompted to make haste and finish our work before the night comes. I leaned over a rail in the twilight on the Walden road, waiting for the evening mail to be distributed, when such thoughts visited me. I seemed to recognize the November evening as a familiar thing come round again, and yet I could hardly tell whether I had ever known it or only divined it. The November twilights just begun! It appeared like a part of a panorama* at which I sat spectator, a part with which I was perfectly familiar just coming into view, and I foresaw how it would look and roll along, and prepared to be pleased. Just such a piece of art merely, though infinitely sweet and grand, did it appear to me, and just as little were any active duties required of me. We are independent [of] all that we see. The hangman whom I have *seen* cannot hang me. The earth which I have *seen* cannot bury me. Such doubleness and distance does sight prove. Only the rich and such as are troubled with ennui are implicated in the maze of phenomena. You cannot see anything until you are clear of it. The long railroad causeway through the meadows west of me, the still twilight in which hardly a cricket was heard, the dark bank of clouds in the horizon long after sunset, the villagers crowding to the post-office, and the hastening home to supper by candle-light, had I not seen all this before! What new sweet was I to extract from it? Truly they mean that we shall learn our lesson well. Nature gets thumbed like an old spelling-book. The almshouse and Frederick were still as last November. I was no nearer, methinks, nor further off from my friends. Yet I sat the bench with perfect contentment, unwilling to exchange the familiar vision that was to be unrolled for any treasure or heaven that could be imagined. Sure to keep just so far apart in our

* A series of pictures of a landscape, historical event, etc., presented on a continuous surface encircling the spectator—popular in Thoreau's day.

orbits still, in obedience to the laws of attraction and repulsion, affording each other only steady but indispensable starlight. It was as if I was promised the greatest novelty the world has ever seen or shall see, though the utmost possible novelty would be the difference between me and myself a year ago. This alone encouraged me, and was my fuel for the approaching winter. That we may behold the panorama with this slight improvement or change, this is what we sustain life for with so much effort from year to year.

And yet there is no more tempting novelty than this new November. No going to Europe or another world is to be named with it. Give me the old familiar walk, post-office and all, with this ever new self, with this infinite expectation and faith, which does not know when it is beaten. We'll go nutting once more. We'll pluck the nut of the world, and crack it in the winter evenings. Theatres and all other sightseeing are puppet-shows in comparison. I will take another walk to the Cliff, another row on the river, another skate on the meadow, be out in the first snow, and associate with the winter birds. Here I am at home. In the bare and bleached crust of the earth I recognize my friend.

    XI, 273-275   1 Nov. 1858

AITING FOR WINTER

The stillness of the woods and fields is remarkable at this season of the year. There is not even the creak of a cricket to be heard. Of myriads of dry shrub oak leaves, not one rustles. Your own breath can rustle them, yet the breath of heaven does not suffice to. The trees have the aspect of waiting for winter. The autumnal leaves have lost their color; they are now truly sere, dead, and the woods wear a sombre color. Summer and harvest are over. The hickories, birches, chestnuts, no less than the maples, have lost their leaves. The sprouts, which had shot up so vigorously to repair the damage which the choppers had done, have stopped short for the winter. Everything stands silent and expectant. If I listen, I hear only the note of a chickadee,—our most common and I may say native bird, most identified with our forests,—or perchance the scream of a jay, or perchance from the solemn depths of these woods I hear tolling far away the knell of one departed. Thought rushes in to fill the vacuum. As you walk, however, the partridge still bursts away. The silent, dry, almost leafless, certainly fruitless woods. You wonder what cheer that bird can find in them. The partridge bursts away from the foot of a shrub oak like its own dry fruit, immortal bird!* This sound still startles us. Dry goldenrods, now turned gray and white, lint our clothes as we walk. And the drooping, downy seed-vessels of the epilobium remind us of the summer. Perchance you will meet with a few solitary asters in the dry fields, with a little color left. The sumach is stripped of everything but its cone of red berries.

. . . A carpet of snow under the pines and shrub oaks will make it look more cheerful. Very few plants have now their spring. But thoughts still spring in man's brain. There are no flowers nor berries to speak of. The grass begins to die at top. In the morning it is stiff with frost. Ice has been discovered in somebody's tub very early this morn, of the thickness of a dollar. The flies are betwixt life and death. The wasps come into the houses and settle on the walls and windows. All insects go into crevices. The fly is entangled in a web and struggles vainly to escape, but there is no spider to secure him; the corner of the pane is a deserted camp. When I lived in the woods the wasps came by thousands to my lodge in November, as to winter quarters, and settled on my windows and on the walls over my head, sometimes deterring visitors from entering. Each morning, when they were numbed with cold, I swept some of them out. But I did not trouble myself to get rid of them. They never molested me, though they bedded with me, and they gradually disappeared into what crevices I do not know, avoiding winter.† I saw a squash-bug go slowly behind a clapboard to avoid winter. As some of these melon seeds come up in the garden again in the spring, so some of these squash-bugs come forth. The flies are for a long time in a somnambulic state. They have too little energy or *vis vitæ* to clean their wings or heads, which

---

* Perhaps Thoreau was remembering Keats's "Ode to a Nightingale" ("Thou wast not born for death, immortal bird!").

† These four sentences on wasps, slightly revised, were incorporated in *Walden* (Ch. 13, "House-Warming").

are covered with dust. They buzz and bump their heads against the windows two or three times a day, or lie on their backs in a trance, and that is all,—two or three short spurts. . . . And so it will go on till the ground freezes. If the race had never lived through a winter, what would they think was coming?

    11, 85-87   8 Nov. 1850

GOING INTO WINTER QUARTERS

A cold and dark afternoon, the sun being behind clouds in the west. The landscape is barren of objects, the trees being leafless, and so little light in the sky for variety. Such a day will almost oblige a man to eat his own heart. A day in which you must hold on to life by your teeth. You can hardly ruck up any skin on Nature's bones. The sap is down; she won't peel. Now is the time to cut timber for yokes and ox-bows, leaving the tough bark on,—yokes for your own neck. Finding yourself yoked to Matter and to Time. Truly a hard day, hard times these! Not a mosquito left. Not an insect to hum. Crickets gone into winter quarters. Friends long since gone there, and you left to walk on frozen ground, with your hands in your pockets. Ah, but is not this a glorious time for your deep inward fires? And will not your green hickory and white oak burn clear in this frosty air? Now is not your manhood taxed by the great Assessor? Taxed for having a soul, a ratable soul. A day when you cannot pluck a flower, cannot dig a parsnip, nor pull a turnip, for the frozen ground! What do the thoughts find to live on? What avails you now the fire you stole from heaven? Does not each thought become a vulture to gnaw your vitals? No Indian summer have we had this November. I see but few traces of the perennial spring. Now is there nothing, not even the cold beauty of ice crystals and snowy architecture, nothing but the echo of your steps over the frozen ground, no voice of birds nor frogs. You are dry as a farrow cow.* The earth will not admit a spade. All fields lie fallow. Shall not your mind? True, the freezing ground is being prepared for immeasurable snows, but there are

*   A cow that is not with calf.

brave thoughts within you that shall remain to rustle the winter through like white oak leaves upon your boughs, or like scrub oaks that remind the traveller of a fire upon the hillsides; or evergreen thoughts, cold even in mid-summer, by their nature shall contrast the more fairly with the snow. Some warm springs shall still tinkle and fume, and send their column of vapor to the skies.

The walker now fares like cows in the pastures, where is no grass but hay; he gets nothing but an appetite. If we must return to hay, pray let us have that which has been stored in barns, which has not lost its sweetness. The poet needs to have more stomachs than the cow, for for him no fodder is stored in barns. He relies upon his instinct, which teaches him to paw away the snow to come at the withered grass.

Methinks man came very near being made a dormant creature, just as some of these animals. The ground squirrel, for instance, which lays up vast stores, is yet found to be half dormant, if you dig him out. Now for the oily nuts of thought which you have stored up.

III, 110-112   13 Nov. 1851

NOVEMBER EAT-HEART

This is November of the hardest kind,—bare frozen ground covered with pale-brown or straw-colored herbage, a strong, cold, cutting northwest wind which makes me seek to cover my ears, a perfectly clear and cloudless sky. The cattle in the fields have a cold, shrunken, shaggy look, their hair standing out every way, as if with electricity, like the cat's. Ditches and pools are fast skimming over, and a few slate-colored snowbirds, with thick, shuffling twitter, and fine-chipping tree sparrows flit from bush to bush in the otherwise deserted pastures. This month taxes a walker's resources more than any. For my part, I should sooner think of going into quarters in November than in the winter. If you do feel any fire at this season out of doors, you may depend upon it, it is your own. It is but a short time, these afternoons, before the night cometh, in which no man can walk.* If you delay to start till three o'clock, there will be hardly time left for a long and rich adventure,—to get fairly out of town. November Eat-heart,—is that the name of it? Not only the fingers cease to do their office, but there is often a benumbing of the faculties generally. You can hardly screw up your courage to take a walk when all is thus tightly locked or frozen up and so little is to be seen in field or wood. I am inclined to take to the swamps or woods as the warmest place, and the former are still the openest. Nature has herself become like the few fruits which she still affords, a very thick-shelled nut with a shrunken meat within. If I find anything to excite or warm my thoughts abroad, it is an agreeable disappointment, for I am obliged to go abroad willfully and against my inclinations at first. The prospect looks so barren, so many springs are frozen up, not a flower perchance and but few birds left, not a companion abroad in all these fields for me, I am slow to go forth. I seem to anticipate a fruitless walk. I think to myself hesitatingly, Shall I go there, or there, or there? and cannot make up my mind to any route, all seem so unpromising, mere surface walking and fronting the cold wind, so that I have to force myself to it often and at random. But then I am often unexpectedly compensated, and the thinnest yellow light of November is more warming and exhilarating than any wine they tell of; and then the mite which November contributes becomes equal in value to the bounty of July. I may meet with something which interests me, and immediately it is as warm as in July, as if it were the south instead of the northwest wind that blowed.

X, 202-204   25 Nov. 1857

WINTERING IN THE PACK

In winter even man is to a slight extent dormant, just as some animals are but partially awake, though not commonly classed with those that hibernate. The summer circulations are to some extent stopped; the range of his afternoon walk is somewhat narrower; he

* A parody of John 9.4: "The night cometh when no man can work."

is more or less confined to the highway and wood-path; the weather oftener shuts him up in his burrow; he begins to feel the access of dormancy and to assume the spherical form of the marmot; the nights are longest; he is often satisfied if he only gets out to the post-office in the course of the day. The arctic voyagers are obliged to invent and willfully engage in active amusements to keep themselves awake and alive. Most men do not now extend their walks beyond the village street. Even our experience is something like wintering in the pack.

VI, 38   30 Dec. 1853

"LET US SING WINTER"

The winter, cold and bound out as it is, is thrown to us like a bone to a famishing dog, and we are expected to get the marrow out of it. While the milkmen in the outskirts are milking so many scores of cows before sunrise these winter mornings, it is our task to milk the winter itself. It is true it is like a cow that is dry, and our fingers are numb, and there is none to wake us up. Some desert the field and go into winter quarters in the city. They attend the oratorios, while the only music that we countrymen hear is the squeaking of the snow under our boots. But the winter was not given to us for no purpose. We must thaw its cold with our genialness. We are tasked to find out and appropriate all the nutriment it yields. If it is a cold and hard season, its fruit, no doubt, is the more concentrated and nutty. It took the cold and bleakness of November to ripen the walnut, but the human brain is the kernel which the winter itself matures. Not till then does its shell come off. The seasons were not made in vain. Because the fruits of the earth are already ripe, we are not to suppose that there is no fruit left for winter to ripen. It is for man the seasons and all their fruits exist. The winter was made to concentrate and harden and mature the kernel of his brain, to give tone and firmness and consistency to his thought. Then is the great harvest of the year, the harvest of thought. All previous harvests are stubble to this, mere fodder and green crop. Now we burn with a purer flame like the stars; our oil is winter-strained. We are islanded in Atlantic and Pacific and Indian Oceans of thought, Bermudas, or Friendly or Spice Islands.

Shall we take refuge in cities in November? Shall the nut fall green from the tree? Let not the year be disappointed of its crop. I knew a crazy man who walked into an empty pulpit one Sunday and, taking up a hymn-book, remarked: "We have had a good fall for getting in corn and potatoes. Let us sing Winter." So I say, "Let us sing winter." What else can we sing, and our voices be in harmony with the season?

VI, 84-86   30 Jan. 1854

THE FROZEN EARTH

Everywhere snow, gathered into sloping drifts about the walls and fences, and, beneath the snow, the frozen ground, and men are compelled to deposit the summer's provision in burrows in the earth like the ground squirrel. Many creatures, daunted by the prospect, migrated in the fall, but man remains and walks over the frozen snow-crust and over the stiffened rivers and ponds, and draws now upon his summer stores. Life is reduced to its lowest terms. There is no home for you now, in this freezing wind, but in that shelter which you prepared in the summer. You steer straight across the fields to that in season. I can with difficulty tell when I am over the river. There is a similar crust over my heart. Where I rambled in the summer and gathered flowers and rested on the grass by the brook-side in the shade, now no grass nor flowers, no brook nor shade, but cold, unvaried snow, stretching mile after mile, and no place to sit.

III, 312-313   18 Feb. 1852

PUTTING AWAY THE SLED

To speak of the general phenomena of March: When March arrives, a tolerably calm, clear, sunny, spring-like day, the snow is so far gone that sleighing ends and our compassion is excited by the sight of horses laboriously dragging wheeled vehicles through mud and water and slosh. We shall no longer hear the jingling of sleigh-bells. The sleigh is housed, or, perchance, converted into a wheeled vehicle by the travelling peddler caught far from home. The wood-sled is perhaps abandoned by the roadside, where the snow ended, with two sticks put under its runners,—there to rest, it may be, while the grass springs up green around it, till another winter comes round. It may be near where the wagon of the careless farmer was left last December on account of the drifted snow. As March approaches, at least, peddlers will do well to travel with wheels slung under their sleighs, ready to convert their sleighs into wheeled vehicles at an hour's warning. Even the boy's sled gets put away by degrees, or when it is found to be in the way, and his thoughts are directed gradually to more earthy games. There are now water privileges for him by every roadside.

The prudent farmer has teamed home, or to market, his last load of wood from the lot, nor left that which was corded a year ago to be consumed by the worms and the weather. He will not have to sell next winter oak wood rotted an inch deep all round, at a reduction in the price if he deals with knowing customers. He has hauled his last logs to mill. No more shall we see the sled-track shine or hear the sled squeak along it.

The boy's sled gets put away in the barn or shed or garret, and there lies dormant all summer, like a woodchuck in the winter. It goes into its burrow just before woodchucks come out, so that you may say a woodchuck never sees a sled, nor a sled a woodchuck,—unless it were a prematurely risen woodchuck or a belated and un-seasonable sled. Before the woodchuck comes out the sled goes in. They dwell at the antipodes of each other. Before sleds rise wood-chucks have set. The ground squirrel too shares the privileges and misfortunes of the woodchuck. The sun now passes from the constellation of the sled into that of the woodchuck.

XIII, 218-219   25 Mar. 1860

THAWING: MAN AND NATURE

It is a genial and reassuring day; the mere warmth of the west wind amounts almost to balminess. The softness of the air mollifies our own dry and congealed substance. I sit down by a wall to see if I can muse again. We become, as it were, pliant and ductile again to strange but memorable influences; we are led a little way by our genius. We are affected like the earth, and yield to the elemental tenderness; winter breaks up within us; the frost is coming out of me, and I am heaved like the road; accumulated masses of ice and snow dissolve, and thoughts like a freshet pour down unwonted channels. A strain of music comes to solace the traveller over earth's downs and dignify his chagrins, the petty men whom he meets are the shadows of grander to come. Roads lead elsewhither than to Carlisle and Sudbury. The earth is uninhabited but fair to inhabit, like the old Carlisle road. Is then the road so rough that it should be neglected? Not only narrow but rough is the way that leadeth to life everlasting.* Our experience does not wear upon us. It is seen to be fabulous or symbolical, and the future is worth expecting. Encouraged, I set out once more to climb the mountain of the earth, for my steps are symbolical steps, and in all my walking I have not reached the top of the earth yet.

v, 34-35   21 Mar. 1853

REBIRTH IN SPRING

This afternoon I throw off my outside coat. A mild spring day. I must hie to the Great Meadows. The air is full of bluebirds. The

---

* Matthew 7.14: "Narrow is the way which leadeth unto life."

ground almost entirely bare. The villagers are out in the sun, and every man is happy whose work takes him outdoors. I go by Sleepy Hollow toward the Great Fields. I lean over a rail to hear what is in the air, liquid with the bluebirds' warble. My life partakes of infinity. The air is as deep as our natures. Is the drawing in of this vital air attended with no more glorious results than I witness? The air is a velvet cushion against which I press my ear. I go forth to make new demands on life. I wish to begin this summer well; to do something in it worthy of it and of me; to transcend my daily routine and that of my townsmen; to have my immortality now, that it be in the *quality* of my daily life; to pay the greatest price, the greatest tax, of any man in Concord, and enjoy the most!! I will give all I am for *my* nobility. I will pay all my days for *my* success. I pray that the life of this spring and summer may ever lie fair in my memory. May I dare as I have never done! May I persevere as I have never done! May I purify myself anew as with fire and water, soul and body! May my melody not be wanting to the season! May I gird myself to be a hunter of the beautiful, that naught escape me! May I attain to a youth never attained! I am eager to report the glory of the universe; may I be worthy to do it; to have got through with regarding human values, so as not to be distracted from regarding divine values. It is reasonable that a man should be something worthier at the end of the year than he was at the beginning.

III, 350-351   15 Mar. 1852

THE MOTIONS OF TIME

How earnestly and rapidly each creature, each flower, is fulfilling its part while its day lasts! Nature never lost a day, nor a moment. As the planet in its orbit and around its axis, so do the seasons, so does time, revolve, with a rapidity inconceivable. In the moment, in the æon, well employed, time ever advances with this rapidity. To an idler the man employed is terribly rapid. He that is not behind his time is swift. The immortals are swift. Clear the track!

The plant that waited a whole year, and then blossomed the instant it was ready and the earth was ready for it, without the conception of delay, was rapid. To the conscience of the idle man, the stillness of a placid September day sounds like the din and whirl of a factory. Only employment can still this din in the air.

IV, 250   13 Sept. 1852

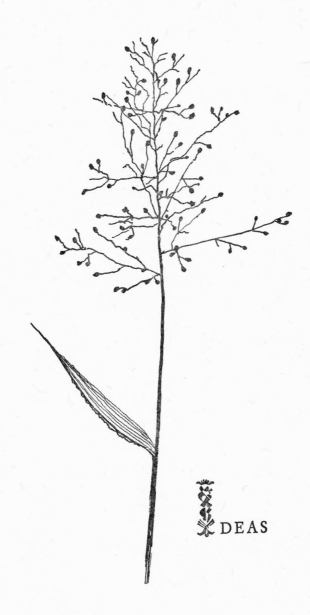

DEAS

ROTATIONS

Nature is constantly original and inventing new patterns, like a mechanic in his shop. When the overhanging pine drops into the water, by the action of the sun, and the wind rubbing it on the shore, its boughs are worn white and smooth and assume fantastic forms, as if turned by a lathe. All things, indeed, are subjected to a rotary motion, either gradual and partial or rapid and complete, from the planet and system to the simplest shellfish and pebbles on the beach; as if all beauty resulted from an object turning on its own axis, or others turning about it. It establishes a new centre in the universe. As all curves have reference to their centres or foci, so all beauty of character has reference to the soul, and is a graceful gesture of recognition or waving of the body toward it.

I, 332   15 Mar. 1842

THE YEAR IS A CIRCLE

For the first time I perceive this spring that the year is a circle. I see distinctly the spring arc thus far. It is drawn with a firm line. Every incident is a parable of the Great Teacher. The cranberries washed up in the meadows and into the road on the causeways now yield a pleasant acid.

Why should just these sights and sounds accompany our life? Why should I hear the chattering of blackbirds, why smell the skunk each year? I would fain explore the mysterious relation between myself and these things. I would at least know what these things unavoidably are, make a chart of our life, know how its shores trend, that butterflies reappear and when, know why just this circle of creatures completes the world. Can I not by expectation affect the revolutions of nature, make a day to bring forth something new?

III, 428   18 Apr. 1852

THE ILLUSION OF TIME

I thank God that the cheapness which appears in time and the world, the trivialness of the whole scheme of things, is in my own cheap and trivial moment. I am time and the world. I assert no independence. In me are summer and winter, village life and commercial routine, pestilence and famine and refreshing breezes, joy and sadness, life and death. How near is yesterday! How far to-morrow! I have seen nails which were driven before I was born. Why do they look old and rusty? Why does not God make some mistake to show to us that time is a delusion? Why did I invent time but to destroy it?

I, 349   25 Mar. 1842

BONE TO DUST

I saw an old bone in the woods covered with lichens, which looked like the bone of an old settler, which yet some little animal had recently gnawed, and I plainly saw the marks of its teeth, so indefatigable is Nature to strip the flesh from bones and return it to dust again. No little rambling beast can go by some dry and ancient bone but he must turn aside and try his teeth upon it. An old bone is knocked about till it becomes dust; Nature has no mercy on it. It was quite too ancient to suggest disagreeable associations. It was like a piece of dry pine root. It survives like the memory of a man. With time all that was personal and offensive wears off. The tooth of envy may sometimes gnaw it and reduce it more rapidly, but it is much more a prey to forgetfulness. Lichens grow upon it, and at last, in what moment no man knows, it has completely wasted away and ceases to be a bone any longer.

II, 93-94   11 Nov. 1850

RENEWAL THROUGH THE SENSES

What is called genius is the abundance of life or health, so that whatever addresses the senses, as the flavor of these berries, or the lowing of that cow, which sounds as if it echoed along a cool mountain-side just before night, where odoriferous dews perfume the air and there is everlasting vigor, serenity, and expectation of perpetual untarnished morning,—each sight and sound and scent and flavor,—intoxicates with a healthy intoxication. The shrunken stream of life overflows its banks, makes and fertilizes broad intervals, from which generations derive their sustenances. This is the true overflowing of the Nile. So exquisitely sensitive are we, it makes us embrace our fates, and, instead of suffering or indifference, we enjoy and bless. If we have not dissipated the vital, the divine, fluids, there is, then, a circulation of vitality beyond our bodies. The cow is nothing. Heaven is not there, but in the condition of the hearer. I am thrilled to think that I owe a perception to the commonly gross sense of taste, that I have been inspired through the palate, that these berries have fed my brain. After I had been eating these simple, wholesome, ambrosial fruits on this high hillside, I found my senses whetted, I was young again, and whether I stood or sat I was not the same creature.

IV, 218-219   11 July 1852

THE FREEDOM OF THE WOODS

How different the ramrod jingle of the chewink or any bird's note sounds now at 5 P.M. in the cooler, stiller air, when also the humming of insects is more distinctly heard, and perchance some impurity has begun to sink to earth strained by the air! Or is it, perchance, to be referred to the cooler, more clarified and pensive state of the mind, when dews have begun to descend in it and clarify it? Chaste eve! A certain lateness in the sound, pleasing to hear, which releases me from the obligation to return in any particular season. I have passed the Rubicon of staying out. I have said to myself, that way is not homeward; I will wander further from what I have called my home—to the home which is forever inviting me. In such an hour the freedom of the woods is offered me, and the birds sing my dispensation. In dreams the links of life are united: we forget that our friends are dead; we know them as of old.

v, 186-187   23 May 1853

ORSHIPING WILDNESS

I see that all is not garden and cultivated field and crops, that there are square rods in Middlesex County as purely primitive and wild as they were a thousand years ago, which have escaped the plow and the axe and the scythe and the cranberry-rake, little oases of wildness in the desert of our civilization, wild as a square rod on the moon, supposing it to be uninhabited. I believe almost in the personality of such planetary matter, feel something akin to reverence for it, can even worship it as terrene, titanic matter extant in my day. We are so different we admire each other, we healthily attract one another. I love it as a maiden. These spots are meteoric, aerolitic, and such matter has in all ages been worshipped. Aye, when we are lifted out of the slime and film of our habitual life, we see the whole globe to be an aerolite, and reverence it as such, and make pilgrimages to it, far off as it is. How happens it that we reverence the stones which fall from another planet, and not the stones which belong to this,—another globe, not this,—heaven, and not earth? Are not the stones in Hodge's wall as good as the aerolite at Mecca? Is not our broad back-door-stone as good as any corner-stone in heaven?

It would imply the regeneration of mankind, if they were to become elevated enough to truly worship stocks and stones. It is the sentiment of fear and slavery and habit which makes a heathenish idolatry. Such idolators abound in all countries, and heathen cross the seas to reform heathen, dead to bury the dead, and all go down to the pit together. If I could, I would worship the parings of my nails. If he who makes two blades of grass grow where one grew be-

fore is a benefactor, he who discovers two gods where there was only
known the one (and such a one!) before is a still greater benefactor.
I would fain improve every opportunity to wonder and worship, as a
sunflower welcomes the light. The more thrilling, wonderful, divine
objects I behold in a day, the more expanded and immortal I become. If a stone appeals to me and elevates me, tells me how many
miles I have come, how many remain to travel,—and the more, the
better,—reveals the future to me in some measure, it is a matter of
private rejoicing. If it did the same service to all, it might well be a
matter of public rejoicing.

    IX, 43-46   30 Aug. 1856

A BROAD MARGIN OF LEISURE

    It is worth the while to apply what wisdom one has to the con-
duct of his life, surely. I find myself oftenest wise in little things and
foolish in great ones. That I may accomplish some particular petty
affair well, I live my whole life coarsely. A broad margin of leisure
is as beautiful in a man's life as in a book. Haste makes waste, no less
in life than in housekeeping. Keep the time, observe the hours of the
universe, not of the cars.* What are threescore years and ten hur-
riedly and coarsely lived to moments of divine leisure in which your
life is coincident with the life of the universe? We live too fast and
coarsely, just as we eat too fast, and do not know the true savor of our
food. We consult our will and understanding and the expectation of
men, not our genius. I can impose upon myself tasks which will crush
me for life and prevent all expansion, and this I am but too inclined
to do.

    One moment of life costs many hours, hours not of business but
of preparation and invitation. Yet the man who does not betake himself at once and desperately to sawing is called a loafer, though he
may be knocking at the doors of heaven all the while, which shall
surely be opened to him. That aim in life is highest which requires
the highest and finest discipline. How much, what infinite, leisure it

    *   Colloquial for railway trains.

requires, as of a lifetime, to appreciate a single phenomenon! You must camp down beside it as for life, having reached your land of promise, and give yourself wholly to it. It must stand for the whole world to you, symbolical of all things. The least partialness is your own defect of sight and cheapens the experience fatally. Unless the humming of a gnat is as the music of the spheres, and the music of the spheres is as the humming of a gnat, they are naught to me. It is not communications to serve for a history,—which are science,—but the great story itself, that cheers and satisfies us.

IV, 433-434   28 Dec. 1852

LIVE IN THE MOMENT

There is a season for everything, and we do not notice a given phenomenon except at that season, if, indeed, it can be called the same phenomenon at any other season. There is a time to watch the ripples on Ripple Lake, to look for arrowheads, to study the rocks and lichens, a time to walk on sandy deserts; and the observer of nature must improve these seasons as much as the farmer his. So boys fly kites and play ball or hawkie * at particular times all over the State. A wise man will know what game to play to-day, and play it. We must not be governed by rigid rules, as by the almanac, but let the season rule us. The moods and thoughts of man are revolving just as steadily and incessantly as nature's. Nothing must be postponed. Take time by the forelock. Now or never! You must live in the present, launch your-self on every wave, find your eternity in each moment. Fools stand on their island opportunities and look toward another land. There is no other land; there is no other life but this, or the like of this. Where the good husbandman is, there is the good soil. Take any other course, and life will be a succession of regrets. Let us see vessels sailing pros-perously before the wind, and not simply stranded barks. There is no world for the penitent and regretful.

XII, 159-160   24 Apr. 1859

* Hockey.

FRESH THOUGHTS, STRANGE SIGHTS

Why can we not oftener refresh one another with original thoughts? If the fragrance of the dicksonia fern is so grateful and suggestive to us, how much more refreshing and encouraging—re-creating—would be fresh and fragrant thoughts communicated to us fresh from a man's experience and life! I want none of his pity, nor sympathy, in the common sense, but that he should emit and communicate to me his essential fragrance, that he should not be forever repenting and going to church (when not otherwise sinning), but, as it were, going a-huckleberrying in the fields of thought, and enrich all the world with his visions and his joys.

Why do you flee so soon, sir, to the theatres, lecture-rooms, and museums of the city? If you will stay here awhile I will promise you strange sights. You shall walk on water; all these brooks and rivers and ponds shall be your highway. You shall see the whole earth covered a foot or more deep with purest white crystals, in which you slump or over which you glide, and all the trees and stubble glittering in icy armor.

XII, 399-400   18 Oct. 1859

SEEING REFLECTIONS

Returning, I see the red oak on R. W. E.'s [Emerson's] shore reflected in the bright sky water. In the reflection the tree is black against the clear whitish sky, though as I see it against the opposite woods it is a warm greenish yellow. But the river sees it against the bright sky, and hence the reflection is like ink. The water tells me how it looks to it seen from below. I think that most men, as farmers, hunters, fishers, etc., walk along a river's bank, or paddle along its stream, without seeing the reflections. Their minds are not abstracted from the surface, from surfaces generally. It is only a reflecting

mind that sees reflections. I am aware often that I have been occupied with shallow and commonplace thoughts, looking for something
superficial, when I did not see the most glorious reflections, though
exactly in the line of my vision. If the fisherman was looking at the
reflection, he would not know when he had a nibble! I know from
my own experience that he may cast his line right over the most elysian
landscape and sky, and not *catch* the slightest notion of them. You
must be in an abstract mood to see reflections however distinct. I was
even startled by the sight of that reflected red oak as if it were a black
water-spirit. When we are enough abstracted, the opaque earth itself
reflects images to us; *i. e.*, we are imaginative, see visions, etc. Such a
reflection, this inky, leafy tree, against the white sky, can only be
seen at this season.

    x, 156-157   2 Nov. 1857

INCIDENTS TRANSCENDING REALITY

Some incidents in my life have seemed far more allegorical than
actual; they were so significant that they plainly served no other use.
That is, I have been more impressed by their allegorical significance
and fitness; they have been like myths or passages in a myth, rather
than mere incidents or history which have to wait to become significant. Quite in harmony with my subjective philosophy. This, for instance: that, when I thought I knew the flowers so well, the beautiful purple azalea or pinxter-flower should be shown me by the hunter
who found it. Such facts are lifted quite above the level of the actual. They are all just such events as my imagination prepares me for,
no matter how incredible. Perfectly in keeping with my life and char-
acteristic. Ever and anon something will occur which my philosophy
has not dreamed of. The limits of the actual are set some thoughts
further off. That which had seemed a rigid wall of vast thickness unexpectedly proves a thin and undulating drapery. The boundaries of
the actual are no more fixed and rigid than the elasticity of our imaginations. The fact that a rare and beautiful flower which we never
saw, perhaps never heard [of], for which therefore there was no place

in our thoughts, may at length be found in our immediate neighbor-hood, is very suggestive.

v, 203-204   31 May 1853

UR LIFE SHOULD BE A JOURNEY

Our life should be so active and progressive as to be a journey. Our meals should all be of journey-cake * and hasty pudding. We should be more alert, see the sun rise, not keep fashionable hours, enter a house, our own house, as a khan, a caravansary. At noon I did not dine; I ate my journey-cake. I quenched my thirst at a spring or a brook. As I sat at the table, the hospitality was so perfect and the repast so sumptuous that I seemed to be breaking my fast upon a bank in the midst of an arduous journey, that the water seemed to be a living spring, the napkins grass, the conversation free as the winds; and the servants that waited on us were our simple desires.

III, 240   28 Jan. 1852

TAYING AT HOME

How many things concur to keep a man at home, to prevent his yielding to his inclination to wander! If I would extend my walk a hundred miles, I must carry a tent on my back for shelter at night or in the rain, or at least I must carry a thick coat to be prepared for a change in the weather. So that it requires some resolution, as well as energy and foresight, to undertake the simplest journey. Man does not travel as easily as the birds migrate. He is not everywhere at home, like flies. When I think how many things I can conveniently carry, I am wont to think it most convenient to stay at home. My home, then, to a certain extent is the place where I keep my thick coat and my tent and some books which I cannot carry; where, next, I can

* A variant of johnny-cake (M. M. Mathews, *Dictionary of Americanisms*).

depend upon meeting some friends; and where, finally, I, even I, have established myself in business. But this last in my case is the least important qualification of a home.

II, 402-403   19 Aug. 1851

AILED DOWN
TO MY NATIVE REGION

I cannot but regard it as a kindness in those who have the steer-ing of me that, by the want of pecuniary wealth, I have been nailed down to this my native region so long and steadily, and made to study and love this spot of earth more and more. What would signify in comparison a thin and diffused love and knowledge of the whole earth instead, got by wandering? The traveller's is but a barren and comfortless condition. Wealth will not buy a man a home in nature,— house nor farm there. The man of business does not by his business earn a residence in nature, but is denaturalized rather. What is a farm, house and land, office or shop, but a settlement in nature under the most favorable conditions? It is insignificant, and a merely negative good fortune, to be provided with thick garments against cold and wet, an unprofitable, weak, and defensive condition, compared with being able to extract some exhilaration, some warmth even, out of cold and wet themselves, and to clothe them with our sympathy. The rich man buys woollens and furs, and sits naked and shivering still in spirit, besieged by cold and wet. But the poor Lord of Creation, cold and wet he makes to warm him, and be his garments.

v, 496-497   12 Nov. 1853

UT OF DOORS"

A great part of our troubles are literally domestic or originate in the house and from living indoors. I could write an essay to be en-titled "Out of Doors,"—undertake a crusade against houses. What a different thing Christianity preached to the house-bred and to a party who lived out of doors! Also a sermon is needed on economy of fuel. What right has my neighbor to burn ten cords of wood, when I burn only one? Thus robbing our half-naked town of this precious covering. Is he so much colder than I? It is expensive to maintain him in our midst. If some earn the salt of their porridge, are we certain that they earn the fuel of their kitchen and parlor? One man makes a little of the driftwood of the river or of the dead and refuse (unmarketable!) [wood] of the forest suffice, and Nature rejoices in him. Another, Herod-like, requires ten cords of the best of young white oak or hickory, and he is commonly esteemed a virtuous man. He who burns the most wood on his hearth is the least warmed by the sight of it growing. Leave the trim wood-lots to widows and orphan girls. Let men tread gently through nature. Let us religiously burn stumps and worship in groves, while Christian vandals lay waste the forest temples to build miles of meeting-houses and horse-sheds and feed their box stoves.

IX, 344 26 Apr. 1857

A NEW WORLD

How novel and original must be each new man's view of the universe! for though the world is so old, and so many books have been written, each object appears wholly undescribed to our experience, each field of thought wholly unexplored. The whole world is an America, a *New World*. The fathers lived in a dark age and throw no light on any of our subjects. The sun climbs to the zenith daily, high over all literature and science. Astronomy, even, concerns us worldlings only, but the sun of poetry and of each new child born into the planet has never been astronomized, nor brought nearer by a telescope. So it will be to the end of time. The end of the world is not yet. Science is young by the ruins of Luxor, unearthing the Sphinx, or Nineveh, or between the Pyramids.

III, 384 2 Apr. 1852

ALONE IN NATURE

With what sober joy I stand to let the water drip from me and feel my fresh vigor, who have been bathing in the same tub which the muskrat uses! Such a medicated bath as only nature furnishes. A fish leaps, and the dimple he makes is observed now. How ample and generous was nature! My inheritance is not narrow. Here is no other this evening. Those resorts which I most love and frequent, numerous and vast as they are, are as it were given up to me, as much as if I were an autocrat or owner of the world, and by my edicts excluded men from my territories. Perchance there is some advantage here not enjoyed in older countries. There are said to be two thousand inhabitants in Concord, and yet I find such ample space and verge, even miles of walking every day in which I do not meet nor see a human being, and often not very recent traces of them. So much of man as there is in your mind, there will be in your eye. Methinks that for a great part of the time, as much as it is possible, I walk as one possessing the advantages of human culture, fresh from society of men, but turned loose into the woods, the only man in nature, walking and meditating to a great extent as if man and his customs and institutions were not. The catbird, or the jay, is sure of the whole of your ear now. Each noise is like a stain on pure glass. The rivers now, those great blue subterranean heavens, reflecting the supernal skies and red-tinted clouds.

II, 437   31 Aug. 1851

RAPPORT WITH NATURE

There are many ways of feeling one's pulse. In a healthy state the constant experience is a pleasurable sensation or sentiment. For instance, in such a state I find myself in perfect connection with nature, and the perception, or remembrance even, of any natural phenomena is attended with a gentle pleasurable excitement. Prevailing sights and sounds make the impression of beauty and music on me.

But in sickness all is deranged. I had yesterday a kink in my back and a general cold, and as usual it amounted to a cessation of life. I lost for the time my *rapport* or relation to nature. Sympathy with nature is an evidence of perfect health. You cannot perceive beauty but with a serene mind. The cheaper your amusements, the safer and saner. They who think much of theatres, operas, and the like, are beside themselves. Each man's necessary path, though as obscure and apparently uneventful as that of a beetle in the grass, is the way to the deepest joys he is susceptible of; though he converses only with moles and fungi and disgraces his relatives, it is no matter if he knows what is steel to his flint.

x, 188   18 Nov. 1857

NDIAN VS. WHITE MAN

The charm of the Indian to me is that he stands free and un-constrained in Nature, is her inhabitant and not her guest, and wears her easily and gracefully. But the civilized man has the habits of the house. His house is a prison, in which he finds himself oppressed and confined, not sheltered and protected. He walks as if he sustained the roof; he carries his arms as if the walls would fall in and crush him, and his feet remember the cellar beneath. His muscles are never re-laxed. It is rare that he overcomes the house, and learns to sit at home in it, and roof and floor and walls support themselves, as the sky and trees and earth.

It is a great art to saunter.

1, 253   26 Apr. 1841

HE TOWN INVADES THE COUNTRY

I hear of pickers ordered out of the huckleberry-fields, and I see stakes set up with written notices forbidding any to pick there. Some let their fields, or allow so much for the picking. *Sic transit gloria ruris.* We are not grateful enough that we have lived part of our lives before these evil days came. What becomes of the true value of country life? What if you must go to market for it? Shall things come to such a pass that the butcher commonly brings round huckleberries in his cart? It is as if the hangman were to perform the marriage ceremony, or were to preside at the communion table. Such is the inevitable tendency of *our* civilization,—to reduce huckleberries to a level with beef-steak. The butcher's item on the door is now "calf's head and huckleberries." I suspect that the inhabitants of England and of the Continent of Europe have thus lost their natural rights with the increase of population and of monopolies. The wild fruits of the earth disappear before civilization, or are only to be found in large markets. The whole country becomes, as it were, a town or beaten common, and the fruits left are a few hips and haws.

XI, 78-79   6 Aug. 1858

MAN ENSLAVES THE HORSE

When I sat on Lee's Cliff the other day (August 29th), I saw a man working with a horse in a field by the river, carting dirt; and the horse and his relation to him struck me as very remarkable. There was the horse, a mere animated machine,—though his tail was brushing off the flies,—his whole existence subordinated to the man's, with no tradition, perhaps no instinct, in him of independence and freedom, of a time when he was wild and free,— completely humanized. No compact made with him that he should have the Saturday afternoons, or the Sundays, or any holidays. His independence never recognized, it being now quite forgotten both by men and by horses that the horse was ever free. For I am not aware that there are any wild horses known surely not to be descended from tame ones. Assisting that man to pull down that bank and spread it over the meadow; only keeping off the flies with his tail, and stamping, and catching a mouthful of grass or leaves from time to time, on his own account,— all the rest for man. It seemed hardly worth while that he should be *animated* for this. It was plain that the man was not educating the horse; not trying to develop his nature, but merely getting work out of him. That mass of animated matter seemed more completely the servant of man than any inanimate. For slaves have their holidays; a heaven is conceded to them, but to the horse none. Now and forever he is man's slave. The more I considered, the more the man seemed akin to the horse; only his was the stronger will of the two. For a little further on I saw an Irishman shovelling, who evidently was as much tamed as the horse. He had stipulated that to a certain extent his independence be recognized, and yet really he was but little more independent. I had always instinctively regarded the horse as a free people somewhere, living wild. Whatever has not come under the sway of man is wild. In this sense original and independent men are wild,—not tamed and broken by society. Now for my part I have such a respect for the horse's nature as would tempt me to let him alone; not to interfere with him,—his walks, his diet, his loves. But by mankind he is treated simply as if he were an engine which must have rest and is sensible of pain. Suppose that every squirrel were made to turn a coffee-mill! Suppose that the gazelles were made to draw milk-carts!

There he was with his tail cut off, because it was in the way, or to suit the taste of his owner; his mane trimmed, and his feet shod with iron that he might wear longer. What is a horse but an animal that has lost its liberty? What is it but a system of slavery? and do you not thus by *insensible* and unimportant degrees come to human slavery? Has lost its liberty!—and has man got any more liberty himself for having robbed the horse, or has he lost just as much of his own, and become more like the horse he has robbed? Is not the other end of the bridle in this case, too, coiled round his own neck? Hence stable-boys, jockeys, all that class that is daily transported by fast horses. There he stood with his oblong square figure (his tail being cut off) seen against the water, brushing off the flies with his tail and stamping, braced back while the man was filling the cart.

II, 447·449   3 Sept. 1851

MAN FOULS HIS NEST

As I went past the Hunt cellar, where Hosmer pulled down the old house in the spring, I thought I would see if any new or rare plants had sprung up in that place which had so long been covered from the light. . . .

It is remarkable what a curse seems to attach to any place which has long been inhabited by man. Vermin of various kinds abide with him. It is said that the site of Babylon is a desert where the lion and the jackal prowl. If, as here, an ancient cellar is uncovered, there springs up at once a crop of rank and noxious weeds, evidence of a certain unwholesome fertility,— by which perchance the earth relieves herself of the poisonous qualities which have been imparted to her. As if what was foul, baleful, grovelling, or obscene in the inhabitants had sunk into the earth and infected it. Certain qualities are there in excess in the soil, and the proper equilibrium will not be attained until after the sun and air have purified the spot. The very shade breeds saltpetre. Yet men value this kind of earth highly and will pay a price for it, as if it were as good a soil for virtue as for vice.

In other places you find henbane and the Jamestown-weed and the like, in cellars,—such herbs as the witches are said to put into their caldron.

It would be fit that the tobacco plant should spring up on the house-site, aye on the grave, of almost every householder of Concord. These vile weeds are sown by vile men. When the house is gone they spring up in the corners of cellars where the cider-casks stood always on tap, for murder and all kindred vices will out. And that rank crowd which lines the gutter, where the wash of the dinner dishes flows, are but more distant parasites of the host. What obscene and poisonous weeds, think you, will mark the site of a Slave State?— what kind of Jamestown-weed?

There are mallows for food,—for cheeses, at least; rich-weed for high living; the nettle for domestic felicity,—a happy disposition; black nightshade, tobacco, henbane, and Jamestown-weed as symbols of the moral atmosphere and influences of that house, the idiocy and insanity of it; dill and Jerusalem-oak and catnep for senility grasping at a straw; and beggar-ticks for poverty. . . .

Not only foul and poisonous weeds grow in our tracks, but our vileness and luxuriance make simple and wholesome plants rank and weed-like. All that I ever got a premium for was a monstrous squash, so coarse that nobody could eat it. Some of these bad qualities will be found to lurk in the pears that are invented in and about the purlieus of great towns. "The evil that men do lives after them." * The corn and potatoes produced by excessive manuring may be said to have, not only a coarse, but a poisonous, quality. They are made food [for] hogs and oxen too. What creatures is the grain raised on the corn-fields of Waterloo food for, unless it be for such as prey upon men? Who cuts the grass in the graveyard? I can detect the site of the shanties that have stood all along the railroads by the ranker vegetation. I do not go there for delicate wild-flowers.

It is important, then, that we should air our lives from time to time by removals, and excursions into the fields and woods,—starve our vices. Do not sit so long over any cellar-hole as to tempt your neighbor to bid for the privilege of digging saltpetre there.

So live that only the most beautiful wild-flowers will spring up where you have dwelt,—harebells, violets, and blue-eyed grass.

XII, 340-343   22 Sept. 1859

NATURE VS. MAN

I love Nature partly *because* she is not man, but a retreat from him. None of his institutions control or pervade her. There a different kind of right prevails. In her midst I can be glad with an entire gladness. If this world were all man, I could not stretch myself, I should lose all hope. He is constraint, she is freedom to me. He makes me wish for another world. She makes me content with this. None of the joys she supplies is subject to his rules and definitions. What he touches he taints. In thought he moralizes. One would think that no free, joyful labor was possible to him. How infinite and pure the least

* Shakespeare, *Julius Caesar*, III.2.80.

pleasure of which Nature is basis, compared with the congratulation
of mankind! The joy which Nature yields is like [that] afforded by
the frank words of one we love.

<blockquote>
Man, man is the devil,
The source of all evil.*
</blockquote>

Methinks that these prosers, with their saws and their laws, do not
know how glad a man can be. What wisdom, what warning, can
prevail against gladness? There is no law so strong which a little
gladness may not transgress. I have a room all to myself; it is nature.
It is a place beyond the jurisdiction of human governments. Pile up
your books, the records of sadness, your saws and your laws. Nature
is glad outside, and her merry worms within will ere long topple
them down. There is a prairie beyond your laws. Nature is a prairie
for outlaws. There are two worlds, the post-office and nature. I know
them both. I continually forget mankind and their institutions, as I
do a bank.

IV, 445-446   3 Jan. 1853

BEAUTY, WITHOUT AND WITHIN

We soon get through with Nature. She excites an expectation
which she cannot satisfy. The merest child which has rambled into a
copsewood dreams of a wilderness so wild and strange and inex-
haustible as Nature can never show him. The red-bird which I saw
on my companion's string on election days I thought but the out-
most sentinel of the wild, immortal camp,—of the wild and dazzling
infantry of the wilderness,—that the deeper woods abounded with
redder birds still; but, now that I have threaded all our woods and
waded the swamps, I have never yet met with his compeer, still less
his wilder kindred. The red-bird which is the last of Nature is but the
first of God. The White Mountains, likewise, were smooth mole-
hills to my expectation. We *condescend* to climb the crags of earth.
It is our weary legs alone that praise them. That forest on whose
skirts the red-bird flits is not of earth. I expected a fauna more infinite

* Probably a bit of early New England doggerel.

and various, birds of more dazzling colors and more celestial song. How many springs shall I continue to see the common sucker (*Catostomus Bostoniensis*) floating dead on our river! Will not Nature select her types from a new fount? The vignette of the year. This earth which is spread out like a map around me is but the lining of my inmost soul exposed. In me is the sucker that I see. No wholly extraneous object can compel me to recognize it. I am guilty of suckers. I go about to look at flowers and listen to the birds. There was a time when the beauty and the music were all within, and I sat and listened to my thoughts, and there was a song in them. I sat for hours on rocks and wrestled with the melody which possessed me. I sat and listened by the hour to a positive though faint and distant music, not sung by any bird, nor vibrating any earthly harp. When you walked with a joy which knew not its own origin. When you were an organ of which the world was but one poor broken pipe. I lay long on the rocks, foundered like a harp on the seashore, that knows not how it is dealt with. You sat on the earth as on a raft, listening to music that was not of the earth, but which ruled and arranged it. Man *should be* the harp articulate. When your cords were tense.

IV, 293-294   23 May 1854

HE BODY IS A VIOLIN

It occurred to me when I awoke this morning, feeling regret for intemperance of the day before in eating fruit, which had dulled my sensibilities, that man was to be treated as a musical instrument, and if any viol was to be made of sound timber and kept well tuned always, it was he, so that when the bow of events is drawn across him he may vibrate and resound in perfect harmony. A sensitive soul will be continually trying its strings to see if they are in tune. A man's body must be rasped down exactly to a shaving. It is of far more importance than the wood of a Cremona violin.

V, 424   12 Sept. 1853

OST YOUTH

Methinks my present experience is nothing; my past experience is all in all. I think that no experience which I have to-day comes up to, or is comparable with, the experiences of my boyhood. And not only this is true, but as far back as I can remember I have unconsciously referred to the experiences of a previous state of existence. "For life is a forgetting," * etc. Formerly, methought, nature developed as I developed, and grew up with me. My life was ecstasy. In youth, before I lost any of my senses, I can remember that I was all alive, and inhabited my body with inexpressible satisfaction; both its weariness and its refreshment were sweet to me. This earth was the most glorious musical instrument, and I was audience to its strains. To have such sweet impressions made on us, such ecstasies begotten of the breezes! I can remember how I was astonished. I said to myself,—I said to others,—"There comes into my mind such an indescribable, infinite, all-absorbing, divine, heavenly pleasure, a sense of elevation and expansion, and [I] have had nought to do with it. I perceive that I am dealt with by superior powers. This is a pleasure, a joy, an existence which I have not procured myself. I speak as a witness on the stand, and tell what I have perceived." The morning and the evening were sweet to me, and I led a life aloof from society of men. I wondered if a mortal had ever known what I knew. I looked in books for some recognition of a kindred experience, but, strange to say, I found none. Indeed, I was slow to discover that other men had had this experience, for it had been possible to read books and to associate with men on other grounds. The maker of me was improving me. When I detected this interference I was profoundly moved. For years I marched as to a music in comparison with which the military music of the streets is noise and discord. I was daily intoxicated, and yet no man could call me intemperate. With all your science can you tell how it is, and whence it is, that light comes into the soul?

II, 306-307   14 July 1851

* Wordsworth, "Ode: Intimations of Immortality" ("Our birth is but a sleep and a forgetting").

ELASTIC YOUTH

It appears to me that at a very early age the mind of man, perhaps at the same time with his body, ceases to be elastic. His intellectual power becomes something defined and limited. He does not
think expansively, as he would stretch himself in his growing days.
What was flexible sap hardens into heart-wood, and there is no further change. In the season of youth, methinks, man is capable of intellectual effort and performance which surpass all rules and bounds;
as the youth lays out his whole strength without fear or prudence and
does not feel his limits. It is the transition from poetry to prose. The
young man can run and leap; he has not learned exactly how far, he
knows no limits. The grown man does not exceed his daily labor. He
has no strength to waste.

III, 203-204   17 Jan. 1852

YOUTH AND AGE

When a man is young and his constitution and body have not
acquired firmness, *i. e.*, before he has arrived at middle age, he is not
an assured inhabitant of the earth, and his compensation is that he is
not quite earthy, there is something peculiarly tender and divine about
him. His sentiments and his weakness, nay, his very sickness and the
greater uncertainty of his fate, seem to ally him to a noble race of
beings, to whom he in part belongs, or with whom he is in com-
munication. The young man is a demigod; the grown man, alas! is
commonly a mere mortal. He is but half here, he knows not the men
of this world, the powers that be. They know him not. Prompted by
the reminiscence of that other sphere from which he so lately arrived,
his actions are unintelligible to his seniors. He bathes in light. He is
interesting as a stranger from another sphere. He really thinks and
talks about a larger sphere of existence than this world.* It takes him

*   This miniature is filled with echoes of Wordsworth's "Ode: Intimations of Immortality."

forty years to accommodate himself to the carapax of this world. This is the age of poetry. Afterward he may be the president of a bank, and go the way of all flesh. But a man of settled views, whose thoughts are few and hardened like his bones, is truly mortal, and his only re-source is to say his prayers.

XIII, 35   19 Dec. 1859

THE SELF, LOST AND FOUND

The value of the recess in any public entertainment consists in the opportunity for self-recovery which it offers. We who have been swayed as one heart, expanding and contracting with the common pulse, find ourselves in the interim, and set us up again, and feel our own hearts beating in our breasts. We are always a little astonished to see a man walking across the room, through an attentive audience, with any degree of self-possession. He makes himself strange to us. He is a little stubborn withal, and seems to say, "I am self-sustained and independent as well as the performer, and am not to be swal-lowed up in the common enthusiasm. No, no, there are two of us, and John's as good as Thomas." In the recess the audience is cut up into a hundred little coteries, and as soon as each individual life has recovered its tone and the purposes of health have been answered, it is time for the performances to commence again.

I, 199   6 Feb. 1841

PLAYING THE FOOL

By spells seriousness will be forced to cut capers, and drink a deep and refreshing draught of silliness; to turn this sedate day of Lucifer's and Apollo's, into an all fools' day for Harlequin and Cornwallis.* The sun does not grudge his rays to either, but they are alike patronized by the gods. Like overtasked schoolboys, all my members and nerves and sinews petition Thought for a recess, and my very thigh-bones itch to slip away from under me, and run and join the mêlée. I exult in stark inanity, leering on nature and the soul. We think the gods reveal themselves only to sedate and musing gentlemen. But not so; the buffoon in the midst of his antics catches unobserved glimpses, which he treasures for the lonely hour. When I have been playing tom-fool, I have been driven to exchange the old for a more liberal and catholic philosophy.

I, 175-176   23-24 Jan. 1841

AKING ETHER

By taking the ether the other day I was convinced how far asunder a man could be separated from his senses. You are told that it will make you unconscious, but no one can imagine what it is to be unconscious—how far removed from the state of consciousness and all that we call "this world"—until he has experienced it. The value of the experiment is that it does give you experience of an interval as between one life and another,—a greater space than you ever travelled. You are a sane mind without organs,—groping for organs, —which if it did not soon recover its old senses would get new ones. You expand like a seed in the ground. You exist in your roots, like a tree in the winter. If you have an inclination to travel, take the ether; you go beyond the furthest star.

It is not necessary for them to take ether, who in their sane and waking hours are ever translated by a thought; nor for them to see with their hindheads, who sometimes see from their foreheads; nor listen to the spiritual knockings, who attend to the intimations of reason and conscience.

II, 194   12 May 1851

* A masquerade commemorating the surrender of Lord Cornwallis at Yorktown in 1781.

WILDERNESS OF BOOKS

The Library a wilderness of books. Looking over books on Canada written within the last three hundred years, could see how one had been built upon another, each author consulting and referring to his predecessors. You could read most of them without changing your leg on the steps. It is necessary to find out exactly what books to read on a given subject. Though there may be a thousand books written upon it, it is only important to read three or four; they will contain all that is essential, and a few pages will show which they are. Books which are books are all that you want, and there are but half a dozen in any thousand. I saw that while we are clearing the forest in our westward progress, we are accumulating a forest of books in our rear, as wild and unexplored as any of nature's primitive wilder-nesses. The volumes of the Fifteenth, Sixteenth, and Seventeenth Centuries, which lie so near on the shelf, are rarely opened, are effectually forgotten and not implied by our literature and newspapers. When I looked into Purchas's Pilgrims,* it affected me like looking into an impassable swamp, ten feet deep with sphagnum, where the monarchs of the forest, covered with mosses and stretched along the ground, were making haste to become peat. Those old books sug-gested a certain fertility, an Ohio soil, as if they were making a hu-mus for new literatures to spring in. I heard the bellowing of bull-frogs and the hum of mosquitoes reverberating through the thick em-bossed covers when I had closed the book. Decayed literature makes the richest of all soils.

III, 352-353   16 Mar. 1852

* Samuel Purchas; the reference is presumably to *Hakluytus Posthu-mus, or Purchas his Pilgrimes, containing a History of the World in Sea Voyages and Land Travel by Englishmen and Others* (1625), the second part of which is concerned with attempts to discover the North-west Passage.

A TRULY GOOD BOOK

A truly good book attracts very little favor to itself. It is so true that it teaches me better than to read it. I must soon lay it down and commence living on its hint. I do not see how any can be written more, but this is the last effusion of genius. When I read an indifferent book, it seems the best thing I can do, but the inspiring volume hardly leaves me leisure to finish its latter pages. It is slipping out of my fingers while I read. It creates no atmosphere in which it may be perused, but one in which its teachings may be practiced. It confers on me such wealth that I lay it down with the least regret. What I began by reading I must finish by acting. So I cannot stay to hear a *good* sermon and applaud at the conclusion, but shall be half-way to Thermopylæ before that.

1, 216   19 Feb. 1841

ASSIMILATING SAADI*

The entertaining a single thought of a certain elevation makes all men of one religion. It is always some base alloy that creates the distinction of sects. Thought greets thought over the widest gulfs of time with unerring freemasonry. I know, for instance, that Sadi entertained once identically the same thought that I do, and thereafter I can find no essential difference between Sadi and myself. He is not Persian, he is not ancient, he is not strange to me. By the identity of his thoughts with mine he still survives. It makes no odds what atoms serve us. Sadi possessed no greater privacy or individuality than is thrown open to me. He had no more interior and essential and sacred self than can come naked into my thought this moment. Truth and a true man is something essentially public, not private. If Sadi were to

* This Persian lyric poet was a favorite of the Transcendentalists. Thoreau probably first learned of him from Emerson, who published a poem, "Saadi," in *The Dial*.

come back to claim a *personal* identity with the historical Sadi, he would find there were too many of us; he could not get a skin that would contain us all. The symbol of a personal identity preserved in this sense is a mummy from the catacombs,—a whole skin, it may [be], but no life within it. By living the life of a man is made common property. By sympathy with Sadi I have embowelled him. In his thought I have a sample of *him*, a slice from his core, which makes it unimportant where certain bones which the thinker once employed may lie; but I could not have got this without being equally entitled to it with himself. The difference between any man and that posterity amid whom he is famous is too insignificant to sanction that he should be set up again in any world as distinct from them. Methinks I can be as intimate with the essence of an ancient worthy as, so to speak, he was with himself.

IV, 290   8 Aug. 1852

CONVERSATION

Men are very generally spoiled by being so civil and well-disposed. You can have no profitable conversation with them, they are so conciliatory, determined to agree with you. They exhibit such long-suffering and kindness in a short interview. I would meet with some provoking strangeness, so that we may be guest and host and refresh one another. It is possible for a man wholly to disappear and be merged in his manners. The thousand and one gentlemen whom I meet, I meet despairingly and but to part from them, for I am not cheered by the hope of any rudeness from them. A cross man, a coarse man, an eccentric man, a silent, a man who does not drill well,—of him there is some hope. Your gentlemen, they are all alike. They utter their opinions as if it was not a man that uttered them. It is "just as you please;" they are indifferent to everything. They will talk with you for nothing. The interesting man will rather avoid [you], and it is a rare chance if you get so far as talk with him. The laborers whom I know, the loafers, fishers, and hunters, I can spin yarns with profitably, for it is hands off; they are they and I am I still; they do not come to me and quarter themselves on me for a day or an hour to be treated politely, they do not cast themselves on me for entertainment, they do not approach me with a flag of truce. They do not go out of themselves to meet me. I am never electrified by my gentleman; he is not an electric eel, but one of the common kind that slip through your hands, however hard you clutch them, and leave them covered with slime.

II, 328-329   21 July 1851

"FINISHING" SCHOOL

Many go to Europe *to finish their education*, and when they have returned their friends remark that the most they have acquired is a correct pronunciation of English. It is a premature hardening but hollowing of the shell. They become valuable utensils of the gourd kind, but have no palatable and nutritious inside. Instead of acquiring nutritious and palatable qualities to their pulp, it is all absorbed into a prematurely hardened shell. They went away squashes, and they return gourds. They are all expressed, or squeezed out; their essential oil is gone. They are pronounced [*pronoun*-ced] for you; they are good to stand before or for a noun or man as handles; not even hollow gourds always, but the handle without the mug. They pronounce with the sharp precise report of a rifle, but the likeness is in the sound only, for they have no bullets to fire.

v, 344-345   30 July 1853

CONSERVATIVES

The way in which men cling to old institutions after the life has departed out of them, and out of themselves, reminds me of those monkeys which cling by their tails,—aye, whose tails contract about the limbs, even the dead limbs, of the forest, and they hang suspended beyond the hunter's reach long after they are dead. It is of no use to argue with such men. They have not an apprehensive intellect, but merely, as it were, a prehensile tail. Their intellect possesses merely the quality of a prehensile tail. The tail itself contracts around the dead limb even after they themselves are dead, and not till sensible corruption takes place do they fall. The black howling monkey, or caraya. According to Azara,* it is extremely difficult to get at them, for "when mortally wounded they coil the tail round a branch, and hang by it with the head downwards for days after death, and until, in fact, decomposition begins to take effect." The commenting naturalist says, "A singular peculiarity of this organ is to contract at its extremity of its own accord as soon as it is extended to its full length." I relinquish argument, I wait for decomposition to take place, for the subject is dead; as I value the hide for the museum. They say, "Though you've got my soul, you sha'n't have my carcass."

II, 401·402   19 Aug. 1851

REE-SOILERS †

I have seen many a collection of stately elms which better deserved to be represented at the General Court than the manikins beneath,—than the barroom and victualling cellar and groceries they overshadowed. When I see their magnificent domes, miles away in the horizon, over intervening valleys and forests, they suggest a village, a community, there. But, after all, it is a secondary consideration whether there are human dwellings beneath them; these may have long since passed away. I find that into my idea of the village has entered more of the elm than of the human being. They are worth many a political borough. They constitute a borough. The poor human representative of his party sent out from beneath their shade will not suggest a tithe of the dignity, the true nobleness and comprehen-

* Don Felix de Azara, whose *Voyage dans l'Amérique méridionale* (1809) contained many observations on the natural history of Paraguay.
† The Free-Soil Party (1848–1856) opposed the spread of slavery into the Territories.

siveness of view, the sturdiness and independence, and the serene beneficence that they do. They look from township to township. A fragment of their bark is worth the backs of all the politicians in the union. They are free-soilers in their own broad sense. They send their roots north and south and east and west into many a conservative's Kansas and Carolina, who does not suspect such underground railroads,—they improve the subsoil he has never disturbed,—and many times their length, if the support of their principles requires it. They battle with the tempests of a century. See what scars they bear, what limbs they lost before we were born! Yet they never adjourn; they steadily vote for their principles, and send their roots further and wider from the *same centre*. They die at their posts, and they leave a tough butt for the choppers to exercise themselves about, and a stump which serves for their monument. They attend no caucus, they make no compromise, they use no policy. Their one principle is growth. They combine a true radicalism with a true conservatism. Their radicalism is not cutting away of roots, but an infinite multiplication and extension of them under all surrounding institutions. They take a firmer hold on the earth that they may rise higher into the heavens. Their conservative heartwood, in which no sap longer flows, does not impoverish their growth, but is a firm column to support it; and when their expanding trunks no longer require it, it utterly decays. Their conservatism is a dead but solid heart-wood, which is the pivot and firm column of support to all this growth, appropriating nothing to itself, but forever by its support assisting to extend the area of their radicalism. Half a century after they are dead at the core, they are preserved by radical reforms. They do not, like men, from radicals turn conservative. Their conservative part dies out first; their radical and growing part survives. They acquire new States and Territories, while the old dominions decay, and become the habitation of bears and owls and coons.

VIII, 139-141   24 Jan. 1856

THE POETRY OF THE JAKES

The rhymes which I used to see on the walls of privies, scribbled by boys, I have lately seen, word for word the same; in spite [of] whitewash and brick walls and admonitions they survive. They are no doubt older than Orpheus, and have come down from an antiquity as remote as mythology or fable. So, too, no doubt corporations have ever struggled in vain to obtain cleanliness in those provinces. Filth and impurity are as old as cleanliness and purity. To correspond to man completely, Nature is even perhaps unchaste herself. Or per-chance man's impurity begets a monster somewhere, to proclaim his sin. The poetry of the jakes,—it flows as perennially as the gutter.

III, 255   30 Jan. 1852

THE DEVIL BEHIND ME

In our holiest moment our devil with a leer stands close at hand. He is a very busy devil. It gains vice some respect, I must confess, thus to be reminded how indefatigable it is. It has at least the merit of industriousness. When I go forth with zeal to some good work, my devil is sure to get his robe tucked up the first and arrives there as soon as I, with a look of sincere earnestness which puts to shame my best intent. He is as forward as I to a good work, and as disinterested. He has a winning way of recommending himself by making himself useful. How readily he comes into my best project, and does his work with a quiet and steady cheerfulness which even virtue may take pat-tern from.

I never was so rapid in my virtue but my vice kept up with me. It always came in by a hand, and never panting, but with a curried coolness halted, as if halting were the beginning not the end of the course. It only runs the swifter because it has no rider. It never was behind me but when I turned to look and so fell behind myself. I never did a charitable thing but there he stood, scarce in the rear, with hat in hand, partner on the same errand, ready to share the smile of gratitude. Though I shut the door never so quick and tell it to stay at home like a good dog, it will out with me, for I shut in my own legs so, and it escapes in the meanwhile and is ready to back and reinforce me in most virtuous deeds. And if I turn and say, "Get thee behind me," * he then indeed turns too and takes the lead, though he seems to retire with a pensive and compassionate look, as much as to say, "Ye know not what ye do."

Just as active as I become to virtue, just so active is my remaining vice. Every time we teach our virtue a new nobleness, we teach our vice a new cunning. When we sharpen the blade it will stab better as well as whittle. The scythe that cuts will cut our legs. We are double-edged blades, and every time we whet our virtue the return stroke straps our vice. And when we cut a clear descending blow, our vice on tother edge rips up the work. Where is the skillful swordsman that can draw his blade straight back out of the wound?

1, 207-208   8 Feb. 1841

DYSPEPTICS AND EUPEPTICS

A wise man is as unconscious of the movements in the body politic as he is of the process of digestion and the circulation of the blood in the natural body. These processes are *infra*-human. I sometimes awake to a half-consciousness of these things going on about me, —as politics, society, business, etc., etc.,—as a man may become conscious of some of the processes of digestion, in a morbid state, and so have the dyspepsia, as it is called. It appears to me that those things which most engage the attention of men, as politics, for instance, are vital functions of human society, it is true, but should [be] unconsciously performed, like the vital functions of the natural body. It is as if a thinker submitted himself to be rasped by the great gizzard of creation. Politics is, as it were, the gizzard of society, full of grit and

* Matthew 16.33. The quotation at the end of the sentence is a subversion of Luke 23.34: "Then said Jesus, Father, forgive them; for they know not what they do."

gravel, and the two political parties are its two opposite halves, which grind on each other. Not only individuals but states have thus a con-firmed dyspepsia, which expresses itself, you can imagine by what sort of eloquence. Our life is not altogether a forgetting,* but also, alas, to a great extent a remembering, of that which perchance we should never have been conscious of,—the consciousness of what should not be permitted to disturb a man's waking hours. As for society, why should we not meet, not always as dyspeptics, but some-times as eupeptics?

III, 103   9 Nov. 1851

PARASITES

We must be very active if we would be clean and live our own life, and not a languishing and scurvy one. The trees, which are stationary, are covered with parasites, especially those which have grown slowly. The air is filled with the fine sporules of countless mosses, algæ, lichens, fungi, which settle and plant themselves on all quiet surfaces. Under the nails and between the joints of the fingers of the idle, flourish crops of mildew, algæ, and fungi, and other vege-table sloths, though they may be invisible,—the lichens where life still exists, the fungi where decomposition has begun to take place. And the sluggard is soon covered with sphagnum. Algæ take root in the corners of his eyes, and lichens cover the bulbs of his fingers and his head, etc., etc., the lowest forms of vegetable life. This is the definition of dirt. We fall a prey to others of nature's tenants, who take possession of the unoccupied house. With the utmost inward activity we have to wash and comb ourselves beside, to get rid of the adhering seeds. Cleanliness is by activity not to give any quiet shelf for the seeds of parasitic plants to take root on.

III, 245-246   29 Jan. 1852

*   An echo of Wordsworth's "Ode: Intimations of Immortality" ("Our birth is but a sleep and a forgetting").

BATHING

Bathing is an undescribed luxury. To feel the wind blow on your body, the water flow on you and lave you, is a rare physical enjoyment this hot day. The water is remarkably warm here, especially in the shallows,—warm to the hand, like that which has stood long in a kettle over a fire. The pond water being so warm made the water of the brook feel very cold; and this kept close on the bottom of the pond for a good many rods about the mouth of the brook, as I could feel with my feet; and when I thrust my arm down where it was only two feet deep, my arm was in the warm water of the pond, but my hand in the cold water of the brook. . . .

I am inclined to think bathing almost one of the necessaries of life, but it is surprising how indifferent some are to it. What a coarse, foul, busy life we lead, compared even with the South-Sea-Islanders, in some respects. Truant boys steal away to bathe, but the farmers, who most need it, rarely dip their bodies into the streams or ponds. M—— was telling me last night that he had thought of bathing when he had done his hoeing,—of taking some soap and going down to Walden and giving himself a good scrubbing,—but something had occurred to prevent it, and now he will go unwashed to the harvesting, aye, even till the next hoeing is over. Better the faith and practice of the Hindoos who worship the sacred Ganges. We have not faith enough in the Musketaquid to wash in it, even after hoeing. Men stay on shore, keep themselves dry, and drink rum. Pray what were rivers made for? One farmer, who came to bathe in Walden one Sunday while I lived there, told me it was the first bath he had had for fifteen years. Now what kind of religion could his be? Or was it any better than a Hindoo's?

SIMPLICITY

By poverty, *i. e.* simplicity of life and fewness of incidents, I am
solidified and crystallized, as a vapor or liquid by cold. It is a singular
concentration of strength and energy and flavor. Chastity is perpetual
acquaintance with the All. My diffuse and vaporous life becomes as
the frost leaves and spiculæ radiant as gems on the weeds and stubble
in a winter morning. You think that I am impoverishing myself by
withdrawing from men, but in my solitude I have woven for myself
a silken web or *chrysalis,* and, nymph-like, shall ere long burst forth
a more perfect creature, fitted for a higher society. By simplicity,
commonly called poverty, my life is concentrated and so becomes
organized, or a κόσμος [cosmos], which before was inorganic and
lumpish.

IX, 246-247   8 Feb. 1857

WHY I LEFT THE WOODS

But why I changed? why I left the woods?* I do not think
that I can tell. I have often wished myself back. I do know any better
how I ever came to go there. Perhaps it is none of my business, even
if it is yours. Perhaps I wanted a change. There was a little stagnation,
it may be. About 2 o'clock in the afternoon the world's axle creaked
as if it needed greasing, as if the oxen labored with the wain and
could hardly get their load over the ridge of the day. Perhaps if I lived
there much longer, I might live there forever. One would think twice
before he accepted heaven on such terms. A ticket to Heaven must
include tickets to Limbo, Purgatory, and Hell. Your ticket to the

* "I left the woods for as good a reason as I went there. Perhaps it
seemed to me that I had several more lives to live, and could not spare
any more time for that one" (*Walden,* p. 355). Thoreau went to the
pond on July 4, 1845, and returned to Concord on September 6,
1847.

boxes admits you to the pit also. And if you take a cabin passage, you can smoke, at least forward of the engine,—you have the liberty of the whole boat. But no, I do not wish for a ticket to the boxes, nor to take a cabin passage. I will rather go before the mast and on the deck of the world. I have no desire to go "abaft the engine."

I must say that I do not know what made me leave the pond. I left it as unaccountably as I went to it. To speak sincerely, I went there because I had got ready to go; I left it for the same reason.

III, 214-216   22 Jan. 1852

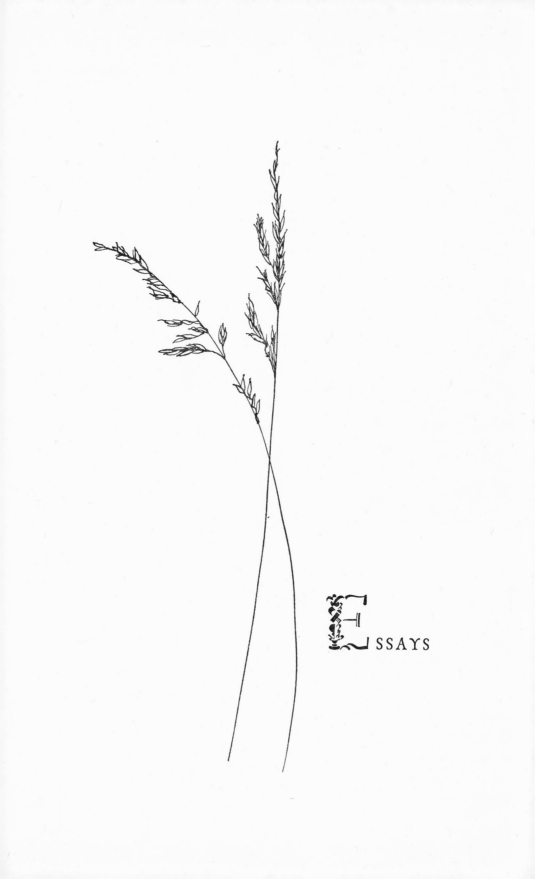

Essays

NON–SELLING AUTHOR

For a year or two past, my *publisher*,* falsely so called, has been writing from time to time to ask what disposition should be made of the copies of "A Week on the Concord and Merrimack Rivers" still on hand, and at last suggesting that he had use for the room they occupied in his cellar. So I had them all sent to me here, and they have arrived to-day by express, filling the man's wagon,— 706 copies out of an edition of 1000 which I bought of Munroe four years ago and have been ever since paying for, and have not quite paid for yet. The wares are sent to me at last, and I have an opportunity to examine my purchase. They are something more sub-stantial than fame, as my back knows, which has borne them up two flights of stairs to a place similar to that to which they trace their origin. Of the remaining two hundred and ninety and odd, seventy-five were given away, the rest sold. I have now a library of nearly nine hundred volumes, over seven hundred of which I wrote myself. Is it not well that the author should behold the fruits of his labor? My works are piled up on one side of my chamber half as high as my head, my *opera omnia*. This is authorship; these are the work of my brain. There was just one piece of good luck in the venture. The unbound were tied up by the printer four years ago in stout paper wrappers, and inscribed,—

H. D. Thoreau's
Concord River
50 cops.

So Munroe had only to cross out "River" and write "Mass." and deliver them to the expressman at once. I can see now what I write for, the result of my labors.

* James Munroe & Co., of Boston, published *A Week on the Con-cord and Merrimack Rivers* in 1849, at Thoreau's expense, but they did agree to let him pay the costs out of sales provided he would guarantee that they eventually receive the full amount. The book cost him $290, and his total income from sales up to the time it was re-maindered (1853) amounted to only $15.

Nevertheless, in spite of this result, sitting beside the inert mass of my works, I take up my pen to-night to record what thought or experience I may have had, with as much satisfaction as ever. Indeed, I believe that this result is more inspiring and better for me than if a thousand had bought my wares. It affects my privacy less and leaves me freer.

v, 459-460   28 Oct. 1853

ISTORY

Two hundred years ago is about as great an antiquity as we can comprehend or often have to deal with. It is nearly as good as two thousand to our imaginations. It carries us back to the days of aborigines and the Pilgrims; beyond the limits of oral testimony, to history which begins already to be enamelled with a gloss of fable, and we do not quite believe what we read; to a strange style of writing and spelling and of expression; to those ancestors whose names we do not know, and to whom we are related only as we are to the race generally. It is the age of our very oldest houses and cultivated trees. Nor is New England very peculiar in this. In England also, a house two hundred years old, especially if it be a wooden one, is pointed out as an interesting relic of the past.

When we read the history of the world, centuries look cheap to us and we find that we had doubted if the hundred years preceding the life of Herodotus seemed as great an antiquity to him as a hundred years does to us. We are inclined to think of all Romans who lived within five hundred years B.C. as *contemporaries* to each other. Yet Time moved at the same deliberate pace then as now. Pliny the Elder, who died in the 79th year of the Christian era, speaking of the paper made of papyrus which was then used,—how carefully it was made, —says, *just as we might say*, as if it were something remarkable: "There are, thus, ancient memorials in the handwriting of Caius and Tiberius Gracchus, almost two hundred years old, which I have seen in the possession of Pomponius Secundus the poet, a very illustrious citizen. As for the handwriting of Cicero, Augustus, and Virgil, we very often meet with it still." This too, according to Pliny, was the age of the oldest wines. "In one year the quality of all kinds of wine was peculiarly good. In the consulship of Lucius Opimius, when Caius Gracchus, disturbing the people with seditions, was killed, there was that bright and serene weather (*ea caeli temperies fulsit*) which they call a *cooking* (of the grape) by the heat of the sun. This was in the year of the city 634. And some of those wines have lasted to this day, almost two hundred years, now reduced to the appearance of candied honey (*in speciem redacta mellis asperi*)." *

How is it that what is actually present and transpiring is commonly perceived by the common sense and understanding only, is bare and bald, without halo or the blue enamel of intervening air? But let it be past or to come, and it is at once idealized. As the man dead is spiritualized, so the fact remembered is idealized. It is a deed ripe and with the bloom on it. It is not simply the understanding now, but the imagination, that takes cognizance of it. The imagination requires a long range. It is the faculty of the poet to see present things as if, in this sense, also past and future, as if distant or universally significant. We do not know poets, heroes, and saints for our contemporaries, but we locate them in some far-off vale, and, the greater and better, the further off we [are] accustomed to consider them. We believe in spirits, we believe in beauty, but not now and here. They have their abode in the remote past or in the future.

XIII, 16-18   8 Dec. 1859

T RAVEL: AT HOME AND ABROAD

A man must generally get away some hundreds or thousands of miles from home before he can be said to begin his travels. Why not begin his travels at home? Would he have to go far or look very closely to discover novelties? The traveller who, in this sense, pursues his travels at home, has the advantage at any rate of a long residence in the country to make his observations correct and profitable. Now the American goes to England, while the Englishman comes to

* Pliny the Elder, *Naturalia Historia*, XIII, 83; XIV, 55.

America, in order to describe the country. No doubt there [are] some advantages in this kind of mutual criticism. But might there not be invented a better way of coming at the truth than this scratch-my-back-and-I-'ll-scratch-yours method? Would not the American, for instance, who had himself, perchance, travelled in England and elsewhere make the most profitable and accurate traveller in his own country? How often it happens that the traveller's principal distinction is that he is one who knows less about a country than a native! Now if he should begin with all the knowledge of a native, and add thereto the knowledge of a traveller, both natives and foreigners would be obliged to read his book; and the world would be absolutely benefited. It takes a man of genius to travel in his own country, in his native village; to make any progress between his door and his gate. But such a traveller will make the distances which Hanno* and Marco Polo and Cook and Ledyard went over ridiculous.

11, 376-377   6 Aug. 1851

RAVELLING

The question is not where did the traveller go? what places did he see?—it would be difficult to choose between places—but who was the traveller? how did he travel? how genuine an experience did he get? For travelling is, in the main, like as if you stayed at home, and then the question is how do you live and conduct yourself at home? What I mean is that it might be hard to decide whether I would travel to Lake Superior, or Labrador, or Florida. Perhaps none would be worth the while, if I went by the usual mode. But if I travel in a simple, primitive, original manner, standing in a truer relation to men and nature, travel away from the old and commonplace, get some honest experience of life, if only out of my feet and homesickness, then it becomes less important whither I go or how far. I so see the world from a new and more commanding point of view. Perhaps it is easier

---

*   A Carthaginian navigator, c. 500 B.C. (The other explorers can be identified in a standard dictionary.)

to live a true and natural life while travelling,—as one can move about less awkwardly than he can stand still. . . .

I sometimes think that I may go forth and walk hard and earnestly, and live a more substantial life and get a glorious experience; be much abroad in heat and cold, day and night; live more, expend more atmospheres, be weary often, etc., etc. But then swiftly the thought comes to me, Go not so far out of your way for a truer life; keep strictly onward in that path alone which your genius points out. Do the things which lie nearest to you, but which are difficult to do. Live a purer, a more thoughtful and laborious life, more true to your friends and neighbors, more noble and magnanimous, and that will be better than a wild walk. To live in relations of truth and sincerity with men is to dwell in a frontier country. What a wild and unfrequented wilderness that would be! What Saguenays of magnanimity that might be explored! Men talk about travelling this way or that, as if seeing were all in the eyes, and a man could sufficiently report what he stood bodily before, when the seeing depends ever on the being. All report of travel is the report of victory or defeat, of a contest with every event and phenomenon and how you came out of it. A blind man who possesses inward truth and consistency will see more than one who has faultless eyes but no serious and laborious astronomer to look through them. As if the eyes were the only part of a man that travelled! Men convert their property into cash, ministers fall sick to obtain the assistance of their parishes, all chaffer with sea-captains, etc., as if the whole object were to get conveyed to some part of the world a pair of eyes merely. A telescope conveyed to and set up at the Cape of Good Hope at great expense, and only a Bushman to look through it. Nothing like a little internal activity called life—if it were only walking much in a day—to keep the eyes in good order; no such collyrium.

III, 183-185   11-12 Jan. 1852

THE SOLITARY VOYAGER

There sits one by the shore who wishes to go with me, but I cannot think of it. I must be fancy-free. There is no such mote in the sky as a man who is not perfectly transparent to you,—who has any opacity. I would rather attend to him earnestly for half an hour, on shore or elsewhere, and then dismiss him. He thinks I could merely take him into my boat and then not mind him. He does not realize that I should by the same act take him into my mind, where there is no room for him, and my bark would surely founder in such a voyage as I was contemplating. I know very well that I should never reach that expansion of the river I have in my mind, with him aboard with his broad terrene qualities. He would sink my bark (not to another sea) and never know it. I could better carry a heaped load of meadow mud and sit on the tholepins. There would be more room for me, and I should reach that expansion of the river nevertheless.

I could better afford to take him into bed with me, for then I might, perhaps, abandon him in my dreams. Ah! you are a heavy fellow, but I am well disposed. If you could go without going, then you might go. There's the captain's stateroom, empty to be sure, and you say you could go in the steerage. I know very well that only your baggage would be dropped in the steerage, while you would settle right down into that other snug recess. Why, I am *going*, not staying. I have come on purpose to sail, to paddle away from such as you, and you have waylaid me at the shore. You have chosen to make your assault at the moment of embarkation. Why, if I thought you were steadily gazing after me a mile off, I could not endure it. It is because I trust that I shall ere long depart from your thoughts, and so you from mine, that I am encouraged to set sail at all. I make haste to put several meanders and some hills between us. This Company is obliged to make a distinction between dead freight and passengers. I will take almost any amount of freight for you cheerfully,—anything, my dear sir, but yourself.

IX, 46-47   31 Aug. 1856

THE SOLITARY WALKER

There is nothing so sanative, so poetic, as a walk in the woods and fields even now, when I meet none abroad for pleasure. Nothing so inspires me and excites such serene and profitable thought. The objects are elevating. In the street and in society I am almost invariably cheap and dissipated, my life is unspeakably mean. No amount of gold or respectability would in the least redeem it,—dining with the Governor or a member of Congress!! But alone in distant woods or fields, in unpretending sprout-lands or pastures tracked by rabbits, even in a bleak and, to most, cheerless day, like this, when a villager would be thinking of his inn, I come to myself, I once more feel myself grandly related, and that cold and solitude are friends of mine. I suppose that this value, in my case, is equivalent to what others get by churchgoing and prayer. I come to my solitary woodland walk as the homesick go home. I thus dispose of the superfluous and see things as they are, grand and beautiful. I have told many that I walk every day about half the daylight, but I think they do not believe it. I wish to get the Concord, the Massachusetts, the America, out of my head and be sane a part of every day. If there are missionaries for the heathen, why not send them to me? I wish to know something; I wish to be made better. I wish to forget, a considerable part of every day, all mean, narrow, trivial men (and this requires usually to forego and forget all personal relations so long), and therefore I come out to these solitudes, where the problem of existence is simplified. I get away a mile or two from the town into the stillness and solitude of nature, with rocks, trees, weeds, snow about me. I enter some glade in the woods, perchance, where a few weeds and dry leaves alone lift themselves above the surface of the snow, and it is as if I had come to an open window. I see out and around myself. Our *skylights* are thus far away from the ordinary resorts of men. I am not satisfied with ordinary windows. I must have a true *skylight*. My true skylight is on the outside of the village. I am not thus expanded, recreated, enlightened, when I meet a company of men. It chances that the sociable, the town and county, or the farmers' club does not prove a skylight to me. I do not invariably find myself translated under those circumstances. They bore me. The man I meet with is not often so instructive as the silence he breaks. This stillness, solitude, wildness of nature is a kind of thoroughwort, or boneset, to my intellect. This is what I go out to seek. It is as if I always met in those places some grand, serene, immortal, infinitely encouraging, though invisible, companion, and walked with him. There at last my nerves are steadied, my senses and my mind do their office. I am aware that most of my neighbors would think it a hardship to be compelled to linger here one hour, especially this bleak day, and yet I receive this sweet and ineffable compensation for it. It is the most agreeable thing I do. Truly, my coins are uncurrent with them. . . .

My fairies invariably take to flight when a man appears upon the scene. In a caucus, a meeting-house, a lyceum, a clubroom, there is nothing like it in my experience. But away out of the town, on Brown's scrub oak lot, which was sold the other day for six dollars an acre, I have company such as England cannot buy, nor afford. . . .

Who shall criticize that companion? It is like the hone to the knife. I bathe in that climate and am cleansed of all social impurities. I become a witness with unprejudiced senses to the order of the universe. *There* is nothing petty or impertinent, none to say, "See what a great man I am!" *There* chiefly, and not in the society of the wits, am I cognizant of wit. Shall I prefer a part, an infinitely small fraction, to the whole? There I get my underpinnings laid and repaired, cemented, levelled. There is my country club. We dine at the sign of the Shrub Oak, the New Albion House.

IX, 208-209, 215-216   7, 11 Jan. 1857

GENTLEMAN TRAVELLER VS. TRUE WAYFARER

I have several friends and acquaintances who are very good companions in the house or for an afternoon walk, but whom I cannot make up my mind to make a longer excursion with; for I discover, all at once, that they are too gentlemanly in manners, dress, and all

their habits. I see in my mind's eye that they wear black coats, considerable starched linen, glossy hats and shoes, and it is out of the
question. It is a great disadvantage for a traveller to be a gentleman
of this kind; he is so ill-treated, only a prey to landlords. It would be
too much of a circumstance to enter a strange town or house with such
a companion. You could not travel incognito; you might get into the
papers. You should travel as a common man. If such a one were to
set out to make a walking-journey, he would betray himself at every
step. Every one would see that he was trying an experiment, as plainly
as they see that a lame man is lame by his limping. The natives would
bow to him, other gentlemen would invite him to ride, conductors
would warn him that this was the second-class car, and many would
take him for a clergyman; and so he would be continually pestered
and balked and run upon. You would not see the natives at all. Instead of going in quietly at the back door and sitting by the kitchen
fire, you would be shown into a cold parlor, there to confront a fire-
board, and excite a commotion in a whole family. The women would
scatter at your approach, and their husbands and sons would go right
up to hunt up their black coats,—for they all have them; they are as
cheap as dirt. You would go trailing your limbs along the highways,
mere bait for corpulent innholders, as a [frog's]* leg is trolled along
a stream [for pickerel], and your part of the profits would be the
frog's. No, you must be a common man, or at least travel as one, and
then nobody will know that you are there or have been there. I
would not undertake a simple pedestrian excursion with one of these,
because to enter a village, or a hotel, or a private house, with such a
one, would be too great a circumstance, would create too great a
stir. You could only go half as far with the same means, for the price
of board and lodgings would rise everywhere; so much you have to
pay for wearing that kind of coat. Not that the difference is in the coat
at all, for the character of the scurf is determined by that of the true
liber † beneath. Innkeepers, stablers, conductors, clergymen, know a
true wayfaring man at first sight and let him alone. It is of no use to
shove your gaiter shoes a mile further than usual. Sometimes it is

* Thoreau's slip of the pen, "a pickerel's leg," has been corrected
to "a [frog's] leg."
† Bast; the inner fiber or bark (NED).

mere shiftlessness or want of originality,—the clothes wear them; sometimes it is egotism, that cannot afford to be treated like a common man,—they wear the clothes. They wish to be at least fully appreciated by every stage-driver and schoolboy. They would like well enough to see a new place, perhaps, but then they would like to be regarded as important public personages. They would consider it a misfortune if their names were left out of the published list of passengers because they came in the steerage,—an obscurity from which they might never emerge.

IX, 400-402   3 June 1857

PROPER CLOTHES FOR THE WALKER

There is certainly a singular propriety in that color for the coat of a farmer or teamster or shepherd or hunter, who is required to be much abroad in our landscape at this season. It is in harmony with nature, and you are less conspicuous in the fields and can get nearer to wild animals for it. For this reason I am the better satisfied with the color of my hat, a drab, than with that of my companion, which is black, though his coat is of the exact tint and better than mine; but again my dusty boots harmonize better with the landscape than his black and glossy india-rubbers.

I had a suit once in which, methinks, I could glide across the fields unperceived half a mile in front of a farmer's windows. It was such a skillful mixture of browns, dark and light properly proportioned, with even some threads of green in it by chance. It was of loose texture and about the color of a pasture with patches of withered sweet-fern and lechea. I trusted a good deal to my invisibility in it when going across lots, and many a time I was aware that to it I owed the near approach of wild animals.

No doubt my dusty and tawny cowhides surprise the street walkers who wear patent-leather or Congress shoes, but they do not consider how absurd such shoes would be in my vocation, to thread the woods and swamps in. Why should I wear *Congress* who walk alone, and not where there is any congress of my kind?

C [Channing] was saying, properly enough, the other day, as we were making our way through a dense patch of shrub oak: "I suppose that those villagers think that we wear these old and worn hats with holes all along the corners for oddity, but Coombs, the musquash hunter and partridge and rabbit snarer, knows better. He understands us. He knows that a new and square-cornered hat would be spoiled in one excursion through the shrub oaks."

The walker and naturalist does not wear a hat, or a shoe, or a coat, to be looked at, but for other uses. When a citizen comes to take a walk with me I commonly find that he is lame,—disabled by his shoeing. He is sure to wet his feet, tear his coat, and jam his hat, and the superior qualities of my boots, coat, and hat appear. I once went into the woods with a party for a fortnight. I wore my old and common clothes, which were of Vermont gray. They wore, no doubt, the best they had for such an occasion,—of a fashionable color and quality. I thought that they were a little ashamed of me while we were in the towns. They all tore their clothes badly but myself, and I, who, it chanced, was the only one provided with needles and thread, enabled them to mend them. When we came out of the woods I was the best dressed of any of them.

XIII, 230-232   26 Mar. 1860

WALKING THE WILD ROAD

Now I yearn for one of those old, meandering, dry, uninhabited roads, which lead away from towns, which lead us away from temptation, which conduct to the outside of earth, over its uppermost crust; where you may forget in what country you are travelling; where no farmer can complain that you are treading down his grass, no gentleman who has recently constructed a seat in the country that you are trespassing; on which you can go off at half-cock and wave adieu to the village; along which you may travel like a pilgrim, going nowhither; where travellers are not too often to be met; where my spirit is free; where the walls and fences are not cared for; where your head is more in heaven than your feet are on earth; which have long reaches

where you can see the approaching traveller half a mile off and be prepared for him; not so luxuriant a soil as to attract men; some root and
stump fences which do not need attention; where travellers have no
occasion to stop, but pass along and leave you to your thoughts; where
it makes no odds which way you face, whether you are going or coming, whether it is morning or evening, mid-noon or midnight; where
earth is cheap enough by being public; where you can walk and think
with least obstruction, there being nothing to measure progress by;
where you can pace when your breast is full, and cherish your moodi-
ness; where you are not in false relations with men, are not dining nor
conversing with them; by which you may go to the uttermost parts of
the earth. It is wide enough, wide as the thoughts it allows to visit
you. Sometimes it is some particular half-dozen rods which I wish to
find myself pacing over, as where certain airs blow; then my life will
come to me, methinks; like a hunter I walk in wait for it. When I am
against this bare promontory of a huckleberry hill, then forsooth my
thoughts will expand. Is it some influence, as a vapor which exhales
from the ground, or something in the gales which blow there, or in
all things there brought together agreeably to my spirit? The walls
must not be too high, imprisoning me, but low, with numerous gaps.
The trees must not be too numerous, nor the hills too near, bounding
the view, nor the soil too rich, attracting the attention to the earth. It
must simply be the way and the life,*—a way that was never known
to be repaired, nor to need repair, within the memory of the oldest
inhabitant. I cannot walk habitually in those ways that are liable to
be mended; for sure it was the devil only that wore them. Never by
the heel of thinkers (of thought) were they worn; the zephyrs could
repair that damage. The saunterer wears out no road, even though he
travel on it, and therefore should pay no highway, or rather *low* way,
tax. He may be taxed to construct a higher way than men travel. A
way which no geese defile, nor hiss along it, but only sometimes their
wild brethren fly far overhead; which the kingbird and the swallow
twitter over, and the song sparrow sings on its rails; where the small
red butterfly is at home on the yarrow, and no boys threaten it with
imprisoning hat. There I can walk and stalk and pace and plod.
Which nobody but Jonas Potter travels beside me; where no cow

* Christ said, "I am the way, the truth and the life" (John 14.6).

but his is tempted to linger for the herbage by its side; where the guide-board is fallen, and now the hand points to heaven significantly, —to a Sudbury and Marlborough in the skies. That's a road I can travel, that's the particular Sudbury I am bound for, six miles an hour, or two, as you please; and few there be that enter thereon. There I can walk, and recover the lost child that I am without any ringing of a bell; where there was nothing ever discovered to detain a traveller, but all went through about their business; where I never passed the time of day with any,—indifferent to me were the arbitrary divisions of time; where Tullus Hostilius* might have disappeared,—at any rate has never been seen. The road to the Corner! the ninety and nine acres that you go through to get there! I would rather see it again, though I saw it this morning, than Gray's churchyard. . . .

It is they who go to Brighton and to market that wear out the roads, and they should pay all the tax. The deliberate pace of a thinker never made a road the worse for travelling on.

II, 322-325   21 July 1851

CRANBERRYING AS AN ADVENTURE

I have come out this afternoon a-cranberrying, chiefly to gather some of the small cranberry, *Vaccinium Oxycoccus*, which Emerson says is the common cranberry of the north of Europe. This was a small object, yet not to be postponed, on account of imminent frosts, *i. e.*, if I would know this year the flavor of the European cranberry as compared with our larger kind. I thought I should like to have a dish of this sauce on the table at Thanksgiving of my own gathering. I could hardly make up my mind to come this way, it seemed so poor an object to spend the afternoon on. I kept foreseeing a lame conclusion,—how I should cross the Great Fields, look into Beck Stow's, and then retrace my steps no richer than before. In fact, I expected little of this walk, yet it did pass through the side of my mind that

---

* According to tradition, the third king of Rome (seventh century B.C.). The allusion three lines below is to Gray's "Elegy Written in a Country Churchyard."

somehow, on this very account (my small expectation), it would turn out well, as also the advantage of having some purpose, however small, to be accomplished,—of letting your deliberate wisdom and foresight in the house to some extent direct and control your steps. If you would really take a position outside the street and daily life of men, you must have deliberately planned your course, you must have business which is not your neighbors' business, which they cannot understand. . . . You shall have your affairs, I will have mine. You will spend this afternoon in setting up your neighbor's stove, and be paid for it; I will spend it in gathering the few berries of the *Vaccinium Oxycoccus* which Nature produces here, before it is too late, and *be paid for it also* after another fashion. I have always reaped unexpected and incalculable advantages from carrying out at last, however tardily, any little enterprise which my genius suggested to me long ago as a thing to be done,—some step to be taken, however slight, out of the usual course. . . .

Both a conscious and an unconscious life are good. Neither is good exclusively, for both have the same source. The wisely conscious life springs out of an unconscious suggestion. I have found my account in travelling in having prepared beforehand a list of questions which I would get answered, not trusting to my interest at the moment, and can then travel with the most profit. Indeed, it is by obeying the suggestions of a higher light within you that you escape from yourself and, in the transit, as it were see with the unworn sides of your eye, travel totally new paths. What is that pretended life that does not take up a claim, that does not occupy ground, that cannot build a causeway to its objects, that sits on a bank looking over a bog, singing its desires?

However, it was not with such blasting expectations as these that I entered the swamp. I saw bags of cranberries, just gathered and tied up, on the banks of Beck Stow's Swamp. They must have been raked out of the water, now so high, before they should rot. I left my shoes and stockings on the bank far off and waded barelegged through rigid andromeda and other bushes a long way, to the soft open sphagnous centre of the swamp.

I found these cunning little cranberries lying high and dry on the firm uneven tops of the sphagnum,—their weak vine considerably on one side,—sparsely scattered about the drier edges of the swamp, or sometimes more thickly occupying some little valley a foot or two over, between two mountains of sphagnum. They were of two varieties, judging from the fruit. The one, apparently the ripest, colored most like the common cranberry but more scarlet, *i. e.* yellow-ish-green, blotched or checked with dark scarlet-red, commonly pear-shaped; the other, also pear-shaped, or more bulged out in the middle, thickly and finely dark-spotted or peppered on yellowish-green or straw-colored or pearly ground,—almost exactly like the smilacina and convallaria berries now, except that they are a little larger and not so spherical,—and with a tinge of purple. A singular difference. They both lay very snug in the moss, often the whole of the long (an inch and a half or more) peduncle buried, their vines very inobvious, pro-jecting only one to three inches, so that it was not easy to tell what vine they belonged to, and you were obliged to open the moss carefully with your fingers to ascertain it; while the common large cranberry there, with its stiff erect vine, was commonly lifted above the sphagnum. The grayish speckled variety was particularly novel and pretty, though not easy to detect. It lay here and there snugly sunk in the sphagnum, whose drier parts it exactly resembled in color, just like some kind of swamp sparrows' eggs in their nest. I was obliged with my finger carefully to trace the slender pedicel through the moss to its vine, when I would pluck the whole together. Like jewels worn on, or set in, these sphag-nous breasts of the swamp,—swamp pearls, call them. One or two to a vine and, on an average, three eighths of an inch in diameter. They are so remote from their vines, on their long thread-like peduncles, that they remind you the more forcibly of eggs, and in May I might mistake them for such. These plants are almost parasitic, resting wholly on the sphagnum, in water instead of air. The sphagnum is a living soil for it. It rests on and amid this, on an acre of sponges. They are evidently earlier than the common. A few are quite soft and red-purple.

I waded quite round the swamp for an hour, my bare feet in the cold water beneath, and it was a relief to place them on the warmer surface of the sphagnum. I filled one pocket with each variety, but sometimes, being confused, crossed hands and put them into the wrong pocket.

I enjoyed this cranberrying very much, notwithstanding the wet and cold, and the swamp seemed to be yielding its crop to me alone, for there are none else to pluck it or to value it. I told the proprietor once that they grew here, but he, learning that they were not abundant enough to be gathered for the market, has probably never thought of them since. I am the only person in the township who regards them or knows of them, and I do not regard them in the light of their pecuniary value. I have no doubt I felt richer wading there with my two pockets full, treading on wonders at every step, than any farmer going to market with a hundred bushels which he has raked, or hired to be raked. I got further and further away from the town every moment, and my good genius seemed [to] have smiled on me, leading me hither, and then the sun suddenly came out clear and bright, but it did not warm my feet. I would gladly share my gains, take one, or twenty, into partnership and get this swamp with them, but I do not know an individual whom this berry cheers and nourishes as it does me. When I exhibit it to them I perceive that they take but a momentary interest in it and commonly dismiss it from their thoughts with the consideration that it cannot be profitably cultivated. You could not get a pint at one haul of a rake, and Slocum would not give you much for them. But I love it the better partly for that reason even. I fill a basket with them and keep it several days by my side. If any-body else—any farmer, at least—should spend an hour thus wading about here in this secluded swamp, barelegged, intent on the sphag-num, filling his pocket only, with no rake in his hand and no bag or bushel on the bank, he would be pronounced insane and have a guardian put over him; but if he'll spend his time skimming and watering his milk and selling his small potatoes for large ones, or gen-erally in skinning flints, he will probably be made guardian of some-body else. I have not garnered any rye or oats, but I gathered the wild vine of the Assabet.

IX, 35-41   30 Aug. 1856

LUEBERRIES

First there is the early dwarf blueberry, the smallest of the whortleberry shrubs with us, and the first to ripen its fruit, not commonly an erect shrub, but more or less reclined and drooping, often covering the earth with a sort of dense matting. The twigs are green, the flowers commonly white. Both the shrub and its fruit are the most tender and delicate of any that we have.

The *Vaccinium Canadense* may be considered a more northern form of the same.

Some ten days later comes the high blueberry, or swamp blueberry, the commonest stout shrub of our swamps, of which I have been obliged to cut down not a few when running lines as a surveyor through the low woods. They are a pretty sure indication of water, and, when I see their dense curving tops ahead, I prepare to wade, or for a wet foot. The flowers have an agreeable sweet and berry-promising fragrance, and a handful of them plucked and eaten have a subacid taste agreeable to some palates.

At the same time with the last the common low blueberry is ripe. This is an upright slender shrub with a few long wand-like branches, with green bark and pink-colored recent shoots and glaucous-green leaves. The flowers have a considerable rosy tinge, of a delicate tint.

The last two more densely flowered than the others.

The huckleberry, as you know, is an upright shrub, more or less stout depending on the exposure to the sun and air, with a spreading, bushy top, a dark-brown bark, and red recent shoots, with thick leaves. The flowers are much more red than those of the others. . . .

In May and June all our hills and fields are adorned with a profusion of the pretty little more or less bell-shaped flowers of this family, commonly turned toward the earth and more or less tinged with red or pink and resounding with the hum of insects, each one the forerunner of a berry the most natural, wholesome, palatable that the soil can produce.

The early low blueberry, which I will call "bluet," adopting the name from the Canadians, is probably the prevailing kind of whortleberry in New England, for the high blueberry and huckleberry are unknown in many sections. In many New Hampshire towns a neighboring mountain-top is the common berry-field of many villages, and in the berry season such a summit will be swarming with pickers. A hundred at once will rush thither from all the surrounding villages, with pails and buckets of all descriptions, especially on a Sunday, which is their leisure day. When camping on such ground, thinking myself quite out of the world, I have had my solitude very unexpectedly interrupted by such an advent, and found that the week-days were the only Sabbath-days there.

For a mile or more on such a rocky mountain-top this will be the prevailing shrub, occupying every little shelf from several rods down to a few inches only in width, and then the berries droop in short wreaths over the rocks, sometimes the thickest and largest along a seam in a shelving rock,—either that light mealy-blue, or a shining black, or an intermediate blue, without bloom. When, at that season, I look from Concord toward the blue mountain-tops in the horizon, I am reminded that near at hand they are equally blue with berries.

The mountain-tops of New England, often lifted above the clouds, are thus covered with this beautiful blue fruit, in greater profusion than in any garden.

What though the woods be cut down, this emergency was long ago foreseen and provided for by Nature, and the interregnum is not allowed to be a barren one. She is full of resources: she not only begins instantly to heal that scar, but she consoles (compensates?) and refreshes us with fruits such as the forest did not produce. To console us she heaps our baskets with berries.

The timid or ill-shod confine themselves to the land side, where they get comparatively few berries and many scratches, but the more adventurous, making their way through the open swamp, which the bushes overhang, wading amid the water andromeda and sphagnum, where the surface quakes for a rod around, obtain access to those great drooping clusters of berries which no hand has disturbed. There is no wilder and richer sight than is afforded from such a point of view, of the edge of a blueberry swamp where various wild berries are intermixed.

XIV, 298-302   30 Dec. 1860

FRUITS, WILD AND CULTIVATED

It is glorious to consider how independent man is of all enervating luxuries; and the poorer he is in respect to them, the richer he is. Summer is gone with all its infinite wealth, and still nature is genial to man. Though he no longer bathes in the stream, or reclines on the bank, or plucks berries on the hills, still he beholds the same inaccessible beauty around him. What though he has no juice of the grape stored up for him in cellars; the air itself is wine of an older vintage, and far more sanely exhilarating, than any cellar affords. It is ever some gouty senior and not a blithe child that drinks, or cares for, that so famous wine. . . .

Most of us are still related to our native fields as the navigator to undiscovered islands in the sea. We can any autumn discover a new fruit there which will surprise us by its beauty or sweetness. So long as I saw one or two kinds of berries in my walks whose names I did not know, the proportion of the unknown seemed indefinitely if not infinitely great.

Famous fruits imported from the tropics and sold in our markets—as oranges, lemons, pineapples, and bananas—do not concern me so much as many an unnoticed wild berry whose beauty annually lends a new charm to some wild walk, or which I have found to be palatable to an outdoor taste.

The tropical fruits are for those who dwell within the tropics; their fairest and sweetest parts cannot be exported nor imported. Brought here, they chiefly concern those whose walks are through the market-place. It is not the orange of Cuba, but the checkerberry of the neighboring pasture, that most delights the eye and the palate of the New England child. What if the Concord Social Club, instead of eating oranges from Havana, should spend an hour in admiring the beauty of some wild berry from their own fields which they never attended to before? It is not the foreignness or size or nutritive qualities of a fruit that determine its absolute value.

It is not those far-fetched fruits which the speculator imports that concerns us chiefly, but rather those which you have fetched yourself in your basket from some far hill or swamp, journeying all the long afternoon in the hold of a basket, consigned to your friends at home, the first of the season.

We cultivate imported shrubs in our front yards for the beauty of their berries, when yet more beautiful berries grow unregarded by us in the surrounding fields.

As some beautiful or palatable fruit is perhaps the noblest gift of nature to man, so is a fruit with which a man has in some measure identified himself by cultivating or collecting it one of the most suitable presents to a friend. It was some compensation for Commodore Porter,* who may have introduced some cannon-balls and bombshells into ports where they were not wanted, to have introduced the Valparaiso squash into the United States. I think that this eclipses his military glory.

As I sail the unexplored sea of Concord, many a dell and swamp and wooded hill is my Ceram and Amboyna. . . .

The bitter-sweet of a white oak acorn which you nibble in a bleak November walk over the tawny earth is more to me than a slice of imported pineapple. We do not think much of table-fruits. They are especially for aldermen and epicures. They do not feed the imagination. That would starve on them. These wild fruits, whether eaten or not, are a dessert for the imagination. The south may keep her pineapples, and we will be content with our strawberries. . . .

The value of these wild fruits is not in the mere possession or eating of them, but in the sight or enjoyment of them. The very derivation of the word "fruit" would suggest this. It is from the Latin *fructus*, meaning that which is *used* or *enjoyed*. If it were not so, then going a-berrying and going to market would be nearly synonymous expressions. Of course it is the spirit in which you do a thing which makes it interesting, whether it is sweeping a room or pulling turnips. Peaches are unquestionably a very beautiful and palatable fruit, but

* David Porter (1780–1843), distinguished but controversial naval officer. During the War of 1812, as commander of a squadron in the Pacific, his operations extended from Valparaiso (Chile) to Ceram and Amboyna (islands in the Moluccas, Indonesia), referred to in the next paragraph.

the gathering of them for the market is not nearly so interesting as the gathering of huckleberries for your own use.

XIV, 259-265, 273   23-24, 26 Nov. 1860

GETTING ONE'S OWN FUEL

I have collected and split up now quite a pile of driftwood,—rails and riders and stems and stumps of trees,—perhaps half or three quarters of a tree. It is more amusing, not only to collect this with my boat and bring [it] up from the river on my back, but to split it also, than it would be to speak to a farmer for a load of wood and to saw and split that. Each stick I deal with has a history, and I read it as I am handling it, and, last of all, I remember my adventures in getting it, while it is burning in the winter evening. That is the most interesting part of its history. It has made part of a fence or a bridge, perchance, or has been rooted out of a clearing and bears the marks of fire on it. When I am splitting it, I study the effects of water on it, and, if it is a stump, the curiously winding grain by which it separates into so many prongs,—how to take advantage of its grain and split it most easily. I find that a dry oak stump will split pretty easily in the direction of its diameter, but not at right angles with it or along its circles of growth. I got out some good knees for a boat. Thus one half the value of my wood is enjoyed before it is housed, and the other half is equal to the whole value of an equal quantity of the wood which I buy.

Some of my acquaintances have been wondering why I took all this pains, bringing some nearly three miles by water, and have suggested various reasons for it. I tell them in my despair of making them understand me that it is a profound secret,—which it has proved,—yet I did hint to them that one reason was that I wanted to get it. I take some satisfaction in eating my food, as well as in being nourished by it. I feel well at dinner-time as well as after it. The world will never find out why you don't love to have your bed tucked up for you,—why you will be so perverse. I enjoy more drinking water at a clear spring than out of a goblet at a gentleman's table. I like best the bread which I have baked, the garment which I have made, the shelter which I have constructed, the fuel which I have gathered. . . .

Instead of walking in the wood-market amid sharp-visaged teamsters, I float over dark reflecting waters in which I see mirrored the stumps on the bank, and am dazzled by the beauty of a summer duck. Though I should get no wood, I should get a beauty perhaps more valuable. The price of this my wood, however high, is the very thing which I delight to pay. What I obtain with the most labor—the most water-logged and heaviest wood which I fish up from the bottom and split and dry—warms the most. The greater, too, the distance from which I have conveyed it, the more I am warmed by it in my thought. All the intervening shores glow and are warmed by it as it passes, or as I repass them in my mind. And yet men will cut their wood with sorrow, and burn it with lucifer matches. This was where I drove my team afield, and, instead of the grey-fly,* I heard the wood tortoises even yet rustling through the sedge to the water, or the gray squirrel coursing from maple to maple. . . .

That big swamp white oak limb or tree which I found prostrate in the swamp was longer than my boat and tipped it well. One whole side, the upper, was covered with green hypnum, and the other was partly white with fungi. That green coat adhered when I split it. Immortal wood! that had begun to live again. Others burn unfortunate trees that lose their lives prematurely. These old stumps stand like anchorites and yogees, putting off their earthy garments, more and more sublimed from year to year, ready to be translated, and then they are ripe for my fire. I administer the last sacrament and purification. I find old pitch pine sticks which have lain in the mud at the bottom of the river, nobody knows how long, and weigh them up,—almost as heavy as lead,—float them home, saw and split them. Their pitch, still fat and yellow, has saved them for me, and they burn like candles. . . . I become a connoisseur in wood at last, take only the best.

> VII, 502-503; VIII, 30-31;   20 Oct.; 18 Nov. 1855;
> X, 116   21 Oct. 1857

* Milton, "Lycidas," lines 27-28:
    "We drove afield, and both together heard
    What time the gray-fly winds her sultry horn."

FOREST FIRE

I once set fire to the woods.* Having set out, one April day, to go to the sources of Concord River in a boat with a single companion, meaning to camp on the bank at night or seek a lodging in some neighboring country inn or farmhouse, we took fishing tackle with us that we might fitly procure our food from the stream, Indian-like. At the shoemaker's near the river, we obtained a match, which we had forgotten. Though it was thus early in the spring, the river was low, for there had not been much rain, and we succeeded in catching a mess of fish sufficient for our dinner before we had left the town, and by the shores of Fair Haven Pond we proceeded to cook them. The earth was uncommonly dry, and our fire, kindled far from the woods in a sunny recess in the hillside on the east of the pond, suddenly caught the dry grass of the previous year which grew about the stump on which it was kindled. We sprang to extinguish it at first with our hands and feet, and then we fought it with a board obtained from the boat, but in a few minutes it was beyond our reach; being on the side of a hill, it spread rapidly upward, through the long, dry, wiry grass interspersed with bushes.

"Well, where will this end?" asked my companion. I saw that it might be bounded by Well Meadow Brook on one side, but would, perchance, go to the village side of the brook. "It will go to town," I answered. While my companion took the boat back down the river, I set out through the woods to inform the owners and to raise the town.

---

* The incident occurred on 30 April 1844, shortly before Thoreau's twenty-seventh birthday. His younger friend and companion, Edward Hoar, was a senior at Harvard home on vacation. The *Concord Freeman*, 3 May 1870, said that more than three hundred acres had been burned over, with a property damage of more than $2000. The owners and other townspeople were understandably angry; there was talk of prosecution, which might have materialized except that Hoar's father was a leading citizen. Thoreau's long *Journal* account, written six years after the event, may have been an attempt to rationalize his behavior, but it makes a fine essay. (Harding, *The Days of Thoreau*, 159–161.)

The fire had already spread a dozen rods on every side and went leaping and crackling wildly and irreclaimably toward the wood. That way went the flames with wild delight, and we felt that we had no control over the demonic creature to which we had given birth. We had kindled many fires in the woods before, burning a clear space in the grass, without ever kindling such a fire as this.

As I ran toward the town through the woods, I could see the smoke over the woods behind me marking the spot and progress of the flames. The first farmer whom I met driving a team, after leaving the woods, inquired the cause of the smoke. I told him. "Well," said he, "it is none of my stuff," and drove along. The next I met was the owner in his field, with whom I returned at once to the woods, running all the way. I had already run two miles. When at length we got into the neighborhood of the flames, we met a carpenter who had been hewing timber, an infirm man who had been driven off by the fire, fleeing with his axe. The farmer returned to hasten more assistance. I, who was spent with running, remained. What could I do alone against a front of flame half a mile wide?

I walked slowly through the wood to Fair Haven Cliff, climbed to the highest rock, and sat down upon it to observe the progress of the flames, which were rapidly approaching me, now about a mile distant from the spot where the fire was kindled. Presently I heard the sound of the distant bell giving the alarm, and I knew that the town was on its way to the scene. Hitherto I had felt like a guilty person,—nothing but shame and regret. But now I settled the matter with myself shortly. I said to myself: "Who are these men who are said to be the owners of these woods, and how am I related to them? I have set fire to the forest, but I have done no wrong therein, and now it is as if the lightning had done it. These flames are but consuming their natural food." (It has never troubled me from that day to this more than if the lightning had done it. The trivial fishing was all that disturbed me and disturbs me still.) So shortly I settled it with myself and stood to watch the approaching flames. It was a glorious spectacle, and I was the only one there to enjoy it. The fire now reached the base of the cliff and then rushed up its sides. The squirrels ran before it in blind haste, and three pigeons dashed into the midst of the smoke. The flames flashed up the pines to their tops, as if they were powder.

When I found I was about to be surrounded by the fire, I re-treated and joined the forces now arriving from the town. It took us several hours to surround the flames with our hoes and shovels and by back fires subdue them. In the midst of all I saw the farmer whom I first met, who had turned indifferently away saying it was none of his stuff, striving earnestly to save his corded wood, his stuff, which the fire had already seized and which it after all consumed.

It burned over a hundred acres or more and destroyed much young wood. When I returned home late in the day, with others of my townsmen, I could not help noticing that the crowd who were so ready to condemn the individual who had kindled the fire did not sympathize with the owners of the wood, but were in fact highly elate and as it were thankful for the opportunity which had afforded them so much sport; and it was only half a dozen owners, so called, though not all of them, who looked sour or grieved, and I felt that I had a deeper interest in the woods, knew them better and should feel their loss more, than any or all of them. The farmer whom I had first con-ducted to the woods was obliged to ask me the shortest way back, through his own lot. Why, then, should the half-dozen owners [and] the individuals who set the fire alone feel sorrow for the loss of the wood, while the rest of the town have their spirits raised? Some of the owners, however, bore their loss like men, but other some declared behind my back that I was a "damned rascal;" and a flibbertigibbet or two, who crowed like the old cock, shouted some reminiscences of "burnt woods" from safe recesses for some years after. I have had nothing to say to any of them. The locomotive engine has since burned over nearly all the same ground and more, and in some measure blot-ted out the memory of the previous fire. For a long time after I had learned this lesson I marvelled that while matches and tinder were contemporaries the world was not consumed; why the houses that have hearths were not burned before another day; if the flames were not as hungry now as when I waked them. I at once ceased to re-gard the owners and my own fault,—if fault there was any in the matter,—and attended to the phenomenon before me, determined to make the most of it. To be sure, I felt a little ashamed when I reflected on what a trivial occasion this had happened, that at the time I was no better employed than my townsmen.

That night I watched the fire, where some stumps still flamed at midnight in the midst of the blackened waste, wandering through the woods by myself; and far in the night I threaded my way to the spot where the fire had taken, and discovered the now broiled fish,— which had been dressed,—scattered over the burnt grass.

11, 21-25   1850

EE–HUNTING

To Fair Haven Pond, bee-hunting,—Pratt, Rice, Hastings, and myself, in a wagon.

A fine, clear day after the coolest night and severest frost we have had. The apparatus was, first a simple round tin box about four and a half inches in diameter and one and a half inches deep, containing a piece of empty honeycomb of its own size and form, filling it within a third of an inch of the top; also another, *wooden* box about two and a half inches square every way, with a glass window occupying two thirds the upper side under a slide, with a couple of narrow slits in the wood, each side of the glass, to admit air, but too narrow for the bees to pass; the whole resting on a circular bottom a little larger than the lid of the tin box, with a sliding door in it. We were earnest to go this week, before the flowers were gone, and we feared the frosty night might make the bees slow to come forth.

After we got to the Baker Farm, to one of the open fields near-est to the tree I had marked, the first thing was to find some flowers and catch some honey-bees. We followed up the bank of the brook for some distance, but the goldenrods were all dried up there, and the asters on which we expected to find them were very scarce. By the pond-side we had no better luck, the frosts perhaps having made flow-ers still more scarce there. We then took the path to Clematis Brook on the north of Mt. Misery, where we found a few of the *Diplopap-*

pus linariifolius (savory-leaved aster) and one or two small white
(bushy?) asters, also *A. undulatus* and *Solidago nemoralis* rarely, on
which they work in a sunny place; but there were only two or three
bumblebees, wasps, and butterflies, yellow and small red, on them.
We had no better luck at Clematis Brook. Not a honey-bee could
we find, and we concluded that we were too late,—that the weather
was too cold, and so repaired at once to the tree I had found, a hemlock two feet and a half in diameter on a side-hill a rod from the
pond. I had cut my initials in the bark in the winter, for custom gives
the first finder of the nest a right to the honey and to cut down the
tree to get it and pay the damages, and if he cuts his initials on it no
other hunter will interfere. Not seeing any signs of bees from the
ground, one of the party climbed the tree to where the leading stem
had formerly been broken off, leaving a crotch at about eighteen feet
from the ground, and there he found a small hole into which he
thrust a stick two or three feet down the tree, and dropped it to the
bottom; and, putting in his hand, he took out some old comb. The
bees had probably died.

After eating our lunch, we set out on our return. By the roadside at Walden, on the sunny hillside sloping to the pond, we saw a
large mass of goldenrod and aster several rods square and comparatively fresh. Getting out of our wagon, we found it to be resounding
with the hum of bees. (It was about 1 o'clock.) There were far more
flowers than we had seen elsewhere. Here were bees in great numbers, both bumblebees and honey-bees, as well as butterflies and wasps
and flies. So, pouring a mixture of honey and water into the empty
comb in the tin box, and holding the lid of the tin box in one hand
and the wooden box with the slides shut in the other, we proceeded
to catch the honey-bees by shutting them in suddenly between the lid
of the tin box and the large circular bottom of the wooden one, cutting off the flower-stem with the edge of the lid at the same time. Then,
holding the lid still against the wooden box, we drew the slide in the
bottom and also the slide covering the window at the top, that the
light might attract the bee to pass up into the wooden box. As soon
as he had done so and was buzzing against the glass, the lower slide
was closed and the lid with the flower removed, and more bees were

caught in the same way. Then, placing the other, tin, box containing
the comb filled with honeyed water close under the wooden one, the
slide was drawn again, and the upper slide closed, making it dark;
and in about a minute they went to feeding, as was ascertained by
raising slightly the wooden box. Then the latter was wholly removed,
and they were left feeding or sucking up the honey in broad daylight.
In from two to three minutes one had loaded himself and commenced leaving the box. He would buzz round it back and forth a
foot or more, and then, sometimes, finding that he was too heavily
loaded, alight to empty himself or clean his feet. Then, starting once
more, he would begin to circle round irregularly, at first in a small
circle only a foot or two in diameter, as if to examine the premises
that he might know them again, till, at length, rising higher and higher
and circling wider and wider and swifter and swifter, till his orbit was
ten or twelve feet in diameter and as much from the ground,—though
its centre might be moved to one side,—so that it was very difficult
to follow him, especially if you looked against a wood or the hill, and
you had to lie low to fetch him against the sky (you must operate in
an open space, not in a wood); all this as if to ascertain the course to
his nest; then, in a minute or less from his first starting, he darts off
in a bee-line, that is, as far as I could see him, which might be eight
or ten rods, looking against the sky (and you had to follow his whole
career very attentively indeed to see when and where he went off at a
tangent), in a waving or sinuous (right and left) line, toward his nest.

    We sent forth as many as a dozen bees, which flew in about
three directions, but all toward the village, or where we knew there
were hives. They did not fly so almost absolutely straight as I had
heard, but within three or four feet of the same course for half a dozen
rods, or as far as we could see. Those belonging to one hive all had
to digress to get round an apple tree. As none flew in the right direction for us, we did not attempt to line them. In less than half an hour
the first returned to the box still lying on the wood-pile,—for not
one of the bees on the surrounding flowers discovered it,—and so
they came back, one after another, loaded themselves and departed;
but now they went off with very little preliminary circling, as if assured of their course. We were furnished with little boxes of red,
blue, green, yellow, and white paint, in dry powder, and with a stick

we sprinkled a little of the red powder on the back of one while he was feeding,—gave him a little dab,—and it settled down amid the fuzz of his back and gave him a distinct red jacket. He went off like most of them toward some hives about three quarters of a mile distant, and we observed by the watch the time of his departure. In just twenty-two minutes red jacket came back, with enough of the powder still on his back to mark him plainly. He may have gone more than three quarters of a mile. At any rate, he had a head wind to contend with while laden. They fly swiftly and surely to their nests, never resting by the way, and I was surprised—though I had been informed of it—at the distance to which the village bees go for flowers.

The rambler in the most remote woods and pastures little thinks that the bees which are humming so industriously on the rare wild flowers he is plucking for his herbarium, in some out-of-the-way nook, are, like himself, ramblers from the village, perhaps from his own yard, come to get their honey for his hives. All the honey-bees we saw were on the blue-stemmed golden-rod (*Solidago cæsia*), which is late, lasts long, which emitted a sweet agreeable fragrance, not on the asters. I feel the richer for this experience. It taught me that even the insects in my path are not loafers, but have their special errands. Not merely and vaguely in this world, but in this hour, each is about its business. If, then, there are any sweet flowers still lingering on the hillside, it is known to the bees both of the forest and the village. The botanist should make interest with the bees if he would know when the flowers open and when they close. Those I have named were the only common and prevailing flowers at this time to look for them on.

Our red jacket had performed the voyage in safety; no bird had picked him up. Are the kingbirds gone? Now is the time to hunt bees and take them up, when the combs are full of honey and before the flowers are so scarce that they begin to consume the honey they have stored. . . .

Forty pounds of honey was the most our company had got hereabouts.

We also caught and sent forth a bumblebee, who manœuvred like the others, though we thought he took time to eat some before he loaded himself, and then he was so overloaded and bedaubed that he had to alight after he had started, and it took him several minutes to clean himself.

It is not in vain that the flowers bloom, and bloom late too, in favored spots. To us they are a culture and a luxury, but to bees meat and drink. The tiny bee which we thought lived far away there in a flower-bell in that remote vale, he is a great voyager, and anon he rises up over the top of the wood and sets sail with his sweet cargo straight for his distant haven. How well they know the woods and fields and the haunt of every flower! The flowers, perchance, are widely dispersed, because the sweet which they collect from the atmosphere is rare but also widely dispersed, and the bees are enabled to travel far to find it. A precious burthen, like their color and fragrance, a crop which the heavens bear and deposit on the earth.

IV, 368-374   30 Sept. 1852

THE ARROWHEAD HUNTER

It is now high time to look for arrowheads, etc. I spend many hours every spring gathering the crop which the melting snow and rain have washed bare. When, at length, some island in the meadow or some sandy field elsewhere has been plowed, perhaps for rye, in the fall, I take note of it, and do not fail to repair thither as soon as the earth begins to be dry in the spring. If the spot chances never to have been cultivated before, I am the first to gather a crop from it. The farmer little thinks that another reaps a harvest which is the fruit of his toil. As much ground is turned up in a day by the plow as Indian implements could not have turned over in a month, and my eyes rest on the evidences of an aboriginal life which passed here a thousand years ago perchance. Especially if the knolls in the meadows are washed by a freshet where they have been plowed the previous fall, the soil will be taken away lower down and the stones left,—the arrowheads, etc., and soapstone pottery amid them,—somewhat as gold is washed in a dish or tom.* I landed on two spots this afternoon and picked up a dozen arrowheads. It is one of the regular pursuits

* A contrivance for washing gold-bearing gravel.

of the spring. As much as sportsmen go in pursuit of ducks, and gun-
ners of musquash, and scholars of rare books, and travellers of adventures, and poets of ideas, and all men of money, I go in search of
arrowheads when the proper season comes round again. So I help myself to live worthily, and loving my life as I should. It is a good collyrium to look on the bare earth,—to pore over it so much, getting
strength to all your senses, like Antæus. If I did not find arrowheads, I
might, perchance, begin to pick up crockery and fragments of pipes,—
the relics of a more recent man. Indeed, you can hardly name a more
innocent or wholesome entertainment. . . .

I have not decided whether I had better publish my experience
in searching for arrowheads in three volumes, with plates and an index, or try to compress it into one. These durable implements seem
to have been suggested to the Indian mechanic with a view to my
entertainment in a succeeding period. After all the labor expended on
it, the bolt may have been shot but once perchance, and the shaft
which was devoted to it decayed, and there lay the arrowhead, sinking into the ground, awaiting me. They lie all over the hills with like
expectation, and in due time the husbandman is sent, and, tempted by
the promise of corn or rye, he plows the land and turns them up to
my view. Many as I have found, methinks the last one gives me about
the same delight that the first did. Some time or other, you would say,
it had rained arrowheads, for they lie all over the surface of America.
You may have your peculiar tastes. Certain localities in your town
may seem from association unattractive and uninhabitable to you. You
may wonder that the land bears any money value there, and pity
some poor fellow who is said to survive in that neighborhood. But
plow up a new field there, and you will find the ominpresent arrow-
points strewn over it, and it will appear that the red man, with other
tastes and associations, lived there too. No matter how far from the
modern road or meeting-house, no matter how near. They lie in the
meeting-house cellar, and they lie in the distant cow-pasture. And
some collections which were made a century ago by the curious like
myself have been dispersed again, and they are still as good as new.
You cannot tell the third-hand ones (for they are all second-hand)
from the others, such is their persistent out-of-door durability; for they
were chiefly made to be lost. They are sown, like a grain that is slow

to germinate, broadcast over the earth. Like the dragon's teeth * which
bore a crop of soldiers, these bear crops of philosophers and poets,
and the same seed is just as good to plant again. It is a stone fruit.
Each one yields me a thought. I come nearer to the maker of it than
if I found his bones. His bones would not prove any wit that wielded
them, such as this work of his bones does. It is humanity inscribed on
the face of the earth, patent to my eyes as soon as the snow goes off,
not hidden away in some crypt or grave or under a pyramid. No dis-
gusting mummy, but a clean stone, the best symbol or letter that could
have been transmitted to me.

At every step I see it, and I can easily supply the "Tahatawan"
or "Mantatuket" that might have been written if he had had a clerk.
It is no single inscription on a particular rock, but a footprint—rather
a mindprint—left everywhere, and altogether illegible. No vandals,
however vandalic in their disposition, can be so industrious as to destroy them.

Time will soon destroy the works of famous painters and sculp-
tors, but the Indian arrowhead will balk his efforts and Eternity will
have to come to his aid. They are not fossil bones, but, as it were,
fossil thoughts, forever reminding me of the mind that shaped them.
I would fain know that I am treading in the tracks of human game,—
that I am on the trail of mind,— and these little reminders never fail
to set me right. When I see these signs I know that the subtle spirits
that made them are not far off, into whatever form transmuted. What
if you do plow and hoe amid them, and swear that not one stone shall
be left upon another? They are only the less like to break in that case.
When you turn up one layer you bury another so much the more securely. They are at peace with rust. This arrow-headed character
promises to outlast all others. The larger pestles and axes may, perchance, grow scarce and be broken, but the arrowhead shall, perhaps, never cease to wing its way through the ages to eternity. It was
originally winged for but a short flight, but it still, to my mind's eye,
wings its way through the ages, bearing a message from the hand that

*   Cadmus, a Phoenician prince, killed a dragon sacred to Mars. From
the dragon's teeth, which he sowed in the earth, armed men sprang up
and fought with one another until only five were left. These helped
Cadmus build the city of Thebes.

shot it. Myriads of arrow-points lie sleeping in the skin of the revolv-ing earth, while meteors revolve in space. The footprint, the mind-print of the oldest men. When some Vandal chieftain has razed to the earth the British Museum, and, perchance, the winged bulls from Nineveh shall have lost most if not all of their features, the arrow-heads which the museum contains will, perhaps, find themselves at home again in familiar dust, and resume their shining in new springs upon the bared surface of the earth then, to be picked up for the thousandth time by the shepherd or savage that may be wandering there, and once more suggest their story to him. Indifferent they to British Museums, and, no doubt, Nineveh bulls are old acquaintances of theirs, for they have camped on the plains of Mesopotamia, too, and were buried *with* the winged bulls.

They cannot be said to be lost nor found. Surely their use was not so much to bear its fate to some bird or quadruped, or man, as it was to lie here near the surface of the earth for a perpetual reminder to the generations that come after. As for museums, I think it is better to let Nature take care of our antiquities. These are our antiquities, and they are cleaner to think of than the rubbish of the Tower of London, and they are a more ancient armor than is there. It is a recom-mendation that they are so inobvious,—that they occur only to the eye and thought that chances to be directed toward them. When you pick up an arrowhead and put it in your pocket, it may say: "Eh, you think you have got me, do you? But I shall wear a hole in your pocket at last, or if you put me in your cabinet, your heir or great-grandson will forget me or throw me out the window directly, or when the house falls I shall drop into the cellar, and there I shall lie quite at home again. Ready to be *found* again, eh? Perhaps some new red man that is to come will fit me to a shaft and make me do his bid-ding for a bow-shot. What reck I?"

xii, 88-93   28 Mar. 1859

INDIANS: HUNTER VS. FARMER

For the Indian there is no safety but in the plow. If he would not be pushed into the Pacific, he must seize hold of a plow-tail and let go his bow and arrow, his fish-spear and rifle. This the only Christianity that will save him.

His fate says sternly to him, "Forsake the hunter's life and enter into the agricultural, the second, state of man. Root yourselves a little deeper in the soil, if you would continue to be the occupants of the country." But I confess I have no little sympathy with the Indians and hunter men. They seem to me a distinct and equally respectable people, born to wander and to hunt, and not to be inoculated with the twilight civilization of the white man. . . .

The Indian, perchance, has not made up his mind to some things which the white man has consented to; he has not, in all respects, stooped so low; and hence, though he too loves food and warmth, he draws his tattered blanket about him and follows his fathers, rather than barter his birthright. He dies, and no doubt his Genius judges well for him. But he is not worsted in the fight; he is not destroyed. He only migrates beyond the Pacific to more spacious and happier hunting-grounds.

A race of hunters can never withstand the inroads of a race of husbandmen. The latter burrow in the night into their country and undermine them; and [even] if the hunter is brave enough to resist, his game is timid and has already fled. The rifle alone would never exterminate it, but the plow is a more fatal weapon; it wins the country inch by inch and holds all it gets.

What detained the Cherokees * so long was the 2923 plows which that people possessed; and if they had grasped their handles more firmly, they would never have been driven beyond the Mis-

* The Cherokees were unique among American Indians in the degree to which they adopted the white man's civilization. Before they were forced to migrate from the "Nation" in north Georgia to Indian Territory in Oklahoma (1838), they had adopted farming, frame houses, roads, etc., and had invented a written language.

sissippi. No sense of justice will ever restrain the farmer from plowing up the land which is only hunted over by his neighbors. No hunting-field was ever well fenced and surveyed and its bounds accurately marked, unless it were an English park. It is a property not held by the hunter so much as by the game which roams it, and was never well secured by warranty deeds. The farmer in his treaties says only, or means only, "So far will I plow this summer," for he has not seed corn enough to plant more; but every summer the seed is grown which plants a new strip of the forest.

The African will survive, for he is docile, and is patiently learn-ing his trade and dancing at his labor; but the Indian does not often dance, unless it be the war dance.

1, 443-446   1837-1847

ICE CRYSTALS

This morning we have something between ice and frost on the trees. The whole earth, as last night, but much more, is encased in ice, which on the plowed fields makes a singular icy coat a quarter of an inch or more in thickness. About 9 o'clock A.M., I go to Lee's *via* Hubbard's Wood and Holden's Swamp and the riverside, for the middle is open. The stones and cow-dung, and the walls too, are all cased in ice on the north side. The latter look like alum rocks. This, not frozen mist or frost, but frozen drizzle, collected around the slight-est cores, gives prominence to the least withered herbs and grasses. Where yesterday was a plain, smooth field, appears now a teeming crop of fat, *icy* herbage. The stems of the herbs on their north sides are enlarged from ten to a hundred times. The addition is so uni-versally on the north side that a traveller could not lose the points of compass to-day, though it should [be] never so dark, for every blade of grass would serve to guide him, telling from which side the storm came yesterday. These straight stems of grasses stand up like white batons or sceptres, and make conspicuous foreground to the landscape, from six inches to three feet high. C. [Channing] thought that these fat, icy branches on the withered grass and herbs had no nucleus, but looking closer I showed him the fine black wiry threads on which they impinged, which made him laugh with surprise. The very cow-dung is incrusted, and the clover and sorrel send up a dull-green gleam through their icy coat, like strange plants. The pebbles in the plowed land are seen as through a transparent coating of gum. Some weeds bear the ice in masses, some, like the trumpet-weed and tansy, in balls for each dried flower. What a crash of jewels as you walk! The most careless walker, who never deigned to look at these humble weeds before, cannot help observing them now. This is why the herbage is left to stand dry in the fields all winter. . . . A clear day; a pure sky with cirrhi. In this clear air and bright sunlight, the ice-covered trees have a new beauty, especially the birches along under the edge of Warren's wood on each side of the railroad, bent quite to the ground in every kind of curve. At a distance, as you are approaching them end-wise, they look like white tents of Indians under the edge of the wood. The birch is thus remarkable, perhaps, because from the feathery form of the tree, whose numerous small branches sustain so great a weight, bending it to the ground, and moreover because, from the color of the bark, the core is less observable. The oaks not only are less pliant in the trunk, but have fewer and stiffer twigs and branches. The birches droop over in all directions, like ostrich-feathers. Most wood-paths are im-passable now to a carriage, almost to a foot traveller, from the number of saplings and boughs bent over even to the ground in them. Both sides of the Deep Cut now shine in the sun, as if silver-plated, and the fine spray of a myriad bushes on the edge of the bank sparkle like sil-ver. The telegraph-wire is coated to ten times its size, and looks like a slight fence scalloping along at a distance. Is merged in nature. When we climb the bank at Stow's wood-lot and come upon the piles of freshly split white pine wood (for he is ruthlessly laying it waste), the transparent ice, like a thick varnish, beautifully exhibits the color of the clear, tender, yellowish wood (pumpkin pine?), and its grain, and we pick our way over a bed of pine boughs and twigs a foot or two deep, covering the ground, each twig and needle thickly incrusted with ice into one vast gelid mass, which our feet cronch as if we were walk-ing through the cellar of some confectioner to the gods. The invigorat-ing scent of the recently cut pines refreshes us, if that is any atonement for this devastation. The beauty of the oak-tops all silvered o'er. Especially now do I notice the hips, barberries, and winter-berries, for their red. The red or purplish catkins of the alders are interesting as a winter fruit, and also of the birch. But few birds about. Apparently their granaries are locked up in ice, with which the grasses and buds are coated. Even far in the horizon the pine-tops are turned to firs or spruce by the weight of the ice bending them down, so that they look like a spruce swamp. No two trees wear the ice alike. The short plumes and needles of the spruce make a very pretty and peculiar figure. I see some oaks in the distance which, by their branches being curved or arched downward and massed, are turned into perfect elms, which suggests that that is the peculiarity of the elm. Few if any other trees are thus wisp-like, the branches gracefully drooping. I mean some slender red and white oaks which have recently been left in a clearing. Just apply a weight to the ends of the boughs, which will cause them to droop on all sides, and to each particular twig, which will mass them together, and you have perfect elms. Seen at the right angle, each ice-incrusted stubble shines like a prism with some color of the rainbow,—intense blue, or violet, and red. The smooth field, clad the other day with a low, wiry grass, is now converted into rough stubble-land, where you walk with cronching feet. It is remarkable that the trees ever recover from this burden which bends them to the ground. I should like to weigh a limb of this pitch pine. The character of the tree is changed.

I have now passed the bars and am approaching the Cliffs. The forms and variety of the ice are particularly rich here, there are so many low bushes and weeds before me as I ascend toward the sun, especially very small white pines almost merged in the ice-incrusted ground. All objects, even the apple trees and rails, are to the eye polished silver. It is a perfect land of faery. As if the world were a great frosted cake with its ornaments. The boughs gleam like silver candlesticks. Le Jeune * describes the same in Canada, in 1636, as *"nos grands bois ne paroissoient qu'une forest de cristal."* The silvery ice stands out an inch by three fourths [of] an inch in width on the north side of every twig of these apple trees, with rich irregularities of its own in its edge. When I stoop and examine some fat icy stubble

* Paul LeJeune, Jesuit missionary to Canada and author of *Briève relation du voyage de la Nouvelle France* (1632, 1636).

in my path, I find for all core a ridiculous wiry russet thread, scarce visible, not a hundredth part its size, which breaks with the ice under my feet; yet where this has a minute stub of a branch only a fortieth of an inch in length, there is a corresponding clumsy icy protuberance on the surface an eighth of an inch off. Nature works with such lux-uriance and fury that she follows the least hint. And on the twigs of bushes, for each bud there is a corresponding icy swelling.

The bells are particularly sweet this morning. I hear more, me-thinks, than ever before. How much more religion in their sound, than they ever call men together to! Men obey their call and go to the stove-warmed church, though God exhibits himself to the walker in a frosted bush to-day, as much as in a burning one to Moses of old.

    IV, 436-443   1-2 Jan. 1853

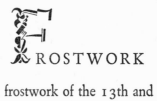

FROSTWORK

That wonderful frostwork of the 13th and 14th was too rare to be neglected,—succeeded as it was, also, by two days of glaze,—but, having company, I lost half the advantage of it. It was remarkable to have a fog for four days in midwinter without wind. We had just had sudden severe cold weather, and I suspect that the fog was occasioned by a warmer air, probably from the sea, coming into contact with our cold ice-and-snow-clad earth. The hoar frost formed of the fog was such a one as I do not remember on such a scale. Apparently as the fog was coarser and far more abundant, it was whiter, less delicate to examine, and of far greater depth than a frostwork formed of dew. We did not have an opportunity to see how it would look in the sun, but seen against the mist or fog it was too fair to be remembered. The trees were the ghosts of trees appearing in their winding-sheets, an intenser white against the comparatively dusky ground of the fog. I rode to Acton in the afternoon of the 13th, and I remember the won-derful avenue of these faery trees which everywhere over-arched my road. The elms, from their form and size, were particularly beautiful. As far as I observed, the frostwork was deepest in the low grounds, especially on the *Salix alba* there. I learn from the papers that this phenomenon prevailed all over this part of the country and attracted the admiration of all. The trees on Boston Common were clad in the same snow-white livery with our Musketaquid trees.

Perhaps the most unusual thing about this phenomenon was its duration. The air seemed almost perfectly still the first day, and I did not perceive that the frosting lost anything; nay, it evidently grew during the first half of the day at least, for it was cold at the same time that it was foggy.

Every one, no doubt, has looked with delight, holding his face low, at that beautiful frostwork which so frequently in winter mornings is seen bristling about the throat of every breathing-hole in the earth's surface. In this case the fog, the earth's breath made visible, was in such abundance that it invested all our vales and hills, and the frostwork, accordingly, instead of being confined to the chinks and crannies of the earth, covered the mightiest trees, so that we, walking beneath them, had the same wonderful prospect and environment that an insect would have in the former case. We, going along our roads, had such a prospect as an insect would have making its way through a chink in the earth which was bristling with hoar frost.

That glaze! I know what it was by my own experience; it was the frozen breath of the earth upon its beard.

But to remember still that frostwork, I do not know why it should build out northward alone, while the twig is perfectly bare on the south side. Is not the phenomenon electrical? You might have guided yourself night or day by observing on which side the twigs it was. Closely examined, it is a coarse aggregation of thin flakes or leafets.

Standing a little east or west of an evergreen, you saw considerable of its greenness, especially the second day, when much had fallen; but in each case successively you were agreeably disappointed when you arrived exactly north of the tree and saw it to best advantage.

Take the most rigid tree, the whole effect is peculiarly soft and spirit-like, for there is no marked edge or outline. How could you draw the outline of these snowy fingers seen against the fog, without exaggeration? There is no more a boundary-line or circumference that can be drawn, than a diameter. Hardly could the New England farmer drive to market under these trees without feeling that his sense of beauty was addressed. He would be aware that the phenomenon called beauty was become visible, if one were at leisure or had had the right culture to appreciate it. A miller with whom I rode actually remarked on the beauty of the trees; and a farmer told me in all sincerity that, having occasion to go into Walden Woods in his sleigh, he thought he never saw anything so beautiful in all his life, and if there had been men there who knew how to write about it, it would have been a great occasion for them.

Many times I thought that if the particular tree, commonly an elm, under which I was walking or riding were the only one like it in the country, it would [be] worth a journey across the continent to see it. Indeed, I have no doubt that such journeys would be undertaken on hearing a true account of it. But, instead of being confined to a single tree, this wonder was as cheap and common as the air itself. Every man's wood-lot was a miracle and surprise to him, and for those who could not go so far there were the trees in the street and the weeds in the yard. It was much like (in effect) that snow that lodges on the fine dead twigs on the lower part of a pine wood, resting there in the twilight commonly only till it has done snowing and the wind arises. But in this case it did not rest *on* the twig, but grew out from it horizontally, and it was not confined to the lowest twigs, but covered the whole forest and every surface.

Looking down the street, you might say that the scene differed from the ordinary one as frosted cake differs from plain bread. In some moods you might suspect that it was the work of enchantment. Some magician had put your village into a crucible and it had crystallized thus.

XI, 402-406   18 Jan. 1859

SNOW FLAKES

The thin snow now driving from the north and lodging on my coat consists of those beautiful star crystals, not cottony and chubby spokes, as on the 13th December, but thin and partly transparent crystals. They are about a tenth of an inch in diameter, perfect little wheels with six spokes without a tire, or rather with six perfect little leafets, fern-like, with a distinct straight and slender midrib, raying from the centre. On each side of each midrib there is a transparent thin blade with a crenate edge. . . . How full of the creative genius is the air in which these are generated! I should hardly admire more if real stars fell and lodged on my coat. Nature is full of genius, full of the divinity; so that not a snowflake escapes its fashioning hand. Nothing is cheap and coarse, neither dewdrops nor snowflakes. Soon the storm increases,—it was already very severe to face,—and the snow comes finer, more white and powdery. Who knows but this is the original form of all snowflakes, but that when I observe these crystal stars falling around me they are but just generated in the low mist next the earth? I am nearer to the source of the snow, its primal, auroral, and golden hour or infancy, but commonly the flakes reach us travel-worn and agglomerated, comparatively without order or beauty, far down in their fall, like men in their advanced age.

As for the circumstances under which this phenomenon occurs, it is quite cold, and the driving storm is bitter to face, though very little snow is falling. It comes almost horizontally from the north. Methinks this kind of snow never falls in any quantity.

A divinity must have stirred within them before the crystals did thus shoot and set. Wheels of the storm-chariots. The same law that shapes the earth-star shapes the snow-star. As surely as the petals of a flower are fixed, each of these countless snow-stars comes whirling to earth, pronouncing thus, with emphasis, the number six. Order, κόσμος [cosmos].

On the Saskatchewan, when no man of science is there to behold, still down they come, and not the less fulfill their destiny, perchance melt at once on the Indian's face. What a world we live in! where myriads of these little disks, so beautiful to the most prying eye, are whirled down on every traveller's coat, the observant and the unobservant, and on the restless squirrel's fur, and on the far-stretching fields and forests, the wooded dells, and the mountain-tops. Far, far away from the haunts of man, they roll down some little slope, fall over and come to their bearings, and melt or lose their beauty in the mass, ready anon to swell some little rill with their contribution, and so, at last, the universal ocean from which they came. There they lie, like the wreck of chariot-wheels after a battle in the skies. Meanwhile the meadow mouse shoves them aside in his gallery, the schoolboy casts them in his snowball, or the woodman's sled glides smoothly over them, these glorious spangles, the sweeping of heaven's floor. And they all sing, melting as they sing of the mysteries of the number six,—six, six, six. He takes up the water of the sea in his hand, leaving the salt; He disperses it in mist through the skies; He recollects and sprinkles it like grain in six-rayed snowy stars over the earth, there to lie till He dissolves its bonds again.

VIII, 87-89   5 Jan. 1856

SEEING THE STARS

I am somewhat oppressed and saddened by the sameness and apparent poverty of the heavens,—that these irregular and few geometrical figures which the constellations make are no other than those seen by the Chaldean shepherds. The same simplicity and unchangeableness which commonly impresses me by wealth sometimes affects me as barrenness. I pine for a new world in the heavens as well as on the earth, and though it is some consolation to hear of the wilderness of stars and systems invisible to the naked eye, yet the sky does not make that impression of variety and wildness that even the forest does, as it ought. It makes an impression, rather, of simplicity and unchangeableness, as of eternal laws; this being the same constellation which the shepherds saw, and obedient still to the same law. It does not affect me as that unhandselled wilderness which the forest is. I seem to see it pierced with visual rays from a thousand observatories. It is more the domain of science than of poetry. But it is the stars as not known to science that I would know, the stars which the lonely traveller knows.

The Chaldean * shepherds saw not the same stars which I see,

* Chaldeans are equated in the Bible with astronomers, astrologers, and magicians. Thoreau may also be alluding to those shepherds who followed the star to Christ's birthplace in Bethlehem.

and if I am elevated in the least toward the heavens, I do not accept their classification of them. I am not to be distracted by the names which they have imposed. The sun which I know is not Apollo, nor is the evening star Venus. The heavens should be as new, at least, as the world is new. This classification of the stars is old and musty; it is as if a mildew had taken place in the heavens, as if the stars so closely packed had heated and moulded there. If they appear fixed, it is because that hitherto men have been thus necessitated to see them. I see not merely old but new testaments in the skies. Do not I stand as near the stars as the Chaldean shepherds? The heavens commonly look as dry and meagre as our astronomies are,—mere troops, as the latter are catalogues, of stars. The Milky Way yields no milk.

A few good anecdotes is our science, with a few imposing statements respecting distance and size, and little or nothing about the stars as they concern man; teaching how he may survey a country or sail a ship, and not how he may steer his life. Astrology contained the germ of a higher truth than this. It may happen that the stars are more significant and truly celestial to the teamster than to the astronomer. Nobody sees the stars now. They study astronomy at the district school, and learn that the sun is ninety-five millions [of miles] distant, and the like,—a statement which never made any impression on me, because I never walked it, and which I cannot be said to believe. But the sun shines nevertheless. Though observatories are multiplied, the heavens receive very little attention. The naked eye may easily see farther than the armed. It depends on who looks through it. No superior telescope to this has been invented. In those big ones the recoil is equal to the force of the discharge. The poet's eye in a fine frenzy rolling ranges from earth to heaven,* but this the astronomer's does not often do. It does not see far beyond the dome of the observatory.

Compared with the visible phenomena of the heavens, the anecdotes of science affect me as trivial and petty. Man's eye is the true star-finder, the comet-seeker. As I sat looking out the window the other evening just after dark, I saw the lamp of a freight-train, and, near by, just over the train, a bright star, which looked exactly like the former, as if it belonged to a different part of the same train. It

---

* *A Midsummer-Night's Dream*, IV.2.49–50 (slightly revised to fit Thoreau's context).

was difficult to realize that the one was a feeble oil lamp, the other
a world.

IV, 469-471   21 Jan. 1853

THE TELEGRAPH HARP

Yesterday and to-day the stronger winds of autumn have begun
to blow, and the telegraph harp has sounded loudly. I heard it especially in the Deep Cut this afternoon, the tone varying with the tension
of different parts of the wire. The sound proceeds from near the posts,
where the vibration is apparently more rapid. I put my ear to one of
the posts, and it seemed to me as if every pore of the wood was filled
with music, labored with the strain,—as if every fibre was affected and
being seasoned or timed, rearranged according to a new and more
harmonious law. Every swell and change or inflection of tone pervaded and seemed to proceed from the wood, the divine tree or wood,
as if its very substance was transmuted. What a recipe for preserving
wood, perchance,—to keep it from rotting,—to fill its pores with music! How this wild tree from the forest, stripped of its bark and set up
here, rejoices to transmit this music! When no music proceeds from
the wire, on applying my ear I hear the hum within the entrails of the
wood,—the oracular tree acquiring, accumulating, the prophetic fury.

The resounding wood! how much the ancients would have
made of it! To have a harp on so great a scale, girdling the very earth,
and played on by the winds of every latitude and longitude, and that
harp were, as it were, the manifest blessing of heaven on a work of
man's! Shall we not add a tenth Muse to the immortal Nine? And
that the invention thus divinely honored and distinguished—on which
the Muse has condescended to smile—is this magic medium of com-
munication for mankind!

To read that the ancients stretched a wire round the earth, at-
taching it to the trees of the forest, by which they sent messages by
one named Electricity, father of Lightning and Magnetism, swifter
far than Mercury, and stern commands of war and news of peace, and
that the winds caused this wire to vibrate so that it emitted a harp-like

and æolian music in all the lands through which it passed, as if to express the satisfaction of the gods in this invention. Yet this is fact, and
we have yet attributed the invention to no god.

III, 11·12   22 Sept. 1851

THE IDEAL AND THE REAL

Looking from the hog-pasture over the valley of Spencer Brook
westward, we see the smoke rising from a huge chimney above a gray
roof amid the woods, at a distance, where some family is preparing
its evening meal. There are few more agreeable sights than this to the
pedestrian traveller. No cloud is fairer to him than that little bluish
one which issues from the chimney. It suggests all of domestic felicity
beneath. There beneath, we suppose, that life is lived of which we
have only dreamed. In our minds we clothe each unseen inhabitant
with all the success, with all the serenity, which we can conceive of.
If old, we imagine him serene; if young, hopeful. Nothing can exceed the perfect peace which reigns there. We have only to see a gray
roof with its plume of smoke curling up amid the trees to have this
faith. There we suspect no coarse haste or bustle, but serene labors
which proceed at the same pace with the declining day. *There* is no
hireling in the barn nor in the kitchen. Why does any distant prospect
ever charm us? Because we instantly and inevitably imagine a life to
be lived there such as is not lived elsewhere, or where we are. We
presume that success is the rule. We forever carry a perfect sampler in
our minds. Why are distant valleys, why lakes, why mountains in the
horizon, ever fair to us? Because we realize for a moment that they
may be the home of man, and that man's life may be in harmony with
them. Shall I say that we thus forever delude ourselves? We do not
suspect that *that* farmer goes to the depot with his milk. *There* the
milk is not watered. We are constrained to imagine a life in harmony
with the scenery and the hour. The sky and clouds, and the earth
itself, with their beauty forever preach to us, saying, Such an abode
we offer you, to such and such a life we encourage you. *There* is not
haggard poverty and harassing debt. There is not intemperance, mo-

roseness, meanness, or vulgarity. Men go about sketching, painting
landscapes, or writing verses which celebrate man's opportunities. To
go into an actual farmer's family at evening, see the tired laborers
come in from their day's work thinking of their wages, the sluttish help
in the kitchen and sink-room, the indifferent stolidity and patient
misery which only the spirits of the youngest children rise above,—
that suggests one train of thoughts. To look down on that roof from a
distance in an October evening, when its smoke is ascending peacefully
to join the kindred clouds above,—that suggests a different train of
thoughts. We think that we see these fair abodes and are elated beyond
all speech, when we see only our own roofs, perchance. We are ever
busy hiring house and lands and peopling them in our imaginations.
There is no beauty in the sky, but in the eye that sees it. Health, high
spirits, serenity, these are the great landscape-painters. Turners,
Claudes, Rembrandts are nothing to them. We never see any beauty
but as the garment of some virtue. Men love to walk in those picture-
galleries still, because they have not quite forgotten their early dreams.
When I see only the roof of a house above the woods and do not know
whose it is, I presume that one of the worthies of the world dwells
beneath it, and for a season I am exhilarated at the thought. I would
fain sketch it that others may share my pleasure. But commonly, if I
see or know the occupant, I am affected as by the sight of the almshouse or hospital.

Consider the infinite promise of a man, so that the sight of his
roof at a distance suggests an idyll or pastoral, or of his grave an Elegy
in a Country Churchyard. How all poets have idealized the farmer's
life! What graceful figures and unworldly characters they have assigned
to them! Serene as the sky, emulating nature with their calm and peaceful lives. As I come by a farmer's to-day, the house of one who died
some two years ago, I see the decrepit form of one whom he had engaged to "carry through," taking his property at a venture, feebly tying
up a bundle of fagots with his knee on it, though time is fast loosening
the bundle that he is. When I look down on that roof I am not reminded of the mortgage which the village bank has on that property,
—that that family long since sold itself to the devil and wrote the deed
with their blood. I am not reminded that the old man I see in the yard
is one who has lived beyond his calculated time, whom the young one

is merely "carrying through" in fulfillment of his contract; that the man at the pump is watering the milk. I am not reminded of the idiot that sits by the kitchen fire.

XII, 366-369   3 Oct. 1859

TWO KINDS OF GOLD

Another, the tenth of these memorable days. We have had some fog the last two or three nights, and this forenoon it was slow to disperse, dog-day-like, but this afternoon it is warmer even than yesterday. I should like it better if it were not so warm. I am glad to reach the shade of Hubbard's Grove; the coolness is refreshing. It is indeed a golden autumn. These ten days are enough to make the reputation of any climate. A tradition of these days might be handed down to posterity. They deserve a notice in history, in the history of Concord. All kinds of crudities have a chance to get ripe this year. Was there ever such an autumn? And yet there was never such a panic and hard times in the commercial world. The merchants and banks are suspending and failing all the country over,* but not the sand-banks, solid and warm, and streaked with bloody blackberry vines. You may run upon them as much as you please,—even as the crickets do, and find their account in it. They are the stockholders in these banks, and I hear them creaking their content. You may see them on change any warmer hour. In these banks, too, and such as these, are my funds deposited, a fund of health and enjoyment. Their (the crickets) prosperity and happiness and, I trust, mine do not depend on whether the New York banks suspend or no. We do not rely on such slender security as the thin paper of the Suffolk Bank. To put your trust in such a bank is to be swallowed up and undergo suffocation. Invest, I say, in these country banks. Let your capital be simplicity and contentment. Withered goldenrod (*Solidago nemoralis*) is no failure, like a broken bank, and yet in its most golden season nobody counterfeits it. Nature needs no counterfeit-detector. I have no compassion for, nor any sympathy with, this miserable state of things. Banks built of granite, after some Grecian

* The Panic of 1857.

or Roman style, with their porticoes and their safes of iron, are not so permanent, and cannot give me so good security for capital invested in them, as the heads of withered hardhack in the meadow. I do not suspect the solvency of these. I know who is their president and cashier.

I take all these walks to every point of the compass, and it is always harvest-time with me. I am always gathering my crop from these woods and fields and waters, and no man is in my way or interferes with me. My crop is not their crop. To-day I see them gathering in their beans and corn, and they are a spectacle to me, but are soon out of my sight. I am not gathering beans and corn. Do they think there are no fruits but such as these? I am a reaper; I am not a gleaner. I go reaping, cutting as broad a swath as I can, and bundling and stacking up and carrying it off from field to field, and no man knows or cares. My crop is not sorghum nor Davis seedlings. There are other crops than these, whose seed is not distributed by the Patent Office.* I go abroad over the land each day to get the best I can find, and that is never carted off even to the last day of November, and I do not go as a gleaner.

The farmer has always come to the field after some material thing; that is not what a philosopher goes there for.

x, 92-94   13 Oct. 1857

PRESERVING NATURAL BEAUTY

Each town should have a park, or rather a primitive forest, of five hundred or a thousand acres, where a stick should never be cut for fuel, a common possession forever, for instruction and recreation. We hear of cow-commons and ministerial lots, but we want *men-commons* and lay lots, inalienable forever. Let us keep the New World *new*, preserve all the advantages of living in the country. There is meadow and pasture and wood-lot for the town's poor. Why not a forest and huckleberry-field for the town's rich? All Walden Wood

---

* During the 1850's the Patent Office, as part of the Department of the Interior, performed some of the functions later taken over by the Department of Agriculture (set up in 1862).

might have been preserved for our park forever, with Walden in its midst, and the Easterbrooks Country, an unoccupied area of some four square miles, might have been our huckleberry-field. If any owners of these tracts are about to leave the world without natural heirs who need or deserve to be specially remembered, they will do wisely to abandon their possession to all, and not will them to some individual who perhaps has enough already. As some give to Harvard College or another institution, why might not another give a forest or huckleberry-field to Concord? A town is an institution which deserves to be remembered. We boast of our system of education, but why stop at schoolmasters and schoolhouses? We are all schoolmasters, and our schoolhouse is the universe. To attend chiefly to the desk or school-house while we neglect the scenery in which it is placed is absurd. If we do not look out we shall find our fine schoolhouse standing in a cow-yard at last.

What are the natural features which make a township hand-some? A river, with its waterfalls and meadows, a lake, a hill, a cliff or individual rocks, a forest, and ancient trees standing singly. Such things are beautiful; they have a high use which dollars and cents never represent. If the inhabitants of a town were wise, they would seek to preserve these things, though at a considerable expense; for such things educate far more than any hired teachers or preachers, or any at present recognized system of school education. I do not think him fit to be the founder of a state or even of a town who does not foresee the use of these things, but legislates chiefly for oxen, as it were. . . .

It would be worth the while if in each town there were a com-mittee appointed to see that the beauty of the town received no detri-ment. If we have the largest boulder in the county, then it should not belong to an individual, nor be made into door-steps.

As in many countries precious metals belong to the crown, so here more precious natural objects of rare beauty should belong to the public.

Not only the channel but one or both banks of every river should be a public highway. The only use of a river is not to float on it.

Think of a mountain-top in the township—even to the minds of the Indians a sacred place—only accessible through private grounds! a temple, as it were, which you cannot enter except by trespassing and at the risk of letting out or letting in somebody's cattle! in fact the temple itself in this case private property and standing in a man's cow-yard,—for such is commonly the case! . . .

It is true we as yet take liberties and go across lots, and steal, or "hook," a good many things, but we naturally take fewer liberties every year, as we meet with more resistance. In old countries, as Eng-land, going across lots is out of the question. You must walk in some beaten path or other, though it may [be] a narrow one. We are tend-ing to the same state of things here, when practically a few will have grounds of their own, but most will have none to walk over but what the few allow them.

Thus we behave like oxen in a flower-garden. The true fruit of Nature can only be plucked with a delicate hand not bribed by any earthly reward, and a fluttering heart. No hired man can help us to gather this crop.

How few ever get beyond feeding, clothing, sheltering, and warming themselves in this world, and begin to treat themselves as human beings,—as intellectual and moral beings! Most seem not to see any further,—not to see over the ridge-pole of their barns,—or to be exhausted and accomplish nothing more than a full barn, though it may be accompanied by an empty head. They venture a little, run some risks, when it is a question of a larger crop of corn or potatoes; but they are commonly timid and count their coppers, when the ques-tion is whether their children shall be educated. He who has the reputation of being the thriftiest farmer and making the best bargains is really the most thriftless and makes the worst. It is safest to invest in knowledge, for the probability is that you can carry that with you wherever you go.

But most men, it seems to me, do not care for Nature and would sell their share in all her beauty, as long as they may live, for a stated sum—many for a glass of rum. Thank God, men cannot as yet fly, and lay waste the sky as well as the earth! We are safe on that side for the present. It is for the very reason that some do not care for those things that we need to continue to protect all from the vandalism of a few.

XII, 387; XIV, 304-307   15 Oct. 1859; 3 Jan. 1861

VOCATIONLESS VACATION

I must not lose any of my freedom by being a farmer and land-holder. Most who enter on any profession are doomed men. The world might as well sing a dirge over them forthwith. The farmer's muscles are rigid. He can do one thing long, not many well. His pace seems determined henceforth; he never quickens it. A very rigid Nemesis is his fate. When the right wind blows or a star calls, I can leave this arable and grass ground, without making a will or settling my estate. I would buy a farm as freely as a silken streamer. Let me not think my front windows must face east henceforth because a particular hill slopes that way. My life must undulate still. I will not feel that my wings are clipped when once I have settled on ground which the law calls my own, but find new pinions grown to the old, and talaria to my feet beside. . . .

I only ask a clean seat. I will build my lodge on the southern slope of some hill, and take there the life the gods send me. Will it not be employment enough to accept gratefully all that is yielded me between sun and sun? Even the fox digs his own burrow. If my jacket and trousers, my boots and shoes, are fit to worship God in, they will do. Won't they, Deacon Spaulding?

. . . My life will wait for nobody, but is being matured still irresistibly while I go about the streets and chaffer with this man and that to secure it a living. It will cut its own channel, like the mountain stream, which by the longest ridges and by level prairies is not kept from the sea finally. So flows a man's life, and will reach the sea water, if not by an earthy channel, yet in dew and rain, overleaping all barriers, with rainbows to announce its victory. It can wind as cunningly and unerringly as water that seeks its level; and shall I complain if the gods make it meander? This staying to buy me a farm is as if the Mississippi should stop to chaffer with a clamshell.

What have I to do with plows? I cut another furrow than you see.

I, 242-245   27 Mar.-7 Apr. 1841

LIVING IN THE IMAGINATION

The world is a fit theatre to-day in which any part may be acted. There is this moment proposed to me every kind of life that men lead anywhere, or that imagination can paint. By another spring I may be a mail-carrier in Peru, or a South African planter, or a Siberian exile, or a Greenland whaler, or a settler on the Columbia River, or a Canton merchant, or a soldier in Florida, or a mackerel-fisher off Cape Sable, or a Robinson Crusoe in the Pacific, or a silent navigator of any sea. So wide is the choice of parts, what a pity if the part of Hamlet be left out!

I am freer than any planet; no complaint reaches round the world. I can move away from public opinion, from government, from religion, from education, from society. Shall I be reckoned a ratable poll in the county of Middlesex, or be rated at one spear under the palm trees of Guinea? Shall I raise corn and potatoes in Massachusetts, or figs and olives in Asia Minor? sit out the day in my office in State Street, or ride it out on the steppes of Tartary? For my Brobdingnag I may sail to Patagonia; for my Lilliput, to Lapland. In Arabia and Persia, my day's adventures may surpass the Arabian Nights' Entertainments. I may be a logger on the head waters of the Penobscot, to be recorded in fable hereafter as an amphibious river-god, by as sounding a name as Triton or Proteus; carry furs from Nootka to China, and so be more renowned than Jason and his golden fleece; or go on a South Sea exploring expedition, to be hereafter recounted along with the periplus of Hanno.* I may repeat the adventures of Marco Polo or Mandeville.

These are but a few of my chances, and how many more things may I do with which there are none to be compared!

Thank Fortune, we are not rooted to the soil, and here is not all the world. The buckeye does not grow in New England; the mockingbird is rarely heard here. Why not keep pace with the day, and not allow of a sunset nor fall behind the summer and the migra-

---

*   A Carthaginian navigator, c. 500 B.C. The two explorers mentioned in the next sentence can be found in any standard dictionary.

tion of birds? Shall we not compete with the buffalo, who keeps pace with the seasons, cropping the pastures of the Colorado till a greener and sweeter grass awaits him by the Yellowstone? The wild goose is more a cosmopolite than we; he breaks his fast in Canada, takes a luncheon in the Susquehanna, and plumes himself for the night in a Louisiana bayou. The pigeon carries an acorn in his crop from the King of Holland's to Mason and Dixon's line. Yet we think if rail fences are pulled down and stone walls set up on our farms, bounds are henceforth set to our lives and our fates decided. If you are chosen town clerk, forsooth, you can't go to Tierra del Fuego this summer.

But what of all this? A man may gather his limbs snugly within the shell of a mammoth squash, with his back to the northeastern boundary, and not be unusually straitened after all. Our limbs, indeed, have room enough, but it is our souls that rust in a corner. Let us migrate interiorly without intermission, and pitch our tent each day nearer the western horizon. The really fertile soils and luxuriant prairies lie on this side the Alleghanies. There has been no Hanno of the affections. Their domain is untravelled ground, to the Mogul's dominions.

I, 129-130   21 Mar. 1840

THE ART OF SPENDING A DAY

We are receiving our portion of the infinite. The art of life! Was there ever anything memorable written upon it? By what disciplines to secure the most life, with what care to watch our thoughts. To observe what transpires, not in the street, but in the mind and heart of me! I do not remember any page which will tell me how to spend this afternoon. I do not so much wish to know how to economize time as how to spend it, by what means to grow rich, that the day may not have been in vain.

What if one moon has come and gone with its world of poetry, its weird teachings, its oracular suggestions? So divine a creature, freighted with hints for me, and I not use her! One moon gone by unnoticed!! Suppose you attend to the hints, to the suggestions, which the moon makes for one month,—commonly in vain,—will they not be very different from anything in literature or religion or philosophy?

The scenery, when it is truly seen, reacts on the life of the seer. How to live. How to get the most life. As if you were to teach the young hunter how to entrap his game. How to extract its honey from the flower of the world. That is my every-day business. I am as busy as a bee about it. I ramble over all fields on that errand, and am never so happy as when I feel myself heavy with honey and wax. I am like a bee searching the livelong day for the sweets of nature. Do I not impregnate and intermix the flowers, produce rare and finer varieties by transferring my eyes from one to another? I do as naturally and as joyfully, with my own humming music, seek honey all the day. With what honeyed thought any experience yields me I take a bee line to my cell. It is with flowers I would deal. Where is the flower, there is the honey,—which is perchance the nectareous portion of the fruit,—there is to be the fruit, and no doubt flowers are thus colored and painted to attract and guide the bee. So by the dawning or radiance of beauty are we advertised where is the honey and the fruit of thought, of discourse, and of action. We are first attracted by the beauty of the flower, before we discover the honey which is a foretaste of the future fruit. Did not the young Achilles (?) spend his youth learning how to hunt? The art of spending a day. If it is possible that we may be addressed, it behooves us to be attentive. If by watching all day and all night I may detect some trace of the Ineffable, then will it not be worth the while to watch? Watch and pray without ceasing,* but not necessarily in sadness. Be of good cheer. Those Jews were too sad: to another people a still deeper revelation may suggest only joy. Don't I know what gladness is? Is it but the reflex of sadness, its back side? In the Hebrew gladness, I hear but too distinctly still the sound of sadness retreating. Give me a gladness which has never given place to sadness.

I am convinced that men are not well employed, that this is not the way to spend a day. If by patience, if by watching, I can secure one new ray of light, can feel myself elevated for an instant upon Pisgah, the world which was dead prose to me become living and divine, shall I not watch ever? shall I not be a watchman henceforth? If by

* Matthew 26.41.

watching a whole year on the city's walls I may obtain a communica-
tion from heaven, shall I not do well to shut up my shop and turn a
watchman? Can a youth, a man, do more wisely than to go where his
life is to [be] found? As if I had suffered that to be rumor which may
be verified. We are surrounded by a rich and fertile mystery. May we
not probe it, pry into it, employ ourselves about it, a little? To devote
your life to the discovery of the divinity in nature or to the eating of
oysters, would they not be attended with very different results? . . .

To watch for, describe, all the divine features which I detect
in Nature.

My profession is to be always on the alert to find God in nature,
to know his lurking-places, to attend all the oratorios, the operas, in
nature.

11, 469-472   7 Sept. 1851

THE TRANSIENT BEAUTY OF THE WORLD

When some rare northern bird like the pine grosbeak is seen
thus far south in the winter, he does not suggest poverty, but dazzles
us with his beauty. There is in them a warmth akin to the warmth that
melts the icicle. Think of these brilliant, warm-colored, and richly war-
bling birds, birds of paradise, dainty-footed, downy-clad, in the midst of
a New England, a Canadian winter. The woods and fields, now somewhat solitary, being deserted by their more tender summer residents, are
now frequented by these rich but delicately tinted and hardy northern
immigrants of the air. Here is no imperfection to be suggested. The
winter, with its snow and ice, is not an evil to be corrected. It is as it
was designed and made to be, for the artist has had leisure to add
beauty to use. My acquaintances, angels from the north. I had a vision
thus prospectively of these birds as I stood in the swamps. I saw this
familiar—too *familiar*—fact at a different angle, and I was charmed
and haunted by it. But I could only attain to be thrilled and enchanted,
as by the sound of a strain of music dying away. I had seen into para-
disaic regions, with their air and sky, and I was no longer wholly or

merely a denizen of this vulgar earth. Yet had I hardly a foothold
there. I was only sure that I was charmed, and no mistake. It is only
necessary to behold thus the least fact or phenomenon, however familiar, from a point a hair's breadth aside from our habitual path or
routine, to be overcome, enchanted by its beauty and significance.
Only what we have touched and worn is trivial,—our scurf, repetition,
tradition, conformity. To perceive freshly, with fresh senses, is to be
inspired. Great winter itself looked like a precious gem, reflecting
rainbow colors from one angle.

My body is all sentient. As I go here or there, I am tickled by
this or that I come in contact with, as if I touched the wires of a
battery. I can generally recall—have fresh in my mind—several
scratches last received. These I continually recall to mind, reimpress,
and harp upon. The age of miracles is each moment thus returned.
Now it is wild apples, now river reflections, now a flock of lesser redpolls. In winter, too, resides immortal youth and perennial summer.
Its head is not silvered; its cheek is not blanched but has a ruby tinge
to it.

If any part of nature excites our pity, it is for ourselves we grieve,
for there is eternal health and beauty. We get only transient and partial
glimpses of the beauty of the world. Standing at the right angle, we
are dazzled by the colors of the rainbow in colorless ice. From the
right point of view, every storm and every drop in it is a rainbow.
Beauty and music are not mere traits and exceptions. They are the
rule and character. It is the exception that we see and hear. Then I
try to discover what it was in the vision that charmed and translated me.
What if we could daguerreotype our thoughts and feelings! for I
am surprised and enchanted often by some quality which I cannot
detect. I have seen an attribute of another world and condition of
things. It is a wonderful fact that I should be affected, and thus deeply
and powerfully, more than by aught else in all my experience,—that
this fruit should be borne in me, sprung from a seed finer than the
spores of fungi, floated from other atmospheres! finer than the dust
caught in the sails of vessels a thousand miles from land! Here the
invisible seeds settle, and spring, and bear flowers and fruits of immortal beauty.

HE DARK ROAD*

There are some things of which I cannot at once tell whether I have dreamed them or they are real; as if they were just, perchance, establishing, or else losing, a real basis in my world. This is especially the case in the early morning hours, when there is a gradual transition from dreams to waking thoughts, from illusions to actualities, as from darkness, or perchance moon and star light, to sunlight. Dreams are real, as is the light of the stars and moon, and theirs is said to be a *dreamy* light. Such early morning thoughts as I speak of occupy a debatable ground between dreams and waking thoughts. They are a sort of permanent dream in my mind. At least, until we have for some time changed our position from prostrate to erect, and commenced or faced some of the duties of the day, we cannot tell what we have dreamed from what we have actually experienced.

This morning, for instance, for the twentieth time at least, I thought of that mountain in the easterly part of our town (where no high hill actually is) which once or twice I had ascended, and often allowed my thoughts alone to climb. I now contemplate it in my mind as a familiar thought which I have surely had for many years from time to time, but whether anything could have reminded me of it in the middle of yesterday, whether I ever before remembered it in broad daylight, I doubt. I can now eke out the vision I had of it this morning with my old and yesterday forgotten dreams.

My way up used to lie through a dark and unfrequented wood at its base,—I cannot now tell exactly, it was so long ago, under what circumstances I first ascended, only that I shuddered as I went along (I have an indistinct remembrance of having been out overnight alone),—and then I steadily ascended along a rocky ridge half clad with stinted trees, where wild beasts haunted, till I lost myself quite in the upper air and clouds, seeming to pass an imaginary line which separates a hill, mere earth heaped up, from a mountain, into a super-

---

*   This dream allegory, suggestive of Bunyan's *Pilgrim's Progress*, makes an interesting contrast to the Transcendental optimism of the day.

terranean grandeur and sublimity. What distinguishes that summit above the earthy line, is that it is unhandselled,* awful, grand. It can never become familiar; you are lost the moment you set foot there. You know no path, but wander, thrilled, over the bare and pathless rock, as if it were solidified air and cloud. That rocky, misty summit, secreted in the clouds, was far more thrillingly awful and sublime than the crater of a volcano spouting fire.

This is a business we can partly understand. The perfect mountain height is already thoroughly purified. It is as if you trod with awe the face of a god turned up, unwittingly but helplessly, yielding to the laws of gravity. And are there not such mountains, east or west, from which you may look down on Concord in your thought, and on all the world? In dreams I am shown this height from time to time, and I seem to have asked my fellow once to climb there with me, and yet I am constrained to believe that I never actually ascended it. It chances, now I think of it,[1] that it rises in my mind where lies the Burying-Hill. You might go through its gate to enter that dark wood,[2] but that hill and its graves are so concealed and obliterated by the awful mountain that I never thought of them as underlying it. Might not the graveyards of the just always be hills, ways by which we ascend and overlook the plain?

But my old way down was different, and, indeed, this was another way up, though I never so ascended. I came out, as I descended, breathing the thicker air. I came out the belt of wood into a familiar pasture, and along down by a wall. Often, as I go along the low side of this pasture, I let my thoughts ascend toward the mount, gradually entering the stinted wood (Nature subdued) and the thinner air, and drape themselves with mists. There are ever two ways up: one is through the dark wood, the other through the sunny pasture. That is,

---

*   Untouched, unimproved (M. M. Mathews, *Dictionary of Americanisms*—citing only Emerson and Thoreau).

[1]   Now *first think of it,* at this stage of my description, which makes it the more singularly symbolical. The interlineations on the last page were made before this. [Thoreau's note.] [The interlineations referred to comprise the words "only that I shuddered . . . overnight alone" in the last paragraph.—Editor.]

[2]   Perchance that was the grave. [Thoreau's note]

I reach and discover the mountain only through the dark wood, but I see to my surprise, when I look off between the mists from its summit, how it is ever adjacent to my native fields, nay, imminent over them, and accessible through a sunny pasture. Why is it that in the lives of men we hear more of the dark wood than of the sunny pasture?

A hard-featured god reposing, whose breath hangs about his forehead.

x, 141-143   29 Oct. 1857

HUNTER OF BEAUTY

If, about the last of October, you ascend any hill in the outskirts of the town and look over the forest, you will see, amid the brown of other oaks, which are now withered, and the green of the pines, the bright-red tops or crescents of the scarlet oaks, very equally and thickly distributed on all sides, even to the horizon. Complete trees standing exposed on the edges of the forest, where you have never suspected them, or their tops only in the recesses of the forest surface, or perhaps towering above the surrounding trees, or reflecting a warm rose red from the very edge of the horizon in favorable lights. All this you will see, and much more, if you are prepared to see it,—if you *look* for it. Otherwise, regular and universal as this phenomenon is, you will think for threescore years and ten that all the wood is at this season sere and brown. Objects are concealed from our view not so much because they are out of the course of our visual ray as because there is no intention of the mind and eye toward them. We do not realize how far and widely, or how near and narrowly, we are to look. The greater part of the phenomena of nature are for this reason concealed to us all our lives. Here, too, as in political economy, the supply answers to the demand. Nature does not cast pearls before swine. There is just as much beauty visible to us in the landscape as we are prepared to appreciate,—not a grain more. The actual objects which one person will see from a particular hilltop are just as different from those which another will see as the persons are different. The scarlet oak must, in a sense, be in your eye when you go forth. We cannot see anything until we are possessed with the idea of it, and then we can hardly see anything else. In my botanical rambles I find that first the idea, or image, of a plant occupies my thoughts, though it may at first seem very foreign to this locality, and for some weeks or months I go think-ing of it and expecting it unconsciously, and at length I surely see it, and it is henceforth an actual neighbor of mine. This is the history of my finding a score or more of rare plants which I could name.

Take one of our selectman and put him on the highest hill in the township, and tell him to look! What, probably, would he see? What would he *select* to look at? Sharpening his sight to the utmost, and putting on the glasses that suited him best, aye, using a spy-glass if he liked, straining his optic nerve to its utmost, and making a full re-port. Of course, he would see a Brocken* spectre of himself. Now take Julius Cæsar, or Emanuel Swedenborg, or a Fiji-Islander, and set him up there! Let them compare notes afterward. Would it appear that they had enjoyed the same prospect? For aught we know, as strange a man as any of these is always at our elbows. It does not appear that anybody saw Shakespeare when he was about in England looking off, but only some of his raiment.

Why, it takes a sharpshooter to bring down even such trivial game as snipes and woodcocks; he must take very particular aim, and know what he is aiming at. He would stand a very small chance if he fired at random into the sky, being told that snipes were flying there. And so it is with him that shoots at beauty. Not till the sky falls will he catch larks, unless he is a trained sportsman. He will not bag any if he does not already know its seasons and haunts and the color of its wing, —if he has not dreamed of it, so that he can *anticipate* it; then, indeed, he flushes it at every step, shoots double and on the wing, with both barrels, even in corn-fields. The sportsman trains himself, dresses, and watches unweariedly, and loads and primes for his particular game. He prays for it, and so he gets it. After due and long preparation, schooling his eye and hand, dreaming awake and asleep, with gun and paddle and boat, he goes out after meadow-hens,—which most of his townsmen never saw nor dreamed of,—paddles for miles against a head wind, and therefore he gets them. He had them half-way into

* A mountain in Germany, scene of the Walpurgis Night (a witches' sabbath).

his bag when he started, and has only to shove them down. The fisherman, too, dreams of fish, till he can almost catch them in his sink-
spout. The hen scratches, and finds her food right under where she
stands; but such is not the way with the hawk.

The true sportsman can shoot you almost any of his game from
his windows. It comes and perches at last on the barrel of his gun;
but the rest of the world never see it, with the feathers on. He will
keep himself supplied by firing up his chimney. The geese fly exactly
under his zenith, and honk when they get there. Twenty musquash
have the refusal of each one of his traps before it is empty.

xi, 284-287   4 Nov. 1858

THE MIGHTY HUNTER

The snow is the great betrayer. It not only shows the tracks of
mice, otters, etc., etc., which else we should rarely if ever see, but the
tree sparrows are more plainly seen against its white ground, and they
in turn are attracted by the dark weeds which it reveals. It also drives
the crows and other birds out of the woods to the villages for food. We
might expect to find in the snow the footprint of a life superior to our
own, of which no zoölogy takes cognizance. Is there no trace of a
nobler life than that of an otter or an escaped convict to be looked for
in the snow? Shall we suppose that that is the only life that has been
abroad in the night? It is only the savage that can see the track of no
higher life than an otter. Why do the vast snow plains give us pleasure,
the twilight of the bent and half-buried woods? Is not all there consonant with virtue, justice, purity, courage, magnanimity? Are we not
cheered by the sight? And does not all this amount to the track of a
higher life than the otter's, a life which has not gone by and left a footprint merely, but is there with its beauty, its music, its perfume, its sweetness, to exhilarate and recreate us? Where there is a perfect government
of the world according to the highest laws, is there no trace of intelligence
there, whether in the snow or the earth, or in ourselves? No other trail
but such as a dog can smell? Is there none which an angel can detect
and follow? None to guide a man on his pilgrimage, which water

will not conceal? Is there no odor of sanctity to be perceived? Is its trail too old? Have mortals lost the scent? The great game for mighty hunters as soon as the first snow falls is Purity, for, earlier than any rabbit or fox, it is abroad, and its trail may be detected by curs of low-est degree. Did this great snow come to reveal the track merely of some timorous hare, or of the Great Hare, whose track no hunter has seen? Is there no trace nor suggestion of Purity to be detected? If one could detect the meaning of the snow, would he not be on the trail of some higher life that has been abroad in the night? Are there not hunters who seek for something higher than foxes, with judgment more discriminating than the senses of fox-hounds, who rally to a nobler music than that of the hunting-horn? As there is contention among the fishermen who shall be the first to reach the pond as soon as the ice will bear, in spite of the cold, as the hunters are forward to take the field as soon as the first snow has fallen, so the observer, or he who would make the most of his life for discipline, must be abroad early and late, in spite of cold and wet, in pursuit of nobler game, whose traces are then most distinct. A life which, pursued, does not earth itself, does not burrow downward but upward, which takes not to the trees but to the heavens as its home, which the hunter pursues with winged thoughts and aspirations,—these the dogs that tree it,— rallying his pack with the bugle notes of undying faith, and returns with some worthier trophy than a fox's tail, a life which we seek, not to destroy it, but to save our own. Is the great snow of use to the hunter only, and not to the saint, or him who is earnestly building up a life? Do the Indian and hunter only need snow-shoes, while the saint sits indoors in embroidered slippers?

VI, 43-45   1 Jan. 1854

THE PROPER STUDY OF MANKIND

It appears to me that, to one standing on the heights of phi-losophy, mankind and the works of man have sunk out of sight al-together; that man is altogether too much insisted on. The poet says the proper study of mankind is man.* I say, study to forget all that; take wider views of the universe. That is the egotism of the race. What is this our childish, gossiping, social literature, mainly in the hands of the publishers? When another poet says the world is too much with us, he means, of course, that man is too much with us. In the promulgated views of man, in institutions, in the common sense, there is narrowness and delusion. It is our weakness that so exaggerates the virtues of philanthropy and charity and makes it the highest human attribute. The world will sooner or later tire of philanthropy and all religions based on it mainly. They cannot long sustain my spirit. In order to avoid delusions, I would fain let man go by and behold a universe in which man is but as a grain of sand. I am sure that those of my thoughts which consist, or are contemporaneous, with social personal connections, however humane, are not the wisest and widest, most universal. What is the village, city, State, nation, aye the civilized world, that it should concern a man so much? the thought of them affects me in my wisest hours as when I pass a woodchuck's hole. It is a comfortable place to nestle, no doubt, and we have friends, some sympathizing ones, it may be, and a hearth, there; but I have only to get up at midnight, aye to soar or wander a little in my thought by day, to find them all slumbering. Look at our literature. What a poor, puny, social thing, seeking sympathy! The author troubles himself about his readers,— would fain have one before he dies. He stands too near his printer; he corrects the proofs. Not satisfied with defiling one another in this world, we would all go to heaven together. To be a good man, that is, a good neighbor in the widest sense, is but little more than to be a good citizen. Mankind is a gigantic institution; it is a community to which most men belong. It is a test I would apply to my companion,—can he forget man? can he see this world slumbering?

I do not value any view of the universe into which man and the institutions of man enter very largely and absorb much of the attention. Man is but the place where I stand, and the prospect hence is infinite. It is not a chamber of mirrors which reflect me. When I reflect, I find that there is other than me. Man is a past phenomenon

* Pope, *Essay on Man*, I, 290. Wordsworth's well-known sonnet, "The World Is Too Much with Us," is quoted four lines below.

to philosophy. The universe is larger than enough for man's abode.
Some rarely go outdoors, most are always at home at night, very few
indeed have stayed out all night once in their lives, fewer still have
gone behind the world of humanity, seen its institutions like toadstools
by the wayside.

III, 381-382   2 Apr. 1852

 AN, THE GOD WE KNOW

I think that we are not commonly aware that man is our contemporary,—that in this strange, outlandish world, so barren, so prosaic, fit not to live in but merely to pass through, that even here so
divine a creature as man does actually live. Man, the crowning fact,
the god we know. While the earth supports so rare an inhabitant,
there is somewhat to cheer us. Who shall say that there is no God, if
there is a *just* man. It is only within a year that it has occurred to me
that there is such a being actually existing on the globe. Now that I
perceive that it is so, many questions assume a new aspect. We have
not only the idea and vision of the divine ourselves, but we have
brothers, it seems, who have this idea also. Methinks my neighbor is
better than I, and his thought is better than mine. There is a representative of the divinity on earth, of [whom] all things fair and noble
are to be expected. We have the material of heaven here. I think that
the standing miracle to man is man. Behind the paling yonder, come
rain or shine, hope or doubt, there dwells a man, an actual being who
can sympathize with our sublimest thoughts.

The revelations of nature are infinitely glorious and cheering,
hinting to us of a remote future, of possibilities untold; but startlingly
near to us some day we find a fellow-man.

The frog had eyed the heavens from his marsh, until his mind
was filled with visions, and he saw more than belongs to this fenny
earth. He mistrusted that he was become a dreamer and visionary.
Leaping across the swamp to his fellow, what was his joy and consolation to find that he too had seen the same sights in the heavens, he
too had dreamed the same dreams!

From nature we turn astonished to this *near* but supernatural fact.

I think that the existence of man in nature is the divinest and most startling of all facts. It is a fact which few have realized.

I can go to my neighbors and meet on ground as elevated as we could expect to meet upon if we were now in heaven. . . .

I do not think that man can understand the *importance* of man's existence, its bearing on the other phenomena of life, until it shall become a remembrance to him the survivor that such a being or such a race once existed on the earth. Imagine yourself alone in the world, a musing, wondering, reflecting spirit, *lost* in thought, and imagine thereafter the creation of man!—man made in the image of God!

11, 207-208   24 May 1851

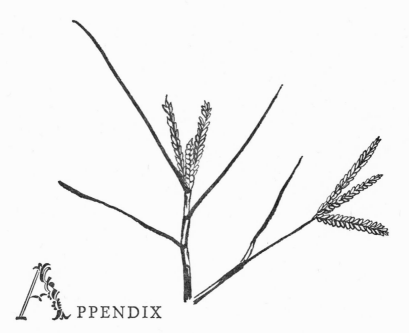

A PPENDIX

EXAMPLES OF·THOREAU'S REVISIONS

THE OYSTERBOAT MEN*
1ST VERSION

Getting into Patchogue late one night in an oysterboat, there was a drunken Dutchman aboard whose wit reminded me of Shakespeare. When we came to leave the beach, our boat was aground, and we were detained three hours waiting for the tide. In the meanwhile two of the fishermen took an extra dram at the beach house. Then they stretched themselves on the seaweed by the shore in the sun to sleep off the effects of their debauch. One was an inconceivably broad-faced young Dutchman,—but oh! of such a peculiar breadth and heavy look, I should not know whether to call it more ridiculous or sublime. You would say that he had humbled himself so much that he was beginning to be exalted. An indescribable mynheerish stupidity. I was less disgusted by their filthiness and vulgarity, because I was compelled to look on them as animals, as swine in their sty. For the whole voyage they lay flat on their backs on the bottom of the boat, in the bilge-water and wet with each bailing, half insensible and wallowing in their vomit. But ever and anon, when aroused by the rude kicks or curses of the skipper, the Dutchman, who never lost his wit nor equanimity, though snoring and rolling in the vomit produced by his debauch, blurted forth some happy repartee like an illuminated swine. It was the earthiest, slimiest wit I ever heard. The countenance was one of a million. It was unmistakable Dutch. In the midst of a million faces of other races it could not be mistaken. It told of Amsterdam. I kept racking my brains to conceive how he could have been born in America, how lonely he must feel, what he did for fellowship. When we were groping up the narrow creek of Patchogue at ten o'clock at night, keeping our boat off, now from this bank, now

---

*   In the summer of 1850 Thoreau had an adventure in going from Fire Island to the little fishing village of Patchogue on the south shore of Long Island. His first literary use of it in the *Journal* is primarily for the portrait of a drunken sailor. The second and shorter version, 27 pages later, concentrates on the incident of the oyster boat going aground, with a variant treatment of the sailor.

from that, with a pole, the two inebriates roused themselves betimes. For in spite of their low estate they seemed to have all their wits as much about them as ever, aye, and all the self-respect they ever had. And the Dutchman gave wise directions to the steerer, which were not heeded. Suddenly rousing himself up where the sharpest-eyed might be bewildered in the darkness, he leaned over the side of the boat and pointed straight down into the creek, averring that the identical hole was a first-rate place for eels. And again he roused himself at the right time and declared what luck he had once had with his pots (not his cups) in another place, which we were floating over in the dark. At last he suddenly stepped on to another boat which was moored to the shore, with a divine ease and sureness, saying, "Well, good-night, take care of yourselves, I can't be with you any longer." He was one of the few remarkable men whom I have met. I have been impressed by one or two men in their cups. There was really a divinity stirred within them, so that in their case I have reverenced the drunken, as savages the insane, man. So stupid that he could never be intoxicated. When I said, "You have had a hard time of it to-day," he answered with indescribable good humor out of the very midst of his debauch, with watery eyes, "Well, it does n't happen every day." It was happening then. He had taken me aboard on his back, the boat lying a rod from the shore, before I knew his condition. In the darkness our skipper steered with a pole on the bottom, for an oysterman knows the bottom of his bay as well as the shores, and can tell where he is by the soundings.

II, 49-51   1850

THE OYSTERBOAT MEN
2ND VERSION

The oystermen had anchored their boat near the shore without regard to the state of the tide, and when we came to it to set sail, just after noon, we found that it was aground. Seeing that they were preparing to push it off, I was about to take off my shoes and stockings in order to wade to it first, but a Dutch sailor with a singular bullfrog or trilobite expression of the eyes, whose eyes were like frog ponds in the broad platter of his cheeks and gleamed like a pool covered with frog-spittle, immediately offered me the use of his back. So mounting, with my legs under his arms, and hugging him like one of [the] family, he set me aboard of the periauger?

They then leaned their hardest against the stern, bracing their feet against the sandy bottom in two feet of water, the Dutchman with his broad back among them. In the most Dutch-like and easy way they applied themselves to this labor, while the skipper tried to raise the bows, never jerking or hustling but silently exerting what vigor was inherent in them, doing, no doubt, their utmost endeavor, while I pushed with a spike pole; but it was all in vain. It was decided to be unsuccessful; we did not disturb its bed by a grain of sand. "Well, what now?" said I. "How long have we got to wait?" "Till the tide rises," said the captain. But no man knew of the tide, how it was. So I went in to bathe, looking out for sharks and chasing crabs, and the Dutchman waded out among the mussels to spear a crab. The skipper stuck a clamshell into the sand at the water's edge to discover if it was rising, and the sailors,—the Dutchman and the other,—having got more drink at Oakes's, stretched themselves on the seaweed close to the water's edge [and] went to sleep. After an hour or more we could discover no change in the shell even by a hair's breadth, from which we learned that it was about the turn of the tide and we must wait some hours longer.

    ii, 78-80   1850

THE LITTLE IRISH BOY*
1ST VERSION

    I have seen, in the form, in the expression of face, of a child three years old, the tried magnanimity and grave nobility of ancient and departed worthies. Just saw a little Irish boy, come from the dis-

---

  * Johnny Riordan, the small son of a poor Irish family living on the outskirts of Concord, prompted Thoreau to a character sketch that ran through three versions. The second—written one month and 90 pages

tant shanty in the woods over the bleak railroad to school this morning, take his last step from his last snow-drift on to the schoolhouse
door-step, floundering still; saw not his face or his profile, only his
mien, and imagined, saw clearly in imagination, his old-worthy face
behind the sober visor of his cap. Ah! this little Irish boy, I know not
why, revives to my mind the worthies of antiquity. He is not drawn,
he never was drawn, in a willow wagon; he progresses by his own
brave steps. Has not the world waited for such a generation? Here
he condescends to his a-b-c without one smile, who has the lore of
worlds uncounted in his brain. He speaks not of the adventures of
the causeway. What was the bravery of Leonidas and his three hundred boys at the pass of Thermopylæ to this infant's? They but dared
to die; he dares to live,—and take his "reward of merit," perchance
without relaxing his face into a smile, that overlooks his unseen and
unrewardable merits. Little Johnny Riordan, who faces cold and routs
it like a Persian army, who, yet innocent, carries in his knees the
strength of a thousand Indras. That does not reward the thousandth
part of his merit. While the charitable waddle about cased in furs, he,
lively as a cricket, passes them on his way to school. I forget for the
time Kossuth and his Hungarians. Here's a Kossuth for you!

III, 149-150   22 Dec. 1851

THE LITTLE IRISH BOY
2ND VERSION

They showed me Johnny Riordan to-day, with one thickness of
ragged cloth over his little shirt for all this cold weather, with shoes
with large holes in the toes, into which the snow got, as he said, without an outer garment, to walk a mile to school every day over the

---

later—is not much of an improvement over the first except that it
substitutes metaphor for historical allusions. The third version, written
at the same time (or some later date?) on loose sheets of MS inclosed
between the leaves of one of his journals, is a fusion of the first two,
with some revisions and some expansion, including verses. It is more
than twice as long and achieves the status of an essay.

bleakest of causeways,—the clothes with countless patches, which hailed from, claimed descent from, were originally identical with, pantaloons of mine, which set as if his mother had fitted them to a tea-kettle first. This little mass of humanity, this tender gobbet for the fates, cast into a cold world with a torn lichen leaf wrapped about him,—Oh, I should rather hear that America's first-born were all slain than that his little fingers and toes should feel cold while I am warm. Is man so cheap that he cannot be clothed but with a mat, a rag, that we should bestow on him our *cold* victuals? Are there any fellow-creatures to whom we abandon our rags, to whom we give our old clothes and shoes when they will not fend the weather from ourselves? Let the mature rich wear the rags and insufficient clothing; let the infant poor wear the purple and fine linen. I shudder when I think of the fate of innocency. Our charitable institutions are an insult to humanity. A charity which dispenses the crumbs that fall from its overloaded tables, which are left after it feasts!

III, 241-242   28 Jan. 1852

THE LITTLE IRISH BOY
3RD VERSION *

They showed me little Johnny Riordan the other day, as bright a boy of five years as ever trod our paths, whom you could not see for five minutes without loving and honoring him. He *lives* in what they call the *shanty* in the woods. He had on, in the middle of January of the coldest winter we have had for twenty years, one thickness only of ragged cloth sewed on to his pantaloons over his little shirt, and shoes with large holes in the toes, into which the snow got, as he was obliged to confess, he who had trodden five winters under his feet! Thus clad he walked a mile to school every day, over the bleakest of railroad causeways, where I knew by experience the grown man would frequently freeze his ears or nose if they were not well protected,—for

---

* Some loose sheets of manuscript inclosed between the leaves of one of Thoreau's journals contain the following more complete sketch of the little Irish boy, made up, with some revision, from the original entries.

his parents have no thermometer,—all to get learning and warmth and there sit at the head of his bench. These clothes, with countless patches, which had for vehicle—O shame! shame! pantaloons that had been mine, they whispered to me, set as if his mother had fitted them to a tea-kettle first.

I glimpsed him the other morning taking his last step from his last snow-drift on to the schoolhouse door-step, floundering still; saw not his face nor his profile, only his mien, but saw clearly in imagination his 'old-worthy' face behind the sober visor of his cap, and he revived to my mind the grave nobility and magnanimity of ancient heroes. He never was drawn in a willow wagon, but progresses by his own brave steps. Has not the world waited for such a generation? Here he condescends to his a-b-c without one smile, who has the lore of worlds uncounted in his brain. He speaks not of the adventures of the causeway. What was the bravery of Leonidas and his three hundred boys at the pass of Thermopylæ to this infant's? They dared but to die; he dares to live, and takes his reward of merit, perchance, without relaxing his face into a smile, that does not reward a thousandth part of his merits, that overlooks his unseen and unrewardable merits,— Little Johnny Riordan, who faces cold and routs it like a Persian army, who, yet innocent, carries in his knees the strength of a thousand Indras. Not to be so tenderly nurtured as you and I forsooth? All day he plays with his coevals and equals, and then they go to their several homes.

I am the little Irish boy,
   That lives in the shanty.
I am five years old to-day,
   And shall soon be one and twenty.

At recess I play
With little Billy Gray,
And when school is done,
Then away I run.

And if I meet the cars,
   I get on the other track,
And then I know, whatever comes,
   I need n't look back.

Having carried off the palm in the intellectual contest with the children of luxury, how bravely he contemplates his destiny: —

I shall grow up
  And be a great man,
And shovel all day
  As hard as I can.

This tender gobbet for the fates, cast into a cold world, with a torn lichen leaf wrapped about him! I would rather hear that America's first-born were all slain than that his little fingers and toes should feel cold while I am warm. Is man so cheap that he cannot be clothed but with a mat or a rag? that we should abandon to him our *worn-out* clothes or our *cold* victuals? Infancy pleads with equal eloquence from all platforms. Rather let the mature rich wear the rags and insufficient clothing, the infant poor and rich, if any, wear the costly furs, the purple and fine linen. Our charitable institutions are an insult to humanity,—a charity which dispenses the crumbs that fall from its overloaded tables! whose waste and whose example helped to produce that poverty!

While the charitable waddle about cased in furs and finery, this boy, lively as a cricket, passes them on his way to school. I see that, for the present, the child is happy, is not puny, and has all the wonders of nature for his toys. Have I not faith that his tenderness will in some way be cherished and protected, as the buds of spring in the remotest wintry dell no less than in the garden and summer-house?

III, 241-244   28 Jan. 1852

ABIN FIT FOR A GOD*
Journal VERSION

July 5. Saturday. Walden.—Yesterday I came here to live. My house makes me think of some mountain houses I have seen, which seemed to have a fresher auroral atmosphere about them, as I fancy

---

* The description of Thoreau's famous cabin (reminding him of a mountain cabin he had seen the year before) is first recorded in his *Journal* on the day after he moved to Walden Pond. The second ver-of the halls of Olympus. I lodged at the house of a saw-miller last summer, on the Caatskill Mountains, high up as Pine Orchard, in the blueberry and raspberry region, where the quiet and cleanliness and coolness seemed to be all one,—which had their ambrosial character. He was the miller of the Kaaterskill Falls. They were a clean and wholesome family, inside and out, like their house. The latter was not plastered, only lathed, and the inner doors were not hung. The house seemed high-placed, airy, and perfumed, fit to entertain a travelling god. It was so high, indeed, that all the music, the broken strains, the waifs and accompaniments of tunes, that swept over the ridge of the Caatskills, passed through its aisles. Could not man be man in such an abode? And would he ever find out this grovelling life? It was the very light and atmosphere in which the works of Grecian art were composed, and in which they rest. They have appropriated to themselves a loftier hall than mortals ever occupy, at least on a level with the mountain-brows of the world. There was wanting a little of the glare of the lower vales, and in its place a pure twilight as became the precincts of heaven. Yet so equable and calm was the season there that you could not tell whether it was morning or noon or evening. Always there was the sound of the morning cricket.

1, 361-362   5 July 1845

ABIN FIT FOR A GOD
Walden VERSION, p. 94

When I first took up my abode in the woods, that is, began to spend my nights as well as days there, which, by accident, was on Independence Day, or the Fourth of July, 1845, my house was not finished for winter, but was merely a defence against the rain, without plastering or chimney, the walls being of rough, weather-stained

---

sion is his revision of this for use in his book. It is hard to say which of two facts is more interesting: that it took Walden cabin as a catalyst to precipitate the mountain cabin into Thoreau's recorded memory or that the *Journal* draft was so magically transformed when it was incorporated in *Walden*.

boards, with wide chinks, which made it cool at night. The upright white hewn studs and freshly planed door and window casings gave it a clean and airy look, especially in the morning, when its timbers were saturated with dew, so that I fancied that by noon some sweet gum would exude from them. To my imagination it retained through-out the day more or less of this auroral character, reminding me of a certain house on a mountain which I had visited a year before. This was an airy and unplastered cabin, fit to entertain a travelling god, and where a goddess might trail her garments. The winds which passed over my dwelling were such as sweep over the ridges of mountains, bearing the broken strains, or celestial parts only, of terrestrial music. The morning wind forever blows, the poem of creation is uninter-rupted; but few are the ears that hear it. Olympus is but the outside of the earth everywhere.

PRING AT THE POND*
Journal VERSION

March 26, 1846. The change from foul weather to fair, from dark, sluggish hours to serene, elastic ones, is a memorable crisis which all things proclaim. The change from foulness to serenity is instantane-ous. Suddenly an influx of light, though it was late, filled my room. I looked out and saw that the pond was already calm and full of hope as on a summer evening, though the ice was dissolved but yesterday. There seemed to be some intelligence in the pond which responded to the unseen serenity in a distant horizon. I heard a robin in the dis-tance,—the first I had heard this spring,—repeating the assurance. The green pitch [pine] suddenly looked brighter and more erect, as if now entirely washed and cleansed by the rain. I knew it would not

---

*   Thoreau's *Journal* description of the coming of spring, written during the first year of his residence at Walden Pond, formed the basis of his description in the chapter entitled "Spring" near the end of his book. At first glance the two seem almost identical. But close readers will find in the *Walden* version numerous revisions to enhance the sense of the miraculous, turning the experience into a kind of epiphany.

rain any more. A serene summer-evening sky seemed darkly reflected in the pond, though the clear sky was nowhere visible overhead. It was no longer the end of a season, but the beginning. The pines and shrub oaks, which had before drooped and cowered the winter through with myself, now recovered their several characters and in the landscape revived the expression of an immortal beauty. Trees seemed all at once to be fitly grouped, to sustain new relations to men and to one another. There was somewhat cosmical in the arrangement of nature. O the evening robin, at the close of a New England day! If I could ever find the twig he sits upon! Where does the minstrel really roost? We perceive it is not the bird of the ornithologist that is heard,—the *Turdus migratorius.*

1, 400-401   26 Mar. 1846

SPRING AT THE POND
Walden VERSION, p. 344

The change from storm and winter to serene and mild weather, from dark and sluggish hours to bright and elastic ones, is a memorable crisis which all things proclaim. It is seemingly instantaneous at last. Suddenly an influx of light filled my house, though the evening was at hand, and the clouds of winter still overhung it, and the eves were dripping with sleety rain. I looked out of the window, and lo! where yesterday was cold gray ice there lay the transparent pond already calm and full of hope as in a summer evening, reflecting a summer evening in its bosom, though none was visible overhead, as if it had intelligence with some remote horizon. I heard a robin in the distance, the first I had heard for many a thousand years, methought, whose note I shall not forget for many a thousand more,—the same sweet and powerful song as of yore. O the evening robin, at the end of a New England summer day! If I could ever find the twig he sits upon! I mean *he;* I mean *the twig.* This at least is not the *Turdus migratorius.*

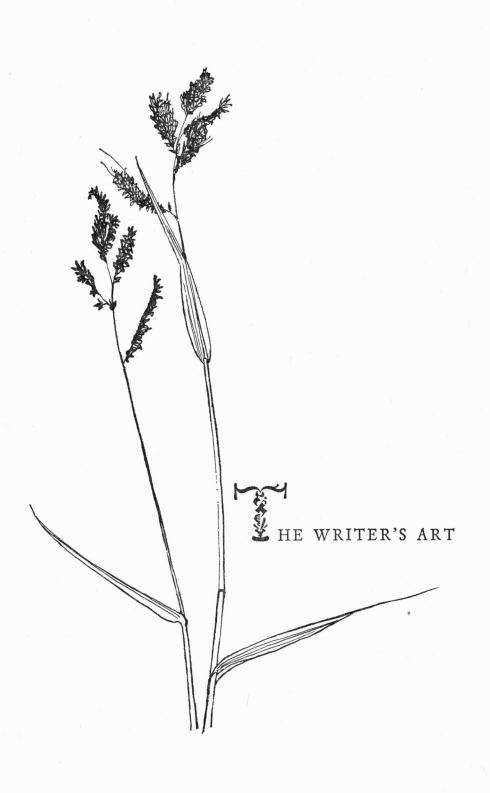

THE WRITER'S ART

THE WRITER'S ART

"My work is writing," Thoreau once remarked in a casual aside. His single-minded dedication, as a matter of fact, set him apart from contemporary American authors, most of whom divided their time between writing books and other occupations such as teaching, editing, lecturing. He filled a large number of volumes with his compositions, the best of which are well known (except for the "miniatures" now first collected from the *Journal*). But his many comments on the theory and techniques of the writer's art have been overlooked by most readers. Brought together here, they make up a significant body of criticism.

Poetry and the Poet

During the Romantic Movement, as in all periods of radical change, there were recurrent efforts to define the nature of poetry. In America this concern continued on down to the middle of the nineteenth century, and Thoreau was caught up in it. His early *Journal* is filled with trial definitions:

The poem is drawn out from under the feet of the poet, his whole weight has rested on this ground.

It has a logic more severe than the logician's.

You might as well go in pursuit of the rainbow, and embrace it on the next hill, as to embrace the whole of poetry even in thought. . . .

Its eccentric and unexplored orbit embraces the system. (1, 114)[1]

When he returned to the problem of defining nearly a decade later in *A Week on the Concord and Merrimack Rivers*, a much more mature writer, he admitted the futility of trying to capture the idea of poetry in an aphorism: "The wisest definition of poetry the poet will instantly prove false, by setting aside its requisitions." (*A Week*, 93)

---

[1] All references in parentheses are to *The Writings of Henry David Thoreau* (Boston, 1906), twenty vols.—to the *Journal* by volume and page only, to the works by short title and page.

But this did not put an end to his discussion of various aspects of the subject.

Since the Romantics were revolting from a tradition that emphasized craftsmanship, they were constantly making distinctions between genius and art, inspiration and talent. Thoreau could not resist this temptation any more than other writers of the period. "A true poem is distinguished not so much by a felicitous expression, or any thought it suggests, as by the atmosphere which surrounds it," he wrote in *A Week:* "Much of our poetry has the best manners, but no character. It is only an unusual precision and elasticity of speech, as if its author had taken, not an intoxicating draught, but an electuary." (*A Week,* 400) In his negative definition, what poetry should not be, he is aptly characterizing the work of several contemporaries: Longfellow (for poetry with good manners but no character), Holmes (for precision and elasticity of speech), Lowell and Whittier (for moral medicine made palatable by the syrup of verse). Yet these were his poetic compatriots who were enjoying popular success while he failed to find an audience. The first American poets who had clearly taken "an intoxicating draught," Whitman and Dickinson, came in the next generation. The affirmative part of Thoreau's definition is less clear. To say that a true poem is distinguished by its "atmosphere" is not very helpful; all we know is that he means something quite different from "felicitous expression."

A much better comparison of finish and depth may be found in a *Journal* passage of 1841. Though it begins with the typical Romantic distinction between them, and his expressed preference for the latter, it ends with acknowledgment of the inescapable relation between the two:

> *The art which only gilds the surface and demands merely a superficial polish, without reaching to the core, is but varnish and filigree. But the work of genius is rough-hewn from the first, because it anticipates the lapse of time and has an ingrained polish, which still appears when fragments are broken off, an essential quality of its substance. Its beauty is its strength. It breaks with a lustre, and splits in cubes and diamonds. Like the diamond, it has only to be cut to be polished, and its surface is a window to its interior splendors.* (1, 275)

Diamond is a happy metaphor for poem, with its suggestion of a many-faceted gem whose surface brilliance is the result of its depth. To the extent that this is emphasizing the interdependence of form and content it is viable theory today. To the extent that it implies a belief in organic form—that form is inherent in substance and merely needs to be released by the poet—it is part of an outmoded Transcendentalism.

When this passage was transcribed into *A Week*, verbatim except for deletion of the diamond metaphor, it was set in the midst of a long discussion of the Man of Genius and the Artist. The former is an originator, Thoreau declares, a demonic man "who produces a perfect work in obedience to laws yet unexplored"; the latter is he who detects and applies the laws. (Both are distinguished from the mere artisan.) The comparison continues:

> There are two kinds of writing, both great and rare,—one that of genius, or the inspired, the other of intellect and taste, in the intervals of inspiration. The former is above criticism, always correct, giving the law to criticism. It vibrates and pulsates with life forever. It is sacred, and to be read with reverence, as the works of nature are studied. There are few instances of a sustained style of this kind. . . . The other is self-possessed and wise. It is reverent of genius and greedy of inspiration. It consists with the most perfect command of the faculties. . . . But the pen is only an instrument in its hand, and not instinct with life, like a longer arm. (*A Week*, 400–401; 350)

Shakespeare is cited as exemplar of the former, Goethe of the latter.

Most of these were issues of real significance when first raised by the Romantic critics, but by mid-century they had become part of a hackneyed tradition which Thoreau had fortunately written out of his system. A final comparison of Genius and Artist, in his first book, takes off in a new direction:

> We talk of genius as if it were a mere knack, and the poet could only express what other men conceived. But in comparison with his task the poet is the least talented of any; the writer of prose has more skill. . . .
>
> Great prose, of equal elevation, commands our respect more than great verse, since it implies a more permanent and level height, a

life more pervaded with the grandeur of the thought. The poet often only makes an irruption, like a Parthian, and is off again, shooting while he retreats; but the prose writer has conquered like a Roman, and settled colonies. (A Week, 364–365)

This is clearly a defense of his own writing career, since his early ambition to be a lyric poet soon gave way to the creation of prose works of a special sort, notably the superb *Walden*. Normally when Thoreau uses the terms poet and poetry in his *Journal*, however, he uses them in their broadest sense so that they include himself and his own best writing, which is always in prose.

There is one more piece of theorizing, a subversion of Romantic theory, that frequently pops up in Thoreau's writing and so must be dealt with before we can discover what is original in his contribution. Several *Journal* entries during 1840 were later brought together in *A Week* and reshaped in this typical statement of the idea:

The true poem is not that which the public read. There is always a poem not printed on paper, coincident with the production of this, stereotyped in the poet's life. It is what he has become through his work. Not how is the idea expressed in stone, or on canvas, or on paper, is the question, but how far has it obtained form and expression in the life of the artist. His true work will not stand in any prince's gallery.

My life has been the poem I would have writ,
But I could not both live and utter it.

(A Week, 365)

This is typical of the confusion of issues about art that so often befogged criticism in mid-Victorian times. It has been invalidated, of course, by all that literary history has shown us about the discrepancy between the artist's life and his works. It can only mean, at best, that one has lived imaginatively, responsive to beauty, concerned with truth or "reality" rather than with false appearances, and so on. Even so, this would not mean that one's life was any more a poem than it was a painting or a sculpture (as Thoreau's own words indicate). Such complete blurring of all distinctions among the arts makes the idea of no use whatever to a student of any one of them, however comforting it may be to the moralist.

It is only when Thoreau escaped from the hackneyed aspects of

Romantic theorizing, and the confusion between life and art indulged in by his contemporaries, that he was able to make any contributions of his own. These usually had to do with specific techniques, rather than with broad principles of criticism. But they can be prefaced by several of his generalizations about the nature and function of the poet that do have a particular interest because they grew out of his unique orientation as a writer. In the very month that *Walden* was going through the press, its hermit author wrote: "The true poet will ever live aloof from society, wild to it, as the finest singer is the wood thrush, a forest bird." (vi, 257) Again, the man who had boasted in this same book that he "travelled a good deal in Concord" makes this strong sense of place a prime requisite for the literary artist in a *Journal* passage of 1857:

> The poet has made the best roots in his native soil of any man, and is the hardest to transplant. The man who is often thinking that it is better to be somewhere else than where he is excommunicates himself. If a man is rich and strong anywhere, it must be on his native soil. Here I have been these forty years learning the language of these fields that I may better express myself. (x, 190–191)

And again: "The poet is no tender slip of fairy stock," he declared, "but the toughest son of earth and Heaven." (*A Week*, 262) While acknowledging his roots in the soil to be his main strength, Thoreau frees himself from the limitations of naturalism with the last two words.

Now for several passages dealing with the inner and outer sources of his writing. Though it is literary nonsense to say that a poet's life is superior to any poem he can write, as noted above, it is a very different thing to say that his internal life furnishes materials for his art:

> The poet sings how the blood flows in his veins. He performs his functions, and is so well that he needs such stimulus to sing only as plants to put forth leaves and blossoms. . . . His song is a vital function like breathing, and an integral result like weight. It is not the overflowing of life, but its subsidence rather, and is drawn from under the feet of the poet. (*A Week*, 94)

In a *Journal* entry of 1851 he once put this cryptically: "A poet writes the history of his body." (iii, 36) Many years later he elaborated his meaning:

A man thinks as well through his legs and arms as his brain. We exaggerate the importance and exclusiveness of the headquarters. Do you suppose they were a race of consumptives and dispeptics who invented Grecian mythology and poetry? The poet's words are, "You would almost say the body thought!" I quite say it. I trust we have a good body then. (XIII, 69–70)

Then in a typical Thoreauvian conceit he fuses flesh and spirit: "The poet's body is not fed like other men's, but he sometimes tastes the genuine nectar and ambrosia of the gods, and lives a divine life." (*A Week*, 365) But unlike the other Transcendentalists Thoreau always returned from such flights to anchor himself back to reality:

It is of no use to plow deeper than the soil is. . . . Yet many a man likes to tackle mighty themes, like immortality, but in his discourse he turns up nothing but yellow sand, under which what little fertile and available surface soil he may have is quite buried and lost. . . . It is a great art in the writer to improve from day to day just that soil and fertility which he has, to harvest that crop which his life yields, whatever it may be, not be straining as if to reach apples or oranges when he yields only groundnuts. He should be digging, not soaring. Just as earnest as your life is, so deep is your soil. If strong and deep, you will sow wheat and raise bread of life in it. (XI, 304)

Just as Thoreau interpreted the subjective aspects of poetry dif-ferently from the Romantics, he also gave a new turn to the next generation's cult of Nature as the poet's chief source of inspiration. His commentary often begins in a rather trite vein, saying for example that the poet "should speak in harmony with nature," but concludes with another emphasis: "The tone and pitch of *his* voice is the main thing." (X, 344). How this paradox can be reconciled is put succinctly in an early *Journal* entry: "Though more than any he stands in the midst of Nature, yet more than any he can stand aloof from her." (1, 289) Indeed at the very beginning of his career Thoreau spells out in con-siderable detail his unique stance with relation to nature, under the rubric of THE POET:

He must be something more than natural,—even supernatural. Nature will not speak through but along with him. His voice will not proceed from her midst, but, breathing on her, will make her the expression of his thought. He then poetizes when he takes a fact out of nature into spirit. He speaks without reference to time or place. His thought is one world, hers another. He is another Nature,—Nature's brother. Kindly offices do they perform for one another. Each publishes the other's truth. (1, 75)

Thoreau had come a long way from Emerson's Transcendental pronouncement about poetic inspiration three years earlier in *Nature* (1836):

Standing on the bare ground,—my head bathed by the blythe air and uplifted into infinite space,—all mean egotism vanishes. I become a transparent eye-ball; I am nothing; I see all; the currents of the Universal Being circulate through me; I am part or parcel of God.[2]

The *Journal* passage of 1839, quoted above, shows Thoreau moving off in another direction, one that could lead to *Walden* just as surely as that of his first and only mentor could not.

The subtle relation between the natural world and the one created by the artist was a central concern of Romantic theorists, beginning with Wordsworth and Coleridge. Thoreau continued to explore the complexities of the problem. Sometimes he merely restated a traditional position—"The poet must bring to Nature the smooth mirror in which she is to be reflected" (v, 183)—but even this is helpful in differentiating his position from Emerson's. At other times he could be far more original, as in the query that grew out of his discussion of galls on oak trees, "Is not Art itself a gall?"—and his conclusion: "The artist changes the direction of Nature and makes her grow according to his idea." (VII, 10) The kind of mirror image of nature he desired and the kind of transformation he hoped to achieve by art are further discussed in terms of tameness and wildness in literature, the former being but another name for dullness, the latter the only kind of writing that attracts us:

Art is not tame, and Nature is not wild, in the ordinary sense. A perfect work of man's art would also be wild or natural in a good sense. Man tames Nature only that he may at last make

[2] *The Complete Works of R. W. Emerson,* ed. E. W. Emerson (1903–1904), 1, 10.

her more free even than he found her, though he may never yet
have succeeded. (A Week, 337)

So he set up the comparison in his first book. Later he elaborated the
idea in a lecture on "Wildness," given several times during the last
decade of his life and finally turned into an essay that was published
posthumously:

I do not know of any poetry to quote which adequately ex-
presses this yearning for the Wild. Approached from this side,
the best poetry is tame. I do not know where to find in any
literature, ancient or modern, any account which contents me of
that Nature with which I am acquainted. You will perceive that
I demand something which no Augustan nor Elizabethan age,
which no culture, in short, can give. Mythology comes nearer
to it than anything. ("Walking," in Excursions, 232)

Homer and the early Greeks had this kind of wildness; English literature has lost it, save for touches in Shakespeare.

This discussion of the wild and the tame is another version of
the familiar genius-talent comparison, with standards now raised to the
highest. Yet Thoreau himself aspired to make just such a translation
of nature into art, implying that it was more likely to be achieved in
America than in England. (II, 144) "He is the richest who has most
use for nature as raw material of tropes and symbols," he wrote in the
Journal for 1853: "If I am overflowing with life, am rich in experience for which I lack expression, then nature will be my language
full of poetry,—all nature will *fable,* and every natural phenomenon
be a myth." (V, 135)

The transforming power of the poet can turn subjective facts, as
well as those drawn from the world of nature, into symbol and myth.
Once when a hunter showed Thoreau a rare and beautiful flower he
had never seen, the purple azalea or pinxter flower, growing right in
his own neighborhood, he commented in his *Journal:*

Some incidents in my life have seemed far more allegorical than
actual; they were so significant that they plainly served no other
use. That is, I have been more impressed by their allegorical
significance and fitness; they have been like myths or passages
in a myth, rather than mere incidents or history which have to
wait to become significant. Quite in harmony with my subjec-

*tive philosophy. . . . Such facts are lifted quite above the level
of the actual. They are all just such events as my imagination
prepares me for, no matter how incredible. . . . The boundaries of the actual are no more fixed and rigid than the elasticity
of our imaginations.* (v, 203)

Here facts from the outer and inner worlds are fused, raw materials
made into symbols available for the poet's use.

On another occasion, his walking companion chided him for recording in his field notebook only concrete and particular facts from
his observations of nature, instead of being concerned with the universal and the ideal. That evening Thoreau confided to his *Journal*:

*I, too, would fain set down something beside facts. Facts should
only be as the frame to my pictures; they should be material to
the mythology which I am writing; not facts to assist men to
make money, farmers to farm profitably, in any common sense;
facts to tell who I am, and where I have been or what I have
thought: as now the bell rings for evening meeting, and its volumes of sound, like smoke from where a cannon is fired, make
the tent in which I dwell. My facts shall be falsehoods to the
common sense. I would so state facts that they shall be significant, shall be myths or mythologic. Facts which the mind perceived, thoughts which the body thought,—with these I deal.*
(III, 99)

Here is the most revealing statement Thoreau ever made about the
kind of writer he aspired to be, especially about the kind of book he
was at that moment creating in *Walden*. It was to be an autobio-
graphic fiction, the myth of Henry Thoreau as poet and seeker. And
there is also in this passage an unexpected new dimension, the metaphysical mode of fusing thought and feeling, which takes him one step
toward explaining how facts can be so mythologized.

Perception

It is all very well to generalize about translating the facts of nature and of one's own life into symbol, fable, and myth. But the all-
important question is, How? Thoreau did not shirk the task of ex-
perimenting with new techniques of perception and expression, then

defining them. "As you *see*, so at length will you *say*," he had written, underscoring to emphasize the importance of this basic formulation of his theory.

In a series of *Journal* entries Thoreau makes explorations to dis-cover the best angles of vision for the poet and argues with himself what are the best modes of seeing. "I must walk more with free senses," he warns himself: "Be not preoccupied with looking. Go not to the object; let it come to you." Then he concludes with a striking phrase: "What I need is not to look at all, but a true sauntering of the eye." (IV, 351) A similar one is "the unconscious side of the eye," with which one can see "rare sights" that are missed by a direct gaze. The idea recurs several times and is clearly set forth in a *Journal* passage of 1853:

> Man cannot afford to be a naturalist, to look at Nature directly, but only with the side of his eye. He must look through and beyond her. To look at her is fatal as to look at the head of Medusa. It turns the man of science to stone. I feel that I am dissipated by so many observations. I should be the magnet in the midst of all this dust and filings. (v, 45)

In a word, man as poet must draw nature to himself and assimilate it to his needs, not as a scientist be drawn into it and lost in its materiality.

Thoreau felt the need of coining new terms to express what he hoped would be a new perspective on nature. But he was also aware of its relation to a long tradition, as revealed by an explicit reference to the first promulgator of the doctrine of "wise passiveness." At the end of a *Journal* commentary on the greater openness to impressions of nature enjoyed by woodchoppers as compared with scientists, be-cause the latter do not spend enough of their "unconscious life" there, he concludes significantly: "(*Mem*. Wordsworth's observations on relaxed attention.)" (III, 123) In what sense, then, is Thoreau pro-posing an original approach, one that goes beyond his heritage from Romanticism? His new terms suggest the quality of the difference, "the side of the eye" and "a true sauntering of the eye." The Words-worthian doctrine was concerned only that poets should attain the proper psychological state of receptivity. Thoreau, on the other hand, is trying to work out new techniques for seeing, moving in the direc-tion of Impressionism and Symbolism.

Further evidence of his modernity may be found in the reason he gives for not caring to front an object and scrutinize it: "I know that the thing that really concerns me is not there, but in my relation to that. *That* is a mere reflecting surface." Most men look at the phenomena of nature as independent of them, whereas for Thoreau the important fact is their effect on him: "With regard to such objects, I find that it is not they themselves (with which the men of science deal) that concern me; the point of interest is somewhere *between* me and them (*i. e.* the objects)." (x, 164–165) Where, indeed, is "*between* me and them" unless it is the point where subject and object meet, and hopefully fuse?

Like the other Transcendentalists, Thoreau stuck to the pre-Newtonian conviction that the perceiver is central. He is the instrument specifically created to see, just as the reason objects exist in nature is for the purpose of being perceived by man. "Wherever I sat," he declares in *Walden,* "the landscape radiated from me accordingly." (90) But the poet is not detached and objective. The meanings of things come to him subjectively, though the things themselves are perceived by the senses. This is the assumption behind a cryptic passage in the *Journal* for 1857:

> *What is the relation between a bird and the ear that appreciates its melody, to whom, perchance, it is more charming and significant than to any else? Certainly they are intimately related, and the one was made for the other. It is a natural fact. If I were to discover that a certain kind of stone by the pond-shore was affected, say partially disintegrated, by a particular natural sound, as of a bird or insect, I see that one could not be completely described without describing the other. I am that rock by the pond-side.* (ix, 274–275)

Thoreau's purpose here is to argue that he becomes part and parcel of nature by the very process of hearing, observing, and participating; the perceiver is merged with the thing perceived. But this is not the same thing as the Transcendental idealization of nature, nor does it mean that he ruled out objective observation. It is his very emphasis on the latter that differentiates him from Emerson and the other Transcendentalists.

Nature itself varies the spectacle presented to man's eyes by

changes in the amount and quality of light, one of the chief elements of
perception. The artist takes advantage of every difference in weather,
season, and time of day. As an alert perceiver, he can become a spectator at many scenes of nature's show without need of inventing new
techniques— simply by being present at the right time and place. In
his *Journal* Thoreau is constantly pointing out what goes unnoticed
by the average person, having only scorn for the fair-weather friends
of nature. One never sees the true beauty of flowers unless he takes a
walk in the pouring rain, he declares. One does not really perceive
what coldness is until he staggers for miles in the face of a biting nor'-
easter. Thoreau goes forth in all kinds of weather: pre-dawn fog,
snowstorm, glowing Indian summer, sun-drenched July in the meadows. He journeys to all kinds of places: the wind-swept cliffs of Cape
Cod, the fly-swarming wilderness of Maine, deserted farms near
Walden, and the middle of Beck Stow's swamp on the outskirts of
Concord. Caught in a spring rain under a large tree, he spends half a
day happily studying the insects in its bark. He records his observations at all times and seasons: moonlight and blackest night, winter
sunset, teeming noon, a drizzly morning in April. His *Journal* is filled
not only with the multitudinous details but also with the infinite variety of nature's spectacle.

Atmospheric conditions that changed the picture, and so in a
sense recreated the world, were particularly interesting to Thoreau—
mist, the haze of dog days in August, moonlight, snow and ice storms.
He had been reading several books by William Gilpin on the relation of the artist to nature, noting in his *Journal* that the "Essay on
Picturesque Beauty" was the key to all Gilpin's writings. But in spite
of numerous experiments to make landscapes resemble pictures, Thoreau did not add anything original to this eighteenth-century concept.
More closely concerned with the techniques of perception are his
many comments on another of nature's ways of transforming itself, as
reflected in river and pond. Looking at the shoreline bushes as he
sails up the Concord, he finds that they appear in the reflection as
they would if actually viewed from that point on the surface from
which they are reflected to his eye. "In the reflection," he concludes,
"you have an infinite number of eyes to see for you and report things
each from its point of view." (XI, 213) The problem becomes more

complicated as the perceiver maneuvers his own position. Looking across the pond at the opposite hillside he compares the substance with its reflection in the water, as he looks at each of them from different angles and then from different levels of the hill he is standing on. Like a true experimenter he tries out all the possibilities that might lead to some new discovery. The one he announces is that nature as imitator-of-itself serves as an exemplar for the artist as "imitator" of nature: "The reflection is never a true copy or repetition of its substance, but a new composition, and this may be the source of its novelty and attractiveness." (x, 97)

A broader application of Thoreau's study of reflections may be found in a passage that contrasts the imaginative perceiver with the practical observer, using a barrage of seemingly frivolous puns to make a serious point about his own methods as a writer:

> I think that most men, as farmers, hunters, fishers, etc., walk along a river's bank, or paddle along its stream, without seeing the reflections. Their minds are not abstracted from the surface, from surfaces generally. It is only a reflective mind that sees reflections. I am aware often that I have been occupied with shallow and commonplace thoughts, looking for something superficial, when I did not see the most glorious reflections, though exactly in the line of my vision. If the fisherman was looking at the reflection, he would not know when he had a nibble! I know from my own experience that he may cast his line right over the most elysian landscape and sky, and not catch the slightest notion of them. You must be in an abstract mood to see reflections however distinct. I was even startled by the sight of that red oak as if it were a black water-spirit. When we are enough abstracted, the opaque earth itself reflects images to us; i.e., we are imaginative, see visions, etc. (x, 156–157)

The most interesting of his observations are those in which the perceiver plays the most active part. In a series of notations he experiments like a landscape painter of a more modern school than the picturesque. For example, here are two contrasting reports, just before sunset, of slanting rays as they penetrate a pine wood. Having seen them from the sunny side on one afternoon he comes around to the opposite side at the same hour two days later to observe the difference:

Then I saw the lit sides of the tree stems all aglow with their
lichens, and observed their black shadows behind. Now I see
chiefly the dark stems massed together, and it is the warm sun-
light that is reduced to a pencil of light; i. e., then light was the
rule and shadow the exception, now shadow the rule and light
the exception. (x, 160)

Such observations were not the result of whim, but were part of a
deliberate program for discovering new ways of looking at the world.
If proof were needed, it could be found in the following memoran-
dum. Boating on the Concord early one morning he records what
he sees when looking upstream—the water is dark—then when looking downstream—it is silvery bright. Then comes the notation:
"*Mem.* Try this experiment again; *i. e.*, look not toward nor from the
sun but athwart this line." (III, 394–395)

A more elaborate experiment in color perception relates to the
dwarf andromeda. Walking around a small pond one spring afternoon Thoreau mistakes the shrubs alongshore for sweet gale because
of their grayish-brown color. Then, realizing that from every position
he has been seeing the sun reflected from the surface of the leaves, he
moves around to the one angle (facing due west) from which he can
discover that they are indeed the andromeda: "from this position
alone I saw, as it were, *through* the leaves which the opposite sun lit
up, giving to the whole this charming warm, what I call Indian, red
color." The conclusion is a reminder to come back at a different hour
and check on this "interesting piece of magic." When he returns to
verify, his joy is recorded in the *Journal*:

The thing that pleases me most within these three days is the
discovery of the andromeda phenomenon. It makes all those parts
of the country where it grows more attractive and elysian to me.
It is a natural magic. These little leaves are the stained windows
in the cathedral of my world. At sight of any redness I am ex-
cited like a cow. . . . How sweet is the perception of a new
natural fact! (III, 430–431, 441–442)

As he says in another connection, we get only transient and partial
glimpses of this world's beauty unless we are alert and responsive: "It
is only necessary to behold the least fact or phenomenon, however
familiar, from a point of view a hair's breadth aside from our habitual

path or routine, to be overcome, enchanted by its beauty and significance." (VIII, 44)

Thoreau was quick to take advantage of all possibilities for a different angle of vision. When winter rain puts a crust of ice on the deep snow firm enough to bear his weight, he is out early the next morning traversing a familiar route to make comparisons. "It is pleasant to walk over the fields raised a foot or more above their summer level," he reports to his *Journal*, "and the prospect is altogether new." (III, 288) There was no end to the experiments he conceived of. In an entry for 16 June 1840 he makes the striking proposal that he should take the stance of a frog: "Would it not be a luxury to stand up to one's chin in some retired swamp for a whole summer's day, scenting the sweet-fern and bilberry blows, and lulled by the minstrelsy of gnats and mosquitoes?" (I, 141) On another occasion he uses the eye trick later made famous by Impressionist painters. Looking at the pitch pines on the opposite shore of Fair Haven Pond, he first compares the reflection with the substance and makes a pencil sketch in his *Journal*. Then the new technique: "By partly closing my eyes and looking through my eyelashes, the wood end appears thus": — followed by another sketch. (III, 402–403)

The starting point for much of this, as for many of Thoreau's ideas, can be found in the early writings of Emerson. In his first little book, *Nature* (1836), one of the evidences brought forward to prove that the meaning of objective reality is dependent on the subjective viewer was his demonstration of how the world can be changed by slight alterations in the observer's position— seeing the shore from a ship, the earth from a balloon, one's own village street from a moving coach. "Turn the eyes upside down, by looking at the landscape through your legs," Emerson said in his chapter on Idealism, "and how agreeable is the picture, though you have seen it any time these twenty years."[3] Thoreau's use of this stunt, in his *Journal*, is strictly esthetic. Like a true experimenter he makes observations from this posture by morning light, then by afternoon light, and concludes like an artist: "The prospect is thus actually a constantly varying mirage, answering to the condition of our perceptive faculties and our fluctuating imaginations." (III, 333, 391)

[3]   Emerson, *Works*, I, 51.

As Thoreau remarked late in life, "I do not in the least care where I get my ideas, or what suggests them." (viii, 135) His originality lay in his expression. The poetic use to which he put Emerson's ideas—and therefore the difference between the two writers—can be illustrated perfectly by tracing from *Nature* (1836) to *Walden* (1854) this very device of looking at the landscape between one's legs. In the former it was used to argue the case for philosophic Idealism. In the latter it is one of the techniques for translating the pond into a symbol. By diverting his attention from the landscape as such, Thoreau can focus on the glassy surface of the water which now seems to have a heaven below as well as a heaven above it:

> *When you invert your head, [the surface] looks like a thread of finest gossamer stretched across the valley, and gleaming against the distant pine woods, separating one stratum of the atmosphere from another. You would think you could walk dry under it to the opposite hills, and that the swallows which skim over might perch on it. Indeed, they sometimes dive below the line, as it were by mistake, and are undeceived. . . . It is like molten glass cooled but not congealed, and the few notes in it are pure and beautiful like the imperfections in glass. . . . Not a fish can leap nor an insect fall but it is reported in circling dimples, in lines of beauty, as it were the constant welling up of its fountain, the gentle pulsing of its life. (Walden, 207–209)*

Some of the finest images and the most significant symbolic meanings in *Walden* follow immediately after this experiment.

Thoreau had been reasoning for some time that all these special effects—from looking at nature in reflections, out of the side of the eye, inverted between the legs—had to do with optics, the relation between light and vision. So he was ready to take part in a three-way Transcendental debate. Channing made a speculation and Emerson passed it on to Thoreau, who recorded his rebuttal in the *Journal*:

> *R. W. E. told me that W. H. Channing conjectured that the landscape looked fairer when we turned our heads, because we beheld it with nerve ends unused before. Perhaps this reason is worth more for suggestion than explanation. It occurs to me that the reflection of objects in still water is in a similar manner fairer than the substance, and yet we do not employ unused nerves to*

behold it. Is it not that we let much more light into our eyes,—
which in the usual position are shaded by the brows,—in the
first case by turning them more to the sky, and in the case of the
reflections by having the sky placed under our feet? i. e. in both
cases we see terrestrial objects with the sky or heavens for a
background or field. Accordingly they are not dark and terrene,
but lit and elysian. (vi, 17)

He excelled all his New England contemporaries in his concern with
esthetic theory and in the practical application of it to his writings.

According to Transcendental doctrine all men are potential poets
and creators, an idea that finds its way indirectly into Thoreau's *Journal*
once. "How novel and original must be each new man's view of the
universe!" he declares: "The whole world is an America, a *new*
World." (iii, 384) But normally he is too tough-minded for such
idealisms. He is convinced that most people are incapable of having
new worlds revealed to them, and that the poet himself has only moments of such creative perception, when all his faculties are receptive
to some new discovery. To be seen an object must fall within the
range of our "intellectual ray" as well as our visual ray, he says: "For
there is no power to see in the eye itself, any more than in any other
jelly."

A large number of *Journal* comments of this sort are gathered
together in a fine late essay. To avoid too much solemnity in discussing an abstract idea, Thoreau begins by giving a witty turn to the
hackneyed illustration of the several subjective interpretations of objective reality by different observers of the same scene. From this he
draws a lesson: "There is just as much beauty visible to us in the
landscape as we are prepared to appreciate,—not a grain more. We
cannot see anything until we are possessed with the idea of it, take it
into our heads,—and then we can hardly see anything else." ("Autumnal Tints," *Excursions*, 285–286) The essay concludes with an
elaborate conceit of the hunter of wild game as symbol of the poet
pursuing beauty in nature:

The sportsman trains himself, dresses, and watches unweariedly,
and loads and primes for his particular game. He prays for it,
and offers sacrifices, and so he gets it. After due and long prepara-
tion, schooling his eye and hand, dreaming awake and asleep,

with gun and paddle and boat, he goes out after meadow-hens,
which most of his townsmen never saw nor dreamed of, and
paddles for miles against a head wind, and wades in water up to
his knees, being out all day without his dinner, and therefore
he gets them. He had them half-way into his bag when he started,
and has only to shove them down. The true sportsman can shoot
you almost any of his game from his windows: what else has he
windows or eyes for? It comes and perches at last on the barrel
of his gun; but the rest of the world never see it with the feathers
on. (Excursions, 287–288)

A seventeenth-century metaphysical poet would have rested his image
there. Being a mid-nineteenth-century one, Thoreau felt it necessary
to spell out the analogy, but he does not ruin the conceit. One can
even be grateful for the tag: "And so it is with him that shoots at
beauty; though he wait till the sky falls, he will not bag any, if he
does not already know its seasons and haunts, and the color of its
wing,— if he has not dreamed of it, so that he can *anticipate* it." Far
better than by abstractions and argument, he uses such emblematic
figures to illustrate his theory of the poet's creative response to beauty.
But sensibility is not enough.

Despite Thoreau's elaborate experiments with angles of perception, hoping he could develop techniques that would help him bring
thing-thought-and-word together, he was not naive enough to believe
he could trap nature with a bag of tricks. He keeps reminding himself
of the essentially ungraspable quality of the external world. Once, for
example, he tries to describe a quite commonplace landscape with
such simple directness and accuracy that he can "possess" it. Admit-
ting his failure, he returns to the same scene three months later and
makes another valiant attempt in his *Journal:*

One afternoon in the fall, November 21st, I saw Fair Haven
Pond with its island and meadow; between the island and the
shore, a strip of perfectly smooth water in the lee of the island;
and two hawks sailing over it; and something more I saw which
cannot easily be described, which made me say to myself that
the landscape could not be improved. I did not see how it could

be improved. Yet I do not know what these things can be; I begin to see such objects only when I leave off understanding them, and afterwards remember that I did not appreciate them before. But I get no further than this. How adapted these forms and colors to our eyes, a meadow and its islands! What are these things? Yet the hawks and the ducks keep so aloof, and nature is so reserved! (11, 160–161)

The point is that no description, however fine-meshed, can ever snare nature. What the writer gets is not the object but his perception of it, something quite different.

One final statement by Thoreau dealing with the relation of thing-thought-and-word will demonstrate how far he went beyond contemporaries in his theory of perception: "Natural objects and phenomena are the original symbols or types which express our thoughts and feelings." (ix, 389) Taken by itself this sounds close to Emerson's theorizing about the "natural" origin of language in his basic little book *Nature*. But taken in conjunction with several other passages in Thoreau's *Journal* it becomes clear that his concern is with esthetic theory rather than Transcendental philosophy. For example, in commenting on some of the naturalists whose writings he read ardently, he says:

As in the expression of moral truths we admire any closeness to the physical fact which in all language is the symbol of the spiritual, so, finally, when natural objects are described, it is an advantage if words derived originally from nature, it is true, but which have been turned (tropes) from their primary significa-tion to a moral sense, are used. . . . Many of the words of the old naturalists were in this sense doubly tropes. (xiii, 145–146)

The next passage takes him one step further: "Is it not as language that all natural objects affect the poet? He sees a flower or other object, and it is beautiful or affecting to him because it is a symbol of his thought. . . . The objects I behold correspond to my mood." (v, 359) The last one is a boast that he has bridged the gap between perception of the object by the mind and its expression in language: "My thought is a part of the meaning of the world, and hence I use a part of the world as a symbol to express my thought." (IV, 410) It remains now to examine Thoreau's highly original commentary on the poet's tech-niques for translating his perceptions of nature into words.

Expression

"As you *see*, so at length will you *say*." This maxim, central to Thoreau's poetics, has already been discussed in relation to perception. Now it will be applied to his theory of expression.

A man must be rich in experience before he can have anything to say; but fullness of life is not always immediately translatable into expression, as he explains in a *Journal* passage of 1851:

> *Our ecstatic states, which appear to yield so little fruit, have this value at least: though in the seasons when our genius reigns we may be powerless for expression, yet, in calmer seasons, when our talent is active, the memory of those rarer moods comes to color our picture and is the permanent paint-pot, as it were, into which we dip our brush. Thus no life or experience goes unreported at last. . . . It is an experience of infinite beauty on which we unfailingly draw.*

These are the states that precede expression. This passage begins with echoes of Wordsworth's great Intimations Ode— "Thus in a season of calm weather," as a time when the poet can draw on his recollected emotions. But with the nearer approach of the "muse," in the next paragraph, the phrasing suggests a new direction:

> *We sometimes experience a mere fullness of life, which does not find any channels to flow into. We are stimulated, but to no obvious purpose. I feel myself uncommonly prepared for some literary work, but I can select no work. I am prepared not so much for contemplation, as for forceful expression. I am braced both physically and intellectually. It is not so much the music as the marching to the music that I feel. I feel that the juices of the fruits which I have eaten, the melons and apples, have ascended to my brain and are stimulating it. They give me a heady force. Now I can write nervously. (II, 467–469)*

Thoreau is using "nervous" here in its original sense, as was frequently done in the nineteenth century, to describe writing that is sinewy and vigorous in expression—his own style, in sharp distinction from that of Wordsworth.

We write well and truly only when we write with gusto, he continues. "Expression is the act of the *whole* man," according to Thoreau: "The intellect is powerless to express thought without the aid of the heart and liver and every other member." (II, 441) This total expression of the inner man, rare and difficult as it is, was the kind of writing he chiefly aimed at. It is even hard to define. Thoreau's best metaphor to describe the process is the result of reworking a *Journal* entry of 1842 for inclusion in his first book, seven years later: "The talent of composition is very dangerous,—the striking out the heart of life at a blow, as the Indian takes off a scalp. I feel as if my life had grown more outward when I can express it." (*A Week*, 351; *Journal*, I, 349) In the privacy of his *Journal* he confessed: "but to give the within outwardness, that is not easy." (I, 189) Then comes a final caution that sets Thoreau apart from the Romantic mode of subjectivity. Though much expression springs from experiences within the self, it must transcend the self. "Say it and have done with it," he declares in the *Journal* of 1851: "Express it without expressing yourself." (III, 85) Again, a few months later: "The peculiarity of a work of genius is the absence of the speaker from his speech. He is but the medium." (III, 236)

One way to get the "fullness of life" flowing into literary channels—to overcome the difficulty of getting started—is to write often and briefly rather than long at a time. "Improve every opportunity to express yourself in writing, as if it were your last," Thoreau urges. (III, 107, 140) An equally recurrent note in his *Journal* is the self-exhortation to write only at the top of his bent. Just as often he is reminding himself how difficult this is: "Though I write every day, yet when I say a good thing it seems as if I wrote but rarely." (I, 223) But his passion for improvement was unremitting. At the very outset of his journal-keeping he began a dialogue on the relative merits of spontaneous and deliberately controlled writing, that which is set down immediately as against that written (or revised) with the aid of perspective. Just a few months after his first entry he queried:

But what does all this scribbling amount to? What is now scrib-
bled in the heat of the moment one can contemplate with some-
what of satisfaction, but alas! tomorrow—aye, tonight—it is
stale, flat, and unprofitable,—in fine, is not, only its shell re-
mains, like some red parboiled lobster-shell which, kicked aside
*never so often, still stares at you in the path. (*1, 34)

On the very next page his faith in inspiration seems restored. "Impulse
is, after all, the best linguist," he says under the heading COMPOSI-
TION: "The nearer we approach to a complete but simple transcript
of our thought the more tolerable will be the piece."

Three years later he takes the more balanced view that what is
written spontaneously is likely to be a mixture, though more of it
may turn out to be valuable than appears at the time:

Of all strange and unaccountable things this journalizing is the
strangest. It will allow nothing to be predicated of it; its good
is not good, nor its bad bad. If I make a huge effort to expose
my innermost and richest wares to light, my counter seems clut-
tered with the meanest homemade stuffs; but after months or
years I may discover the wealth of India, and whatever rarity
is brought overland from Cathay, in that confused heap, and
what perhaps seemed a festoon of dried apple or pumpkin will
prove a string of Brazilian diamonds, or pearls from Coromandel.
(1, 182)

The emphasis here is on the value of setting down impressions immediately as material for future writings, rather than any assumption that
a finished piece of writing can be produced by the spontaneous
method. The passage also deals with recording inner experiences
rather than outer ones. Thoreau clearly has the former in mind when
making his most extravagant claims for spontaneous writing. In a
letter of 1857 he says:

As for style of writing—if one has any thing to say, it drops from
him simply & directly, as a stone falls to the ground, for there are
no two ways about it, but down it comes, and he may stick in the
points and stops wherever he can get a chance. New ideas come
into this world somewhat like falling meteors, with a flash and
an explosion, and perhaps somebody's castle roof perforated. To
try to polish the stone in its descent, to give it a particular turn

and make it whistle a tune perchance, would be of no use, if it were possible. Your polished stuff turns out not to be meteoric, but of this earth.[4]

It should be noted that he took this extreme stance in reaction against the vague and insipid style of a minor contemporary, Wilson Flagg, about whom a correspondent had inquired.

Yet on occasion, and in sober earnest, Thoreau comes close to the idea of intuitive utterance as expounded by Emerson, and claimed by Whitman in his role of vatic poet. Here is a *Journal* passage from 1860:

The fruit a thinker bears is sentences,—statements or opinions. He seeks to affirm something as true. I am surprised that my affirmations or utterances come to me ready-made,—not fore-thought,—so that I occasionally awake in the night simply to let fall ripe a statement which I had never consciously considered before, and as surprising and novel and agreeable to me as any-thing can be. As if we only thought by sympathy with the uni-versal mind, which thought while we were asleep. (xiii, 238)

How can one reconcile this with the equally emphatic declaration at the beginning of his career: "Every sentence is the result of a long probation. . . . Nothing goes by luck in composition. It allows of no tricks." (i, 225–226) The answer is quite simple; he is talking about two different kinds of writing, even two parts of the same piece of writing. The difference is put memorably in another late *Journal* entry:

We must walk consciously only part way toward our goal, and then leap in the dark to our success. What we do best or most perfectly is what we have most thoroughly learned by the longest practice, and at length it falls from us without our notice, as a leaf from a tree. (xii, 39)

This commentary on the creative process seems more valid today than the Transcendental one about "sympathy with the universal mind" quoted above. Many modern poets have used images like "leap in the dark" to describe those parts of their compositions—often the best—which they have no memory of having labored to create. Such "un-

[4] *The Correspondence of Henry David Thoreau*, ed. Walter Harding and Carl Bode (1958), 489.

conscious" writing is usually the expression of some inner experience.

Adequate recording of outer experiences sometimes poses another kind of difficulty, as Thoreau sets it forth in *A Week*. During the famous river trip by the two brothers that furnished the staple of this book, they made it a rule to put down all their experiences in their journals. But they found this resolution hard to keep. Frequently the important experience so absorbed them that trivial and indifferent things got recorded instead: "It is not easy to write in a journal what interests us at any time, because to write it is not what interests us." (*A Week*, 354) Many an author has been faced with such a dilemma. One way of coping with this problem is to live the experience to the full at the time, then explore its meaning in writing later through memory. Looking back in 1857 on his whole career as an author, Thoreau phrases it as follows: "Often I can give the truest and most interesting account of any adventure I have had after years have elapsed, for then I am not confused, only the most significant facts surviving in my memory." (IX, 311) This is a perfect description of how the ultimate transformation of experience into words was achieved in his two books: through the perspective of a decade between the river trip and the publication of *A Week*— almost a decade between the beginning of his experiment at the pond and *Walden*.

There are many steps in the writing process much closer to the experience itself, however, that must take place before such a final transformation is possible. For the keeper of a journal they are likely to be very close indeed, though some perspective is needed. "I succeed best when I *recur* to my experience not too late, but within a day or two," Thoreau declares at the height of his creative period; "when there is some distance, but enough of freshness." (IV, 20) Since his best writing is a fusion of outer and inner experience—precise recording of events or things seen and symbolic rendering of their impact on him—both methods of getting things down are indispensable. In his discrimination of the two, which follows, "today" and "tomorrow" should be taken figuratively for immediate and delayed composition:

> I would fain make two reports in my Journal, first the incidents
> and observations of today; and by tomorrow I review the same
> and record what was omitted before, which will often be the

*most significant and poetic part. I do not know at first what it is
that charms me. The men and things of today are wont to lie
fairer in tomorrow's memory.* (IX, 306)

Closely related to the problem of spontaneous versus controlled
writing is the matter of revision. With the aid of perspective the tal-
ented author can often return to what he has set down spontaneously
and improve it by excision, reordering, and rewriting. For all his high
talk about the intuitions of genius, Thoreau has much more to say
about craftsmanship than the other Transcendentalists. For example,
in the *Journal* of 1852, when the manuscript of *Walden* was being
transformed from a prosaic to a poetic book, he said:

*Whatever wit has been produced on the spur of the moment will
bear to be reconsidered and reformed with phlegm. The arrow
had best not be loosely shot. The most transient and passing
remark must be reconsidered by the writer, made sure and war-
ranted, as if the earth had rested on its axle to back it, and all the
natural forces lay behind it. The writer must direct his sentences
as carefully and leisurely as the marksman his rifle, who shoots
sitting and with a rest, with patent sights and conical balls beside.
He must not merely seem to speak the truth. He must really
speak it. If you foresee that a part of your essay will topple down
after the lapse of time, throw it down now yourself.* (III, 231)

The pain as well as the difficulty of cutting out what one has
written makes him lament, with an obvious grimace: "I wish that I
could buy at the shops some kind of india-rubber that would rub
out at once all that in my writing which it now costs me so many
perusals, so many months if not years, and so much reluctance, to
erase." (VI, 30) On 1 March 1854, while finishing the seventh version of *Walden*, Thoreau comments on another problem connected
with excision:

*In correcting my manuscripts, which I do with sufficient phlegm,
I find that I invariably turn out much that is good along with the
bad, which it is then impossible for me to distinguish—so much
for keeping bad company; but after the lapse of time, having purified the main body and thus created a distinct standard for comparison, I can review the rejected sentences and easily detect
those which deserve to be readmitted.* (VI, 146)

A writer cannot always wait for the "lapse of time," however. When perspective is not possible, he must exercise his sharpest powers of discrimination. "In composition it is the greatest art to find out which are the best passages you have written, and tear the rest away to come at them," he admonishes himself. (xi, 452) But this procedure is too ruthless, so he modifies it a few weeks later: "Find out as soon as possible what are the best things in your composition, and then shape the rest to fit them." (xii, 39) In the case of Thoreau's masterpiece there was no end to his revising. By the middle of March, 1854, he was sending off installments of the eighth and final draft of *Walden*, the printer's "fair copy." On March 28 the first batch of proofs arrived, and three days later he confided in his *Journal*:

> *In criticising your writing, trust your fine instinct. There are many things which we come very near questioning, but do not question. When I have sent off my manuscripts to the printer, certain objectionable sentences or expressions are sure to obtrude themselves on my attention with force, though I had not consciously suspected them before. My critical instinct then at once breaks the ice and comes to the surface.* (v i, 179)

So the page proof offered him one more opportunity for making a number of small revisions. After publication he continued to make a few corrections in his copy of *Walden*—not to be incorporated in the printed text until the second (posthumous) edition.[5]

In Thoreau's commentary on expression much of his concern is with diction, naturally enough, since words are the pigments for a writer's brush. Scattered through the *Journal* are a number of interesting generalizations, such as his distinction between the spoken and written language: "The one is transient, a sound, a tongue, a dialect, and all men learn it of their mothers. It is loquacious, fragmentary, —raw material. The other is a reserved, select, matured expression, a deliberate word addressed to the ear of nations and generations." (i, 369) Again, he sets up a rule for avoiding wordiness; he will follow nature, who is a plain writer, uses few modifiers, and no expletives. As to himself, on the contrary: "I find that I use many words for the

[5]   See the account in J. L. Shanley, *The Making of Walden* (1957), 32–33.

sake of emphasis which really add nothing to the force of my sentences, and they look relieved the moment I have cancelled them." (III, 233) But he is most original and incisive when he focuses on specific matters like diction.

A writer's first concern is a negative one, what kinds of language to avoid— the hackneyed, the pompous, and so on. Thoreau has very sharp opinions on the subject and expresses them frequently. In 1852 he notes in his *Journal:* "A writer who does not speak out of a full experience uses torpid words, wooden or lifeless words, such words as 'humanitary,' which have a paralysis in their tails." (IV, 225) Again, in 1858:

> There are many words which are genuine and indigenous and have their root in our natures, not made by scholars, and as well understood by the illiterate as others. There are also a great many words which are spurious and artificial, and can only be used in a bad sense, since the thing they signify is not fair and substantial, —such as the church, the judiciary, to impeach, etc., etc. They who use them do not stand on solid ground. It is in vain to try to preserve them by attaching other words to them as the true church, etc. It is like towing a sinking ship with a canoe. (x, 233)

A few weeks later he returns to the subject:

> Some men have a peculiar taste for bad words, mouthing and licking them into lumpish shapes like the bear her cubs,—words like "tribal" and "ornamentation," which drag a dead tail after them. They will pick you out of a thousand the still-born words, the falsettos, the wing-clipped and lame words, as if only the false notes caught their ears. (x, 261–262)

From the words he chooses for condemnation it is clear that Thoreau not only sets himself against jargon but includes the whole vocabulary of the Establishment in that category, as befits a radical and one who knows that words and ideas are inseparable.

Rejecting the language of the old orthodoxies, such as church and state, he turns to science as the possible source of a language closer allied to reality. "I can see that there is a certain advantage in these hard and precise terms, such as the lichenist uses, for instance," he says in the *Journal* of 1852: "No man writes on lichens, using the terms of the science intelligibly, without having something to say, but every one thinks himself competent to write on the relation of the soul to the body, as if that were a *phaenogamous* subject." (III, 326–327) Throughout most of his career Thoreau was trying to bring the poet and scientist together because of their common interest in nature and their concern with modes of perception. Now he found an added incentive, the possibility of fusing their language. There are many *Journal* passages like the following:

> *How copious and precise the botanical language to describe the leaves, as well as the other parts of a plant! Botany is worth study-ing if only for the precision of its terms,—to learn the value of words and of system. . . . Suppose as much ingenuity (per-haps it would be needless) in making a language to express the sentiments! . . . [a] language applied to the description of moral qualities!* (11, 409–410)

But by mid-century it was becoming apparent that the language of science was less usable for poetry than had been hoped, that it was in fact moving in the direction of a new orthodoxy of technological jargon.

About this time Thoreau discovered the writings of James J. G. Wilkinson, an extraordinary contemporary who began as a medical scientist, then devoted the better part of his life to editing and inter-preting the works of Swedenborg, the philosopher-scientist-mystic. Influenced by Blake, Wilkinson in turn influenced Emerson, Carlyle, and other literary men. Since he was also a skilled linguist, Wilkinson had a special appeal for Thoreau, as will be apparent from this *Journal* passage:

> *Wilkinson's book*[6] *to some extent realizes what I have dreamed of,—a return to the primitive analogical and derivative senses of words. . . . The man of science discovers no world for the mind of man to inhabit. Wilkinson finds a home for the imagina-tion, and it is no longer outcast and homeless. All perception of truth is the detection of an analogy; we reason from our hands to our head.* (11, 462–463)

Wilkinson made no attempt to bridge the gap between scientist and poet. On the contrary, his writing helped to show Thoreau the in-

[6]   Of James Wilkinson's many books, the one here referred to was probably *The Human Body and Its Connection with Man* (1851).

adequacies of scientific language for his own purposes, and pointed the way back to more viable models.

Thoreau's desire to go back to the "primitive analogical" meanings of words is a clue to his admiration of certain seventeenth-century writers. Eulogies of them can be found scattered through the *Journal*, as in this paragraph on the well-known English diarist:

> *Evelyn and others wrote when the language was in a tender, nascent state and could be moulded to express the shades of meaning; when sesquipedalian words, long since cut and dried and drawn to mill,—not yet to the dictionary lumber-yard,— put forth a fringe of green sprouts here and there along in the angles of their rugged bark, their very bulk insuring some sap remaining; some florid suckers they sustain at least. Which words, split into shingles and laths, will supply poets for ages to come.* (v, 43)

Thoreau's metaphysical conceit, appropriate to the period he is talking about, makes it clear that he wants to incorporate in his own writing the vigor and vitality of seventeenth-century authors, not their proneness to polysyllables. This is emphasized by the one quality he singles out for praise in Francis Quarles, a Jacobean poet whom he finds fault with otherwise: "He presses able-bodied and strong-backed words into his service, which have a certain rustic fragrance and force, as if now first devoted to literature, after having served sincere and stern uses." (I, 458–459) What could better characterize one outstanding quality of Thoreau's writing than "a certain rustic fragrance and force"?

When he moves nearer home, to seventeenth-century New England writers, the phrasing of his eulogy points up a major source of his own famous style, previously unsuspected:

> *What a strong and hearty but reckless, hit-or-miss style had some of the early writers of New England, like [John] Josselyn and William Wood and others elsewhere in those days; as if they spoke with a relish, smacking their lips like a coach-whip, caring more to speak heartily than scientifically true. They are not to be caught napping by the wonders of Nature in a new country, and perhaps are often more ready to appreciate them than she is to exhibit them. They give you one piece of nature, at any rate, and that is themselves. (Cotton Mather, too, has a rich phrase.)*

They use a strong, coarse, homely speech which cannot always be found in the dictionary, nor sometimes be heard in polite society, but which brings you very near to the thing itself described. The strong new soil speaks through them. I have just been reading some in Wood's "New England's Prospect." . . . Certainly that generation stood nearer to nature, nearer to the facts, than this, and hence their books have more life in them. . . .

Expressions he [Wood] uses which you now hear only in kitchens and barrooms, which therefore sound particularly fresh and telling, not book-worn. They speak like men who have backs and stomachs and bowels, with all the advantages and disadvantages that attach to them. . . . Most admirable when they most outrage taste and the rules of composition. (VII, 108–110)

With some modification, Thoreau seems here to be describing the salient characteristics of his own writing. (In referring to barrooms he means language that is unconventional, even coarse, but probably not obscene or profane.) In the light of this passage the reader will find it profitable to reread a number of Miniatures in the present volume, such as "Reformers," "The Town Drunkard," and "Lightning."

In these seventeenth-century New England writers, and perhaps those in the Southern colonies, can be found the beginnings of the American language, as it came gradually to differentiate itself from the British mother tongue. Thoreau did not quite think of it as a separate "language," but he was aware that conditions in the new country were producing a new vocabulary. Several *Journal* passages pay tribute to the high significance for the poet of "Americanisms":

Talk about learning our letters and being literate! Why, the roots of letters are things. Natural objects and phenomena are the original symbols or types which express our thoughts and feelings, and yet American scholars, having little or no root in the soil, commonly strive with all their might to confine themselves to the imported symbols alone. All the true growth and experience, the living speech, they would fain reject as Americanisms. It is the old error, which the church, the state, the school ever commit, choosing darkness rather than light, holding fast to the old and to tradition. A more intimate knowledge, a deeper experience, will

surely originate a word. When I really know that our river pur-
sues a serpentine course to the Merrimack, shall I continue to
describe it by referring to some other river no older than itself
which is like it, and call it a meander? *It is no more meandering*
than the Meander is musketaquidding.[7] *As well sing of the night-*
ingale here as the Meander. What if there were a tariff on words,
on language, for the encouragement of home manufactures? Have
we not the genius to coin our own? Let the schoolmaster dis-
tinguish the true from the counterfeit. (ix, 389–390)

Thoreau was convinced that he had found this kind of American
language in the speeches and writings of John Brown. In the second
of his eulogies on that martyr he declares:

Literary gentlemen, editors, and critics think that they know how
to write because they have studied grammar and rhetoric; but the
art of composition is as simple as the discharge of a bullet from a
rifle, and its masterpieces imply an infinitely greater force behind
it. This unlettered man's speaking and writing is standard English.
Some words and phrases deemed vulgarisms and Americanisms
before, he has made standard American. . . . It suggests that
the one great rule of composition—and if I were a professor of
rhetoric I should insist on this—is to speak the truth. *This first,*
this second, this third. (xiii, 11)

His own masterpiece, *Walden*, has sufficient force behind it to make
a powerful impact on readers more than a century after publication
precisely because it was written in a new "American language," such
as he describes above.

Thoreau's interest in Americanisms is part of his larger concern
to develop a "natural" as opposed to an "artificial" style, that is, one
drawn from experience rather than from previous literature. His *Jour-*
nal, essays, and books are filled with discussions like the following:

When I hear the hypercritical quarrelling about grammar and
style, . . . I see that they forget that the first requisite and rule is
that expression shall be vital and natural, as much as the voice of
a brute or an interjection; first of all, mother tongue; and last of
all, artificial or father tongue. Essentially your truest poetic sen-

---

[7]   Musketaquid was the Indian name for Concord River.

tence is as free and lawless as a lamb's bleat. The grammarian is often one who can neither cry nor laugh, yet thinks that he can express human emotions. So the posture-masters tell you how you shall walk,—turning your toes out, perhaps, excessively,—but so the beautiful walkers are not made. (x1, 386)

Some of Thoreau's most extreme statements along this line gain authority when one remembers that he was speaking from experience rather than from some romantic idealism. "The scholar rarely writes as well as the farmer talks," declares the man who was both scholar and farmer, so to speak, and who drew his friends about equally from the two groups: "I like better the surliness with which the woodchopper speaks of his woods, handling them as indifferently as his axe, than the mealy-mouthed enthusiasm of the lover of nature." (1, 237)

Since Thoreau was a lover of nature as well as a woodchopper, his principle is phrased convincingly when applied to himself:

I find incessant labor with the hands, which engrosses the attention also, the best method to remove palaver out of one's style. One will not dance at his work who has wood to cut and cord before the night falls in the short days of winter; but every stroke will be husbanded, and ring soberly through the wood; and so will his lines ring and tell on the ear, when at evening he settles the accounts of the day. (1, 312–313)

This was written in mid-winter of 1842. Three months later, in spring, he added a postscript: "I am sure I write the tougher truth for these calluses on my palms." (1, 345) And when the passage was greatly expanded for inclusion in his first book, he applied his dictum to the writings of those who are manual laborers by vocation:

We are often struck by the force and precision of style to which hard-working men, unpractised in writing, easily attain when required to make the effort. As if plainness and vigor and sincerity, the ornaments of style, were better learned on the farm and in the workshop than in the schools. The sentences written by such rude hands are nervous and tough, like hardened thongs, the sinews of the deer, or the roots of the pine. (A Week, 109; cf. 108–112)

Since no such writings have come down to the student of literature, there is no way to test the truth of Thoreau's claim. One can discount it as a lapse into sentimentalism. Or one can take the whole passage as figurative. Certainly the images in the last sentence describe the writing of at least one man who learned his style "on the farm and in the workshop [rather] than in the schools," symbolically if not literally— the author of *Walden*.

Two more passages on the natural style will complete Thoreau's attempt at a definition. The first comes from a posthumous essay on the theme of "wildness":

> *He would be a poet who could impress the winds and streams into his service, to speak for him; who nailed words to their primitive senses, as farmers drive down stakes in the spring, which the frost has heaved; who derived his words as often as he used them, —transplanted them to his page with earth adhering to their roots; whose words were so true and fresh and natural that they would appear to expand like the buds at the approach of spring, though they lay half smothered between two musty leaves in a library.* ("Walking," *Excursions*, 232)

The second comes from the *Journal*, drawing its imagery from Greek mythology. Here the earth represents reality and flying symbolizes a mortal mistake:

> *[Do not try] to turn too many feeble somersets in the air,—and so come down on your head at last. Antaeus-like, be not long absent from the ground. Those sentences are good and well discharged which are like so many little resiliencies . . . springing from terra firma. . . . Those are the admirable bounds when the performer has lately touched the springboard. A good bound into the air from the [ground] is a good and wholesome experience, but what shall we say to a man's leaping off precipices in the attempt to fly? He comes down like lead . . . , an ever memorable Icarian fall, in which [his] helpless wings are expanded by [his] swift descent into the pelagos beneath. . . . Better one effective bound upward with elastic limbs from the valley than a jumping from the mountain-tops in the attempt to fly.* (iii, 107–108)

Almost all of Thoreau's theoretical formulations are presented in similes and metaphors, sufficient evidence that he was a poet interested in theory rather than a critic with a minor interest in writing poetry.

What he was trying to work out was a dialectic to support and confirm his own style of writing.

In view of all this figurative language, only the literal-minded would take at face value Thoreau's proposal that he was a "natural" writer unrelated to the tradition. He learned all he could from his predecessors, mainly the Classical and Renaissance authors, and from his contemporaries, chief of whom were Wordsworth and Emerson, as has been shown. But there were two more nineteenth-century influences of importance, one negative and the other positive. The contrast between his reactions to them charts the development of his own style in one of its most important characteristics. Of a well-known early nineteenth-century master of the familiar essay Thoreau says:

> It is the fault of some excellent writers—De Quincey's first impressions on seeing London suggest it to me—that they express themselves with too great fullness and detail. They give the most faithful, natural, and lifelike account of their sensations, mental and physical, but they lack moderation and sententiousness. They do not affect us by an ineffectual earnestness and a reserve of meaning, like a stutterer; they say all they mean. Their sentences are not concentrated and nutty. Sentences which suggest far more than they say, which have an atmosphere about them, which do not merely report an old, but make a new, impression; sentences which suggest as many things and are as durable as a Roman aqueduct; to frame these, that is the art of writing. Sentences which are expensive, towards which so many volumes, so much life, went; which lie like boulders on the page, up and down or across; which contain the seed of other sentences, not mere repetition, but creation; which a man might sell his grounds and castle to build. If De Quincey had suggested each of his pages in a sentence and passed on, it would have been far more excellent writing. His style is nowhere kinked and knotted up into something hard and significant, which you could swallow like a diamond, without digesting. (11, 418–419)

Of the burly Scotsman, Thomas Carlyle, who broke ground for a new generation of writers, Thoreau speaks like a potential disciple:

One wonders how much, after all, was expressed in the old way, so much here depends upon the emphasis, tone, pronunciation, style, and spirit of the reading. No writer uses so profusely all the aids to intelligibility which the printer's art affords. You wonder how others had contrived to write so many pages without emphatic, italicized words, they are so expressive, so natural and indispensable, here. As if none had ever used the demonstrative pronoun demonstratively. In another's sentences the thought, though immortal, is, as it were, embalmed and does not strike you, but here it is so freshly living, not purified by the ordeal of death, that it stirs in the very extremities, the smallest particles and pronouns are all alive with it. —You must not say it, but it. . . . This style is worth attending to as one of the most important features of the man we at this distance know. (1, 425–426)

By 1847, when Thoreau gathered together his relevant *Journal* jottings of the past two years on Carlyle and published them in a forty-page essay, he was committed:

Who cares what a man's style is, so it is intelligible,—as intelligible as his thought. Literally and really, the style is no more than the stylus, the pen he writes with. . . . The question for us is, not whether Pope had a fine style, wrote with a peacock's feather, but whether he uttered useful thoughts. . . . We believe that Carlyle has, after all, more readers, and is better known today for his very originality of style, and that posterity will have reason to thank him for emancipating the language, in some measure, from the fetters which a merely conservative, aimless, and pedantic literary class had imposed upon it, and setting an example of greater freedom and naturalness. No man's thoughts are new, but the style of their expression is the never-failing novelty which cheers and refreshes men. ("Thomas Carlyle and his Works," *Cape Cod*, 330–331)

One of Thoreau's most effective stylistic devices was learned directly from Carlyle. To an intimate correspondent he confided in 1853: "I trust that you realize what an exaggerater I am,—that I lay myself out to exaggerate whenever I have an opportunity,—pile Pelion upon Ossa, to reach heaven so. Expect no trivial truth from me."[8]

[8] Thoreau, *Correspondence*, 304.

The next year, near the end of *Walden*, he announced his new mode of writing, first suggested by Carlyle but now assimilated into a wholly different style:

> *I fear chiefly lest my expression may not be* extra-vagant *enough, may not wander far enough beyond the narrow limits of my daily experience, so as to be adequate to the truth of which I have been convinced.* Extra vagance! *. . . I desire to speak somewhere without* bounds; *like a man in a waking moment, to men in their waking moments; for I am convinced that I cannot exaggerate enough even to lay the foundation of a true expression.* (*Walden*, 357)

Certainly a large part of the shock impact of *Walden* comes from its use of extravagance and exaggeration.

Thoreau's really distinctive voice speaks to us in paradoxes, a mode closely related to that described above. Emerson objected to this quality in his style. Once, in accepting an essay of Thoreau's for publication in the *Dial* (1843), he wrote to say that he had made numerous omissions in order to remove this "*mannerism.*" In the privacy of his journal he was more critically outspoken:

> *Henry Thoreau sends me a paper with the old fault of unlimited contradiction. The trick of his rhetoric is soon learned: it consists in substituting for the obvious word and thought its diametrical antagonist. He praises wild mountains and winter forests for their domestic air; snow and ice for their warmth; villagers and wood-choppers for their urbanity, and the wilderness for resembling Rome and Paris. . . . It makes me nervous and wretched to read it.*[9]

A decade later Emerson was still complaining of his friend: "Always some weary captious paradox to fight you with . . . all his resources of wit and invention are lost to me." Thoreau's response to this is recorded in his *Journal* on 12 March 1854:

> *My companion tempts me to certain licenses of speech, i. e. to reckless and sweeping expressions which I am wont to regret that I have used. That is, I find that I have used more harsh, extrava-*

[9] *The Journals of Ralph Waldo Emerson*, ed. E. W. Emerson and W. E. Forbes (1909–1914), VI, 440. The quotation in the next sentence is from IX, 15.

gant, and cynical expressions concerning mankind and individuals than I have intended. . . . He asks for a paradox, an eccentric statement, and too often I give it to him. (VI, 165)

When Emerson read *Walden* he probably squirmed at one sentence in the "Conclusion," realizing that the author's finger was pointed at him: "In this part of the world it is considered grounds for complaint if a man's writings admit of more than one interpretation." (*Walden,* 358) But when Thoreau himself reread his book shortly after publication, interestingly enough, he entered in his *Journal* a list of his faults, headed by: "Paradoxes,—saying just the opposite,—a style which may be imitated." (VII, 7–8) And yet, paradoxically, he kept on using them. The truth of the matter is quite simple. Paradoxes, when indulged in indiscriminately, become a perverse and exasperating mannerism. Yet they can be extraordinarily effective when made a disciplined and meaningful part of an author's style, as they are in *Walden.* There the first use of paradox is satirical, making readers doubt the values of their own world, item by item; its second use is to make the narrator's world transcend the conventional world by subverting key terms in its language to new meanings.

By the time Thoreau composed *Walden* all the theoretical principles he had laid down for others, if they would master the art of writing, had been assimilated into his own style. What gave this its final distinction was his use of paradox and extravagance, the techniques for creating his most effective wit and metaphor. Thoreau's final achievement of style in his masterpiece has long been famous. Readers can now study its evolution over the years in the Miniatures of the present volume.

Form

The Romantic reaction against what was felt to be artificial in Neoclassical literature, not only diction but structure, was carried to extremes by the New England Transcendentalists. Hence their off-hand attitude toward form, treating it as something that would hopefully take care of itself, since ideal form is "organic" and grows naturally out of the chosen subject. The negative impulse behind this revolt was salutary, because it opened the way for the new and experimental in nineteenth-century American literature, the poetry of Whitman and Dickinson, the prose of Thoreau himself. But on the positive side this break-away produced ambiguous results. Authors who turned their backs on traditional forms were not always successful in creating new ones; then, blurring the distinction between nature and art, they tended to minimize the whole problem of form. By the end of the century the general looseness—free verse, naturalism, polyphonic prose—provoked a counter-revolution led by authors such as James and Eliot and Joyce, who revived the artist's respect for discipline and control by transforming traditional structures to suit a changed modern world. Thoreau stands in the middle of this century of change and, as regards form, his writings must be measured in relation to it.

Among Transcendentalists, Emerson was the chief proponent of organic form. His faith in it was shown, among other ways, by the meager attention he gave to esthetic theory in general. He preferred to think of himself as seer rather than sayer, inspirer not artist, being more concerned with the matter than with the manner of his writings. When he did comment on the processes of art it was likely to be in Transcendental instead of technical terms. In his key essay on esthetics, "The Poet," Emerson made the often quoted statement: "For it is not metres but a metre-making argument that makes a poem,—a thought so passionate and alive that like the spirit of a plant or an animal it has an architecture of its own." Then, a few pages later, the less well-known dictum: "So when the soul of the poet has come to ripeness of thought, [his Genius] detaches and sends away from it its poems and songs." And again: "The poet also resigns himself to his mood, and that thought which agitated him is expressed . . . in a manner wholly new. The expression is organic, or the new type which things themselves take when liberated." [10] The problem of organic form in Emerson's theory and practice is much more complicated than this oversimple summary can indicate, of course. In a long chapter Vivian Hopkins defines his aim as "a *freeing* of the possible plan contained within matter itself" rather than " an *imposing* of form from without," though he was aware that the artist can never make his work grow all

[10] *The Complete Works of Ralph Waldo Emerson,* ed. E. W. Emerson (1903–4), III, 9 ff.

at once, in the living way of a flower or a tree. The chief lack in Emerson's concept of form, she admits in conclusion, is the gap between the intuition in the artist's mind and its transference to objective matter—that is, the whole business of technique, how form is actually achieved.[11]

Comments similar to those of Emerson, above, can be found in a couple of passages from Thoreau's *Journal* quoted previously in this essay (pp. 338–339), but they refer only to the briefest compositions such as his aphorisms and epigrammatic sentences. It is also true that very short lyrics, like Emerson's "Days" and Thoreau's "Smoke," often seem to have been created in the same spontaneous way, though critical explications of such compositions usually reveal far more craftsmanship than was suspected.[12] In the matter of theory, however, Thoreau was not committed to faith in organic form to the degree that Emerson was, though he tended to fall back on the possibility of it when he became concerned lest too much craftsmanship might result in artifice. This partly explains his shifting from one side to the other of the theoretical argument, and his recurrent struggles to achieve form of some sort in his various writings.

Another important difference between the two authors can be found in their practice. Emerson never attempted any compositions longer than the extended essay, even volumes like *English Traits* and *Society and Solitude* being mere collections of separate pieces loosely related by subject matter. For the essays themselves, if he could not make the form grow organically from the chosen subject, he could always rely on the well-known one-two-three sequence of the sermon he had used so often before shifting from pulpit to authorship as a career, though his best essays are shaped by craftsmanship to a greater extent than he was aware. On the other hand, Thoreau's high reputation as a literary author is based on his full-scale books, whose unity cannot be satisfactorily explained by the Transcendental concept of organic form, whether one is referring to the simple narrative-thematic

[11] Vivian Hopkins, *Spires of Form: A Study of Emerson's Aesthetic Theory* (1951), Ch. 2, pp. 63–146.

[12] For "Smoke," see *The Magic Circle of Walden*, pp. 274–276; for "Days," see the articles listed in Frederic I. Carpenter's *Emerson Handbook*.

patterns of *Cape Cod* and *The Maine Woods* or to the symbolic structures of *Walden* and *A Week*. It has often been held that these books, as well as Thoreau's essays, were composed by the "mosaic method," which is curiously related to the concept of organic form and must be discussed at some length now.

Thoreau filled his *Journal* with random observations and ideas, spontaneously shaped by the impulse of the moment, so the thesis goes. Afterwards, choosing some theme that interested him, he would search out all the relevant bits and pieces he had jotted down over the years, then tinker them together in a unified whole—this being the point where craftsmanship supplemented organic form. The inadequacy of this method of composition is the basis of Margaret Fuller's complaint about Thoreau's first ambitious essay, "The Service," submitted in 1840 for publication in the Transcendental magazine, *The Dial*. It was rich in thoughts, she admitted in her letter of rejection, but they were "so out of their natural order" that she could not read it without pain: "I never once feel myself in a stream of thought, but hear the grating of tools on the mosaic." [18]

Of course the mosaic had long ago proved a superb art form, especially under the Byzantine Empire, when the same man was both the craftsman who assembled the colored fragments and the artist who had created the design to adorn the walls of some church or palace. There is, however, a major difference in applying the mosaic method to the creation of literature. A bit of blue stone or glass, cut to fit the space requirements, can be used indifferently for the sky or the Madonna's robe. But a sentence or paragraph has its own inherent meaning in relation to a particular topic and cannot be shifted at will from one part of the artist's composition to another, no matter how he may trim its size. In a limited way it is possible for an author to use some such method in drawing materials from his notebooks. But the point is that Thoreau did not use it extensively in his best work, though the issues raised by the term "mosaic" are central to an understanding of form in his writings.

The relation of his *Journal* to the essays and books Thoreau prepared for publication is much more complicated than is usually thought, and it needs to be understood. "The Service" was indeed a

[18]   Thoreau, *Correspondence*, 42.

poor essay, as he himself admitted by never trying again to get it published, but not because it was a mosaic. The fault was that its parts were gathered together from brief sententious utterances scattered through the *Journal* over a four-year period without any compelling design to fuse them into a whole. Other essays, like "Moonlight" and "Autumnal Tints," were put together in a somewhat different way, from longer passages written down periodically as the moon waxed full again or as the fall season returned with its brilliant colors; but there is the all-important difference that in both cases he had a chosen theme in mind from the start. That one is a failure and the other a success is not because of the method of composition, which is the same for both, but because facts in the latter are transformed by the imagination whereas in the former they are in the service of fancy.[14]

Still another essay, "Walking," was composed in a fairly close sequence of *Journal* entries during 1850–1851, for use as a lecture. Then during the next decade, as Thoreau continued his walking and his lecturing, he polished and reshaped it until finally, during his last illness, he prepared it for publication as one of his finest essays. Its excellence is partly the result of these disciplined revisions, partly because the theme was close to the center of his concern—his explorations of wild nature in his walks around Concord. Finally, an occasional essay like his "Plea for Captain John Brown" was written out almost completely in one continuous journal-draft, this one during the trial and execution of his martyr-hero in 1859.

Thoreau has much to say in the *Journal* itself about all these methods of composition. During his residence at Walden Pond—when he was preparing lectures for the Concord Lyceum, writing essays for the New York magazines, and beginning his first book, *A Week on the Concord and Merrimack Rivers*—he was thinking

---

[14] In addition to the fanciful passages on moonlight referred to above, which run all through Volume III, it should be noted that the *Journal* here and there shows many of the usual faults of writers. For example, Thoreau was capable of using purple rhetoric in describing a sunset (v, 332–333); of being trite in an account of a squirrel's activity (x, 65); of turning sentimental about early spring (xii, 147); of writing romantically about the "telegraph harp" in passages that recur in several volumes.

about all aspects of the writer's craft and trying to formulate his principles. One passage, undated but from the period of 1845–1847,
deals specifically with the mosaic method:

> *From all points of the compass, from the earth beneath and the*
> *heavens above, have come these inspirations and been fully en-*
> *tered in the order of their arrival in the journal. Thereafter, when*
> *the time arrived, they were winnowed into lectures, and again,*
> *in due time, from lectures into essays. And at last they stand, like*
> *the cubes of Pythagoras, firmly on either basis; like statues on*
> *their pedestals, but the statues rarely take hold of hands. There*
> *is only such connection and series as is attainable in the galleries.*
> (1, 413)

The main problem arising from the mosaic method (how to attain
"connection and series" between the parts) clearly applies to the difficulty he was having with his early essays like "The Service," how to
give them enough coherence to make them acceptable to the magazines. But the passage just quoted relates even more specifically to
Thoreau's effort to make the separate parts of *A Week*—then in
progress—"take hold of hands" and become a book. Though it is
usually thought of as a typical Transcendental gathering of loosely related essays, at least one critic has made a plausible interpretation of it
as a unified whole.[15]

Another passage in the *Journal*, near the end of his career, seems
more nearly concerned with his efforts to perfect such a late essay as
"Walking" by revising and rearranging:

> *The writer must to some extent inspire himself. Most of his sen-*
> *tences may at first lie dead in his essay, but when all are arranged,*
> *some life and color will be reflected on them from the mature and*
> *successful lines; they will appear to pulsate with fresh life, and*
> *he will be able to eke out their slumbering sense, and make them*
> *worthy of their neighborhood. In his first essay on a given theme,*
> *he produces scarcely more than a frame and groundwork for his*
> *sentiment and poetry. Each clear thought that he attains to draws*
> *in its train many divided thoughts or perceptions. The writer has*
> *much to do even to create a theme for himself. Most that is first*

---

[15]   See Sherman Paul, *The Shores of America: Thoreau's Inward Ex-*
ploration (1958).

written on any subject is a mere groping after it, mere rubble-stone and foundation. It is only when many observations of different periods have been brought together that he begins to grasp his subject and can make one pertinent and just observation. (x i, 438–439)

By some such process, the accretion of *Journal* passages and their integration into a new whole by revision upward, his essay on the joys of walking was turned into an essay celebrating a new principle: "In wildness is the preservation of the world."

One more long passage on literary techniques must be quoted here. It has application to the composition of essays, but it may well apply also to the rewriting of *Walden,* which was going forward at the time it was formulated, in the winter of 1852. During his residence at the pond, 1845–1847, and the years immediately following, Thoreau had completed a short first draft of his book, but this was mostly confined to an expository account of his experiment in economy there. From 1849 to 1852 he did little work on it. Then he began an elaborate revision and extension of his manuscript that transformed it into the symbolic creation we now know as *Walden.* At exactly this point, in the context of numerous reworkings of old passages and the addition of new ones that were being written for inclusion in his book, he speculated on compositional method in his *Journal,* 22 January 1852:

> *To set down such choice experiences that my own writings may inspire me and at last I may make wholes of parts. Certainly it is a distinct profession to rescue from oblivion and to fix the senti-*
> *ments and thoughts which visit all men more or less generally,*
> that the contemplation of the unfinished picture may suggest its
> harmonious completion. *Associate reverently and as much as you*
> *can with your loftiest thoughts. Each thought that is welcomed*
> *and recorded is a nest egg, by the side of which more will be*
> *laid. Thoughts accidentally thrown together become a frame in*
> *which more may be developed and exhibited. Perhaps this is*
> *the main value of a habit of writing, of keeping a journal,—that*
> *so we remember our best hours and stimulate ourselves. My*
> *thoughts are my company. They have a certain individuality and*
> *separate existence, aye, personality. Having by chance recorded*

a few disconnected thoughts and then brought them into juxta-
position, they suggest a whole new field in which it was possible
to labor and to think. Thought begat thought. (III, 217; my
emphasis)

But this was only one of the ways by which he brought his masterpiece to "its harmonious completion." Though *Walden* is still all too
frequently treated as a series of separable essays, there have been
several strong advocates of its unity. The most thorough-going study
is the one by the present writer, *The Magic Circle of Walden* (1968).

"The Making of *Walden*," through seven successive versions,
has been described in a recent book by J. L. Shanley with that title,
based upon an ingenious unscrambling of the surviving manuscripts.[16]
This account of the elaborate revisions of his book manuscript is fasci-
nating for students of Thoreau, but it is tangential to the present volume. What are pertinent to my inquiry, however, are the *Journal*
passages that were reworked for inclusion in his book, such as have
survived. The record for the early period is a mere fragment of what
it once was, presumably because the *Journal* was raided for both
Walden and *A Week* as well as for essays and poems. Only one volume has come down for the first twelve years of his journalizing, as
compared with an average of five hundred pages for every year after
1850— a ration of one to fifteen. However, much of what went into
Walden was first written between 1850 and 1854, so that passages
which found their way into the book come not only from the first
stripped volume but from the next five richest volumes of the *Journal*.
There are nearly a hundred such passages usually of a paragraph or
more, and they are of two sorts: those transcribed almost verbatim and
those that are significantly changed. Samples of each will now be
analyzed.

In the *Journal* for 29 March 1853 there is a long paragraph of
more than fifty lines that is used almost without change in Chapter 9,
"The Village." It begins: "Two or three times, when a visitor stayed
into the evening, and it proved a dark night, I was obliged to conduct

---

[16]   J. L. Shanley, *The Making of Walden* (Chicago, 1957). He
gives the first version entire, describes the other six, then discusses all of
them in relation to the eighth and final version— the printer's "fair
copy."

him to the cart-path in the rear of my house," and then goes on to re-
count several anecdotes of people getting lost in the dark. (v, 62–64)
In the *Walden* version there are few alterations and all concern minor
matters of phrasing, for example: "Several times, when a visitor
chanced to stay into evening," and so on. (*Walden*, 188–190) All
but one. In the concluding sentence, after speaking of the advantages
of being lost, he wrote in the *Journal:* "In fact, not till we are lost do
we begin to realize where we are, and the infinite extent of our relations." In the book he inserts in the middle of this sentence: "not
till we have lost the world, do we begin to find ourselves." These
dozen words add a whole new dimension of meaning to the paragraph, with their parody of New Testament doctrine to play up the
Transcendental virtue of self-reliance.

Another interesting point about the above quotation is that it
suddenly occurs in the midst of *Journal* notations for 29 March 1853,
when Thoreau was living in his family's house in Concord, yet it
clearly refers to the Walden residence over six years before ("the cart-
path in the rear of my house" followed by the anecdote of "the two
young men who had been fishing in the pond" and who stopped at
his cabin to ask directions through the dark woods). This is further
evidence that the mosaic method of composition was not the customary
one Thoreau used in writing *Walden*. The paragraph is not a random
one jotted down in the *Journal* to be picked up later by a craftsman
looking for material to illustrate a theme; it was a conscious draft for
a particular chapter in *Walden* which was being written at exactly
this time, Thoreau simply using the blank pages of his *Journal* instead
of a pad of paper for his composition.

A somewhat different demonstration can be made with a *Journal*
passage dated 27 August 1852, which was transcribed directly into
"The Ponds." Apparently Thoreau did not decide to add this central
chapter to his book until he began the fourth version of *Walden*, in
that year.[17] Consequently, since the earlier *Journal* had little material
on the pond, he made a number of trips during 1852 from Concord

[17]   The first version, written during his residence at the pond, contained only about two pages out of what eventually became a thirty-page
chapter; nothing was added in the second or third versions, 1849–
1851.

back out to Walden for the specific purpose of taking down observations and impressions to use in his new chapter, again using the blank
pages of his *Journal* for his first drafts, then transcribing them shortly
afterwards into the manuscript of *Walden*. In the passage from 1852,
here chosen for illustration (IV, 320–322), the principal change was
to break it into four parts and distribute it through the chapter.[18] There,
mingled with other passages from the *Journal*, all was amalgamated
into a coherent whole. Revision by rearrangement, but not the mosaic
method, since the theme was chosen before any of the parts were
written.[19]

Still another method of transcribing *Journal* into book can be
illustrated by Thoreau's use of his anecdote of a visit to the shanty
Irishman John Field, recorded on 23 August 1845. Since this was
less than two months after he moved into his cabin at Walden Pond,
and presumably before he even conceived the book which came to be
called *Walden*, one must assume that the anecdote was written for its
own sake and that it was probably the report of an actual visit. However this may be, it was incorporated in the book almost without
change, as the central third of the chapter titled "Baker Farm," with an
appended homily in which he tried to show how he had succeeded in
a situation analogous to the one in which Field had failed. But if the
"argument" of Chapter 10 turns on this case history of a poor family
who are solving incorrectly the basic problem of acquiring the necessaries of life, then Thoreau's comparison with his own solution is fatally
vulnerable. For he had enough capital to build his cabin ($28.12½),
a college education, a well-placed friend (Emerson) whose land he
was allowed to squat on, and no dependents to support since he was a
bachelor. Because John Field had none of these advantages, one could
argue that the economic lesson of "Baker Farm" is invalidated. But the
visit to Field is only an illustrative episode. The chapter's real meaning
is to be found in its opening and closing pages, which have no counter-
part in the *Journal*. These are filled with striking imagery: the rainbow

18   The first fourteen lines to *Walden*, p. 198, the next three to
p. 196, the next seventeen to p. 200, and the final three to p. 195.
19   From the tables in Shanley (see note 16), 30–32, 72–73, one
can determine when the parts of the several versions of *Walden* were
composed.

in which Thoreau finds himself standing (symbolizing the path from earth to heaven); the dolphin into which he is momentarily transformed (the messenger who guided souls to immortality); the *talaria* which he will clap to his heels (the winged sandals worn by Iris, goddess of the rainbow). All of this was missing in the *Journal* draft.

Those who think of *Walden* as a pastiche, scissored from the *Journal*, might still argue that the imagery is mere decoration borrowed from the realm of poetry and added to the autobiographical experience to give it color. But those who learn to read *Walden* as a poem would say that the chapter was conceived as a quest, its meaning to be rendered by an image cluster. If so then the factual episode was borrowed from the *Journal* merely to serve as a counterweight to the aspiring imagery. There is a vast difference between the two methods: one for an expository essay, the other for a work of art. The real theme of "Baker Farm" is a contrast between the elevated and the degraded life, between freedom through imagination and serfdom through stupidity, between a poet's desire to soar into the life of the spirit and a clod's resignation to being bogged down in squalid materialism.[20] By such techniques the magical world of *Walden* was created. Two other examples of such "translation" from *Journal* to book may be found in the Appendix, above. Both versions are given in full because the revisions are too intricate and subtle to be illustrated by summary comment. In one Thoreau transforms his cabin into a mythical abode, in the other he turns the advent of spring into a miracle of rebirth.

These demonstrations of Thoreau's theory and practice make it clear that oversimplified formulas like "mosaic method" and "organic form" are inadequate to explain how he created his masterpiece. Form was always a major problem for Thoreau, but he solved it once brilliantly in the symbolic structure of *Walden*, again with real success in *A Week* and in his best essays— "Walking," "Wild Apples," "Autumnal Tints," "Civil Disobedience," "Life Without Principle." In shaping his lesser books and essays he probably relied to a considerable extent on the method of choosing a theme and then composing pas-

[20]   A detailed interpretation of "Baker Farm" can be found in my book, *The Magic Circle of Walden* (1968), 131–143.

sages from the *Journal* into a mosaic, though the evidence for this is not always conclusive.

The Miniatures, on the other hand, seem to have been created as unified wholes, not tinkered together from fragments scattered through the *Journal*. Some of them may have been shaped "organically," especially the simple narratives and naturally framed vignettes— even those essays compact enough to be controlled, without conscious effort, by a strong generative idea. A few of them have survived in several versions, however, showing the busy hand of the craftsman revising his first "spontaneous" composition. Two of these, "The Oysterboat Men" and "The Little Irish Boy," are reproduced in the Appendix, above; many others may have been similarly reworked, though all traces of the author's travail have vanished. Even those Miniatures that seem most simple and natural are often subtly complex, as my analysis of "Fox Chase" (pp. 146–147, above) has indicated.

Perception, expression, and form—the three principal elements of the writer's art—reach their peak in the Miniatures of *Thoreau's World* as well as in his universally admired *Walden*.

---

*   The index of people and places in Thoreau's Journal (1906, 14 vols.) is inclusive, and since readers can refer to that, the present index of people and places mentioned in the "Miniatures" is selective. For subjects one can refer to the preceding List of Miniatures.

For my two essays, "The Journal" and "The Writer's Art," I have aimed at a complete index of proper names and subjects.

A NOTE ON THE TYPE

The type used in this text is called Eldorado and was designed by W. A. Dwiggins between 1942 and 1953. Its compactness of setting and evenness of color combine to create a gracefulness uncommon to contemporary old-style letters. The initials used were designed by the same master of types especially for The Plimpton Press. The title page is composed in Palatino, designed by Hermann Zapf. These types all share the vital quality of retaining their heritage of and relation to writing with the pen.